WHAT'S
ARE Y

Thirty years of experience and research led A. T. Mann to a
startling realization: your horoscope should begin at
conception—not birth. His revolutionary astrological
paradigm—"life time astrology"—goes beyond conventional
horoscope systems.

In *A New Vision of Astrology,* he offers

- an easy-to-follow time scale that extends from conception
  to old age and helps to explain the forces that affect each
  phase of life,

- critical insights into the roles that significant people are
  destined to play at every stage,

- practical tools for using astrology to eliminate unwanted
  behaviors and patterns in order to improve your quality
  of life . . . and much, much more!

A NEW VISION
OF
ASTROLOGY

A. T. Mann

POCKET BOOKS
New York   London   Toronto   Sydney   Singapore

An *Original* Publication of POCKET BOOKS

POCKET BOOKS, a division of Simon & Schuster, Inc.
1230 Avenue of the Americas, New York, NY 10020

ISBN: 0-7434-5341-7

First Pocket Books trade paperback printing December 2002

10 9 8 7 6 5 4 3 2 1

POCKET and colophon are registered trademarks of
Simon & Schuster, Inc.

For information regarding special discounts for bulk purchases,
please contact Simon & Schuster Special Sales at 1-800-456-6798 or
business@simonandschuster.com

Printed in the U.S.A.

ACKNOWLEDGMENTS

Astrology challenges our imagination, emotions, desires, and ideas. We are complex humans—that is our nature. When we activate our deeper and often dormant senses, we become more alive, more awake, and more present to ourselves and others. Astrology provokes a broader and deeper vision of reality, and encourages us to work with our lives, our relationships, and our world. This is a lifelong task, and we must understand it as such. I thank my astrological colleagues for their psychological and mythological revisioning of this ancient art and science in the last century.

Astrology is a study of human nature amid the cosmos and is as complex as we are. While a reader can learn much about astrology from this book, it is valuable to utilize one of the many astrology schools in the United States to further enhance one's understanding of this ancient science and art. There is no substitute for good teaching, study, and interchange with other seekers. I would particularly mention Kepler College in Seattle as the first accredited school to offer BA and MA degrees in Astrological Studies.[1]

I thank Lady Diana Whitmore for the insights and experiences embodied by the Psychosynthesis & Education Trust in London, where twenty years ago I experienced techniques that have become integral to my understanding, practice, and teaching of astrology.

Thanks to Gillian and David Helfgott for their helpful feedback and encouragement. I thank Michael Erlewine and Matrix Software for permission to use the WinStar2+ computer program for all the horoscopes in this book. I thank my literary agent, Sandra Martin, for her support, persistence, and heart in initiating this project. Charles Williams is a great support and made helpful suggestions throughout the project. Thanks to Joan Goodkind for her reading of the work. I thank my colleague in Universal Quest, Raja Choudhury, for his design and computer genius in bringing the website www.newvisionastrology.com into being. I thank my friend Judith Taylor Wheelock for her support, friendship, and most valuable feedback.

A. T. Mann
Hudson, New York
June 2002

CONTENTS

INTRODUCTION

A June 2001 Gallup Poll showed that 28 percent of American adults (about 50 million people) believe in astrology. Many millions more regularly look at their sun signs in newspapers and magazines. Many people want to know more about astrology and its meaning for their lives, but few take their understanding of this revelatory tool to a higher stage. This entails having your own horoscope calculated for the exact time and place of your birth; learning about the signs, the houses, and the planets; and learning to read the horoscope wheel. Astrological writings reflect this dilemma: Some are addressed to the few who take astrology more seriously and already know the fundamentals, but most are limited to the popular sun-sign level. *A New Vision of Astrology* provides a method for you to learn astrology and an easy way to calculate and create your horoscope via the Internet.

Most people know only the rudimentary meanings of the Sun in the twelve signs of the zodiac—the sun signs. They like the language of astrology and want to know more about it, and realize that we are more complex than a sun sign can possibly describe. Yet how do they advance their knowledge of themselves by learning the more advanced tools of astrology?

In the last half of the 1960s, while working as an architect in

New York City, I had my horoscope done by a computer on the main concourse of Grand Central Terminal in New York City. The "Astro-Flash" interpretation was simplistic and fragmented, but what intrigued me most was the horoscope diagram upon which the interpretation was based. I realized that this was my "cosmic signature," and I vowed to understand the significance of those symbols. My journey of discovery, which that vow engendered, has continued to this day.

In the late 1960s I left New York and traveled in Europe, Morocco, central Asia, and India. I met a number of astrologers and interested amateurs along the way who gave me glimpses of astrology. Previously I had had no more than a general idea of the twelve sun signs, but I wanted to know more, particularly to put the experiences of my journey to the East into a perspective that would enhance my understanding of my life. I resolved to discover myself through astrology and felt that I had to go back to the basics to do this. I needed to start from the beginning with myself and my astrology. The process of discovery has occupied the last thirty years of my life, and I wish to pass its benefits on to you.

In the years when I first started going deeper into myself, I became aware that my mind and feelings provided inherently different and occasionally disparate perspectives on my life. Due to my upbringing and education, my mental reality had prevailed and been dominant up until that time. I learned that this mental identification happens when we allow our minds to dominate our other equally valuable ways of being. Our thinking can suppress our feelings and overrule our body's needs, and it can diminish or subvert our spirituality. Conversely, our feelings can dominate our body and mind when we react emotionally in situations when we really need to be logical or composed. We must redress the balance to be whole.

Plato's four-body model postulates that we have successively finer physical, emotional, mental, and spiritual bodies that describe levels of our being. Astrology uses this model, with the four elements corresponding to the four bodies: Earth is the physical body, Water the emotional body, Air the mental body, and Fire the spiritual or intuitive body. As you will see, these four bodies also unfold in time throughout our lives in four octaves of development.

Exploring my life in therapy was like dredging my fingers through a murky pond. I wondered what would emerge to the surface of my consciousness next. Are psychological contents connected to each other like dream fragments that struggle for coherence? I tried to understand the relative importance of the images and symbols that appeared to me by reading Carl Jung, contemporary psychologists and astrologers, and alchemists and mystics stretching back to ancient times. I felt compelled to discover the origin and nature of this process that fascinated me. I needed a guide, but I intuitively felt I must be my own guide: Astrology seemed to be the perfect vehicle for this investigation.

We are an integral part of the wolf around us. It is essential that we recognize and work with the connectedness of all things. Astrology is one of the most ancient expressions of the human mind and spirit that recognizes the principle "As above, so below." Even physics tells us that we come from the stars: Our body's chemical composition reflects the cosmos and contains traces of every element, confirming the ancient wisdom.

The path of self-discovery often leads in strange directions. I now realize that my education and practice as an architect uniquely prepared me to be an astrologer. My knowledge of physics, mathematics, and art interfaces with a more subtle and elusive feeling for the essence of myself and others, and enables my being as a guide of souls. Astrology is unique in that it contains everything: psychology, physics, mathematics, biology, sociology, history, art, science, rhythm, the music of the spheres, color, health, and more.

Astrology confirms that I need not be anyone but true to myself; for me, this is the greatest gift of understanding.

The ancients knew that astrology is a system of correspondences. Using its unique symbols we can see correlations between individuals, times (of the day, month, year, lifetime, and world age), colors, psychological types and traits, ways of acting, ways of being, body parts and organs, chakras, rays, images, numbers, geometric shapes, letters in the alphabet, gods and goddesses, and many others. Studying and using astrology enables a higher and more profound comprehension of our world and also provides tools for integrating seemingly disparate qualities. We need these tools, and they can be found here.

It was my good fortune to learn astrology while I became a parent. Just before my daughter's conception, my studies began, and by the time of her birth, I was practicing astrology professionally. The creative learning process that occurred during her gestation led me to a transformed vision of what astrology could be and, in my subsequent life as a single-parent father, was an invaluable guide to raising my child as well as my child within.

My first foray into learning astrology was frustrating. I lived in the Berkshires, in western Massachusetts, in a house owned by friends who were peripherally interested in astrology. Through reading a good sampling of books that approached astrology from various viewpoints, I immediately saw barriers to my understanding. Although I could easily understand that we all contain qualities that the signs of the zodiac describe and that, after a little practice, we can identify people we know as, say, Leos or Cancers, I found myself wondering: What part of us do the signs show and how do we know this? Moreover, I wondered: How can we structure and present the resultant interpretative material in a way that makes sense? This led me to explore the structure and meaning of the horoscope diagram itself and to decode the symbols of astrology. As an architect, I feel the need to visualize astrological ideas in order to understand how they really work. I believe that this brings universality to the concepts and makes them more readily understandable. My way of seeing astrology led to the unique insights and original methods described in this book.

Although I have been a professional astrologer for many years, I realize that in the beginning it was an advantage not to know other astrologers. It forced me to look at astrology without the encumbrance of prevailing attitudes. While much of astrology remains valid, I feel that it is necessary to change its perspective to reflect our time. We can benefit from following this process of discovery into the art and science of astrology. I say "art and science" because astrology is both of these. It is a science in that it describes a language and set of rules that symbolize our life in time. As the word *science* means most simply "knowledge," astrology is a way of knowing and communicating through its unique symbolic language how we as humans live in our world, interact with each other, interact within ourselves, and relate to the cosmos of which we are an integral part.

There are some points upon which I focus in this book. They represent unique ways of learning to use astrology that will extend your understanding from the meaning of sun signs to embracing our richer complexity. This is embodied in the Moon and eight planets, the houses and aspects.

We are complex beings in a world synchronized by cosmic cycles. We can only occasionally affect or change these powerful cycles, but we can always understand them in new and deeper ways. It is like traveling through life with a map; having the map does not change the territory, but it provides us with a way to relate to our surroundings, to know where we have been, and to recognize when we are revisiting known territory. Learning the language of astrology is not only enjoyable; it expands and enhances our life.

We express and record our lives as stories that gradually crystallize as our life myths. We are part of an ancient tradition in this respect. Our story is a continually edited text that has arisen from the important events of our lives. It is how we express who we are to others, and also how we store memories within us. When we meet someone, we tell him or her about ourselves through stories. We tell different sequences of stories and modify our stories to fit the circumstances and what we wish to convey. All our stories are told from our viewpoint; indeed, they *are* our viewpoint. As in postmodern literary criticism, there is no objective reality because all of our texts are inherently subjective—they are uniquely ours. No one interpretation of our text is inherently superior to another, nor is any text superior to any other text. We continue to refine, redefine, enrich, and learn to accept ourselves through our life stories. Our new vision of astrology enables us to receive feedback about our life through our stories, to model them, and to see the relationships between them.

We will use an astrological time scale and a unique understanding of the dynamic of time to expand and enrich our basic knowledge of astrological tools. We will learn to accept and nurture those relationships that created us, continue to sustain us, and continue to affect our health and well-being. Those who experience this integrated wisdom recognize its sublime and powerful value as a great gift that we can give ourselves—the understanding and acceptance of who we truly are. This book will enable our quest for identity and give us useful tools with which to understand our surface and our depths.

As a purchaser of this book you are entitled to a series of horoscope diagrams and a list of dates in your life that you can download from the Internet, either at home, at work, or through the Internet café. All you must do is find your unique number at the front of this book, go online to the site www.newvisionastrology.com, and follow the instructions. You will need to provide your name, date, and place of birth, as well as the exact time when you were born. Ideally, to ensure the greatest accuracy, you should get this information from your birth certificate. Throughout the book we will use these materials to allow you to interpret and understand your astrological life in time.

As you read the book, windows such as this one will guide you through the process of interpreting your life with your horoscope. You will discover, by accumulating information throughout the book, to model the stories and influences that bring you into being. Remember that we are complex and that the paradoxes and contradictions that arise are integral to us and provide richness and depth to our lives. What we consider difficult or traumatic events in our lives often hold the potential for transformation if we can recognize them and work through them. We must be kind to ourselves and not expect too much. Astrology is a lifetime process.

ONE

BEYOND THE SUN SIGNS

Our birth is but a sleep and a forgetting:
The Soul that rises with us, our life's Star,
Hath had elsewhere its setting,
And cometh from afar:
Not in entire forgetfulness,
And not in utter nakedness,
But trailing clouds of glory do we come
From God, who is our home.

WILLIAM WORDSWORTH,
"ODE: INTIMATIONS OF IMMORTALITY"

The sun signs are our first introduction to astrology. We realize immediately that there is a profound simplicity and wisdom in the sequence of twelve zodiac signs, despite our logical resistance to the fact that we are categorical and predictable. As if by osmosis we gradually learn this ancient set of symbols and their qualities, especially if we are interested in relationship, in our feelings, in why we do what we do, or why others do what they do. In time we learn the qualities of our own sun sign and also the meaning of the other signs. It even seems that signs other than our own are relevant to us. We wonder why this is the case.

The qualities of the twelve signs resonate with us on some deep level. We read that Leos are proud and self-centered or that Aquarians are idealistic and join groups, and we nod our heads in assent without really knowing why. What is not made clear is that the

Sun is symbolically the father, the masculine principle, vitality, consciousness, and objectivity. The sun signs really tell us only about the masculine qualities and the equivalent parts of us that derive from our father, our father figures, or the masculine influences in our lives. Where can we discover the symbols that signify our feminine side and our emotional life? To do so, we must explore the Moon, our mother, our feelings, our values, and the feminine principle in the same sequence of twelve signs. The twelve astrological signs are types that apply to the Moon and the other planets.

The sun signs are places in the cycle of the solar year, which is why we associate them with our birthday. The sequence of their twelve values has a seasonal and a symbolic coherence. It is logical that the summer sign Leo is warmer and more outgoing than the winter sign Capricorn, which is more reserved and introverted. The reasons are obvious and simply explain when in the seasonal cycle we are born. By extending the logic of sun signs that we have already learned to the other planets, we bring a new richness of relationship to the familiar.

What are the zodiac signs and what do they mean? The zodiac is a ring of constellations functioning as a 360° measuring circle against which the Sun, Moon, and planets move through the heavens. By convention, measurement starts with the Spring Equinox around March 21 each year, when day is exactly equal to night. The yearly cycle of nature starts with Aries in the spring and proceeds through to Pisces at the end of winter, before the process starts over again. The signs are also a metaphor for the psychological stages that we experience in life. They also correspond to the twelve houses of the horoscope. The fact that they are a process rather than random associations is important.

The twelve signs are associated with body parts and organs (Figure 1.1). Aries is the head and brain; Taurus the neck, throat,

From Kircher's *Œdipus Ægyptiacus*.

FIGURE 1.1: ASTROLOGY AND THE BODY

Each sign of the zodiac corresponds to a part of our body and an organ system, from Aries at our head to Pisces at our feet.

and ears; Gemini the shoulders, arms, and lungs; Cancer the breast and stomach; Leo the spine and heart; Virgo the abdomen and the intestines; Libra the solar plexus and colon; Scorpio the sexual organs and reproductive system; Sagittarius the thighs and sciatic nerves; Capricorn the knees and skeletal system; Aquarius the ankles and sympathetic nervous system; and Pisces the feet and lymphatic system. When we have planets in a sign, we often experience health strengths, weaknesses, or specific physical traits in the equivalent body parts or organs. For example, we might have a mole or scar on the area of our body that corresponds to the sign of our Sun or Moon or Mars. I have Sun in the sign Leo and was born with a mole on the Leo (dorsal) part of my spine. The Taurean Sigmund Freud died of throat cancer. Our health and potential for illness work through the dominant signs in our horoscope.

The art of astrology is in the interpretation and integration of zodiac signs, the planets, and the aspect relationships between them. Astrological interpretation requires vision, wisdom, understanding, and, most important, the ability to look within ourselves, to question why we do what we do and how we do it, and to consider deeply the implications of our actions. While we ostensibly learn astrology to help others, our study must begin with our own life, explored in depth. Of course, it is always easier to see others more clearly than we can see ourselves. The more honest and penetrating we are with our own life and ourselves, the more effective and valuable our relationship will be to others.

Figure 1.2 below shows a horoscope like the one you can receive for buying this book. The various components of the horoscope wheel are shown together with the chapters in the book that allow you to interpret them. We will follow this sequence to learn about astrology and to create your life process.

The sun signs in a newspaper or magazine are presented as unrelated to each other, but they have an internal logic because of their location around the circle, which has its own internal geom-

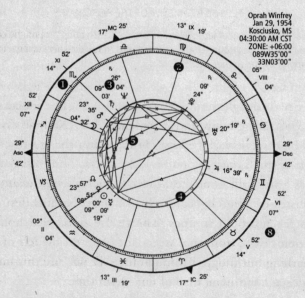

FIGURE 1.2: HOROSCOPE OF OPRAH WINFREY

There are five components of the horoscope: ❶ zodiac signs (chapter 1), ❷ twelve houses (chapter 5), ❸ planets in a sign and house (chapter 6), ❹ ring of time-scale dates (chapter 4), and ❺ aspects connecting planets to each other (chapter 7).

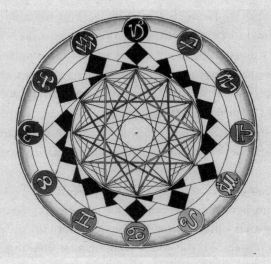

1.3: THE GEOMETRY OF THE HOROSCOPE

The zodiac signs have geometric relationships with each other around the circle. They are linked by triangles, squares, and other shapes that have specific meanings. *Mandala painting by the author, 1995.*

etry, such as triangles and squares (Figure 1.3). The zodiac signifies a cycle of soul growth and experience. The Natural Zodiac, or World Horoscope, has the First House equivalent to Aries, the Second House to Taurus, etc., around the circle. *The signs are divisions in space* and qualities of life, while *the houses are divisions in time* and phases of life. The signs tell us about the qualities, and the houses tell us about timings. The twelve numbered houses step counterclockwise from the Ascendant (Asc) on the left of the circle, marking our progress through life. We will use this important sequence as a temporal map of our life in time.

Each season starts with equinoxes and solstices that are cardinal signs (Aries = spring, Cancer = summer, Libra = autumn, and Capricorn = winter). The fixed signs maintain the middle of each season (Taurus = mid-spring, Leo = mid-summer, Scorpio = mid-autumn, and Aquarius = mid-winter). The mutable signs end each season and are transitional to the next quadrants (Gemini = spring to summer, Virgo = summer to autumn, Sagittarius = autumn to winter, and Pisces = winter to spring). These three *modes* help us understand how the signs act. The cardinal signs are initiatory and originate behavior; the fixed signs are permanent and stable, and maintain behavior; and the mutable signs are changeable and unstable and modify behavior, within each of the four seasons.

We divide the twelve signs into four *elements:* fire, earth, air, and water. The elements are principles of action in the world. The psychologist Carl Jung related them to the four psychological functions: Fire is intuition, earth is sensation, air is thinking, and water is feeling. They correspond to Plato's four bodies, where fire is the spiritual body, earth is the physical body, air is the mental body, and water is the emotional body. They correlate with the modern view of the world as seen by physicists, in which fire is energy, earth is the particle nature of matter, water is the wave nature of matter, and air is the complementarity between particle and wave.[2] The fire signs Aries, Leo, and Sagittarius are energetic, intuitive, and hot. The earth signs Taurus, Virgo, and Capricorn are physical, sensitive, and substantial. The air signs Gemini, Libra, and Aquarius are mental, thinking, and mobile. The water signs Cancer, Scorpio, and Pisces are emotional, feeling, and fluid.

On the horoscope form you receive from newvisionastrology.com you will see on the lower right a grid that shows the element and mode distribution of the nine planets, the Ascendant, and the Midheaven. You can see at a glance which element dominates and which ones are less strong. The distribution may be very meaningful because it shows us the qualities with which we are most comfortable, and the ones for which we must compensate. When we lack an element we often seek that quality in others. If we lack fire,

	C	F	M
F	0	1	2
E	0	0	2
A	2	3	1
W	1	2	0

1.4: ELEMENT AND MODE DISTRIBUTION

Oprah Winfrey lacks the grounding element earth, but has six planets and angles in communicative air signs. Her physical insecurity is compensated for by communication. She also has six planets and angles in the fixed mode, showing her inherent stability and fixedness.

we are attracted to fire-sign types as partners, friends, associates, or even our children. Figure 1.4 shows the distribution for Oprah Winfrey, who lacks the grounding element earth, but compensates with her communicative air.

When we discover the dominant element and mode—as, in Oprah's case, air and fixed—we can surmise that she functions much like the fixed air sign Aquarius, the sign of idealism, eccentric yet popular communication, and networking. She is a perfect figure for our Aquarian Age.

Planets in each sign partake of the mode and element of the sign in which they reside, which qualifies how they act and which part of our psychology they signify. The signs are behavioral lenses that modify how we see the planets. For example, when the Moon is in Virgo, describing our mother and our feelings, the mutable mode will make our feelings about her and our emotions changeable and dualistic, while the element earth will make our feelings more realistic and substantial. We will therefore tend to classify and organize our emotional life as if it were something tangible.

The box "The Zodiac Signs" presents the signs in their natural sequence, related to the qualities derived from their times in the year, together with their traditional meanings. These meanings apply not only to sun signs, but to other planets as well.

THE ZODIAC SIGNS

♈ *Aries the Ram*　　Cardinal, Masculine, Fire Sign　　First House

00°–30°　　　　　　March 21 to April 20　　　　Ruled by Mars

Iron

Lime

Germinating time; unfolding energy. Adventure; daring; impatience; the personality. Aries is pure spirit and energy, leading onward and bringing joy and irresistible will to everything that they do. Aries people are often pioneers or inventors, certainly seeking adventure in their lives. Aries is self-assertive and initiatory, directed energy, and independent without foresight. *Irrepressable will, self-directed.*

Desire

♉ *Taurus the Bull*　　Fixed, Feminine, Earth Sign　　Second House

30°–60°　　　　　　April 20 to May 21　　　　　Ruled by Venus

Copper

Invigoration and strengthening; form creation; preservation. Physical world; matter; fertility; security; finances; stewardship; form; endurance. Taurus is pure substance or undifferentiated matter, receiving the initiatory energy of Aries and stabilizing and grounding it in the physical world and the body. Taurus creates permanence and often builds structures that manifest a materialistic worldview, all the while acting with patience and attention to nature and animals. It is our property, money, and possessions, *attachment to and attitude towards.*

♊ *Gemini the Twins*　　Mutable, Masculine, Air Sign　Third House

60°–90°　　　　　　May 21 to June 22　　　　　Ruled by Mercury

Mercury

Diversity; multiplication; vitality; adaptability. Instinctive mind; imitation; communication; duality; versatility; mobility; facility. Gemini is instinctive self-expression and communication in all its forms, the energy of Aries applied to Taurean matter, producing movement and change. Gemini observes, connects, modifies, gathers, and ranges over short distances to accumulate experience and pass it on to others in face-to-face sibling relationships. It is pure intelligence, facility, and verbal skills.

♋ *Cancer the Crab*　　Cardinal, Feminine, Water Sign　Fourth House

90°–120°　　　　　　June 22 to July 23　　　　　Ruled by the Moon

Silver

Mothering; fecundation; fertilization. Feeling; emotions; mother; home and family; the unconscious; dreams; protective urge. Cancer is our emotional response to communication and the primary relationships of Gemini, acting through the parents and especially the mother, the family, and home life. Cancer protects, nurtures, conserves, and identifies with origins and roots, dissolving differences, and possesses through guilt.

Gold

♌ *Leo the Lion*   Fixed, Masculine, Fire Sign   Fifth House

120°–150°   July 23 to August 24   Ruled by the Sun

Ripening; summer heat; full energy; extroversion; harvest. Self-expression; personal love; games; pleasure; ruling; vanity; arrogance. Leo goes beyond the family to exteriorize the Self into the world through education, game-playing, selfish love, and pure creativity. Leo shows and tells, is proud of achievement, seeks admiration, and radiates love and support for others.

Magnesium

♍ *Virgo the Virgin*   Mutable, Feminine, Earth Sign   Sixth House

150°–180°   August 24 to September 23   Ruled by Mercury

Ripe fruit; orderly storage and collection; selection. Discrimination; work; perfectionism; health and hygiene; analysis; prudence; diet. Virgo is differentiated matter, critical and analytical of spirit, refining and narrowing matter with mind. Virgo organizes, purifies, and creates structures compounded of details and techniques. Virgo chooses, serves, maintains health, teaches secondary education, and works.

Palladium

♎ *Libra the Balance*   Cardinal, Masculine, Air Sign   Seventh House

180°–210°   September 23 to October 24   Ruled by Venus

Balance and adjustment; thanksgiving; social equilibration. Partnership; marriage; public relations; enemies; persuasion; sublimation; yielding. Libra is ideal relationships, the marriage of opposites, attempting to achieve balance and justice, and being willing to sublimate to make it work. Libra adjusts, equilibrates, and encourages a more harmonious environment, and takes these relationships into the outer world.

Nickle

♏ *Scorpio the Scorpion*   Fixed, Feminine, Water Sign   Eighth House

210°–240°   October 24 to November 23   Ruled by Mars and Pluto

Vegetation death; seed life; survival; endurance. Death and regeneration; passion; separation; others; losses; inheritance; metaphysical. Scorpio is deep and hidden emotional power used for either regeneration or destruction, even self-destruction. It is separate from others, internally alone and isolated, detached even unto death. Scorpio controls and directs emotions, experiences backlashes of tension, and carries intense inner passion and sexuality.

Tin

♐ *Sagittarius the Centaur*   Mutable, Masculine, Fire Sign   Ninth House

240°–270°   November 23 to December 22   Ruled by Jupiter

Hibernation; advent; inner life; meditation; expansion. Realization; higher mind; religion and philosophy; sport; freedom; long journeys; action; rebirth. Sagittarius is initiation into the universal through philosophy, psychology, and illumination. Sagittarius explores life abroad as within, aspires to broaden perspectives, searches for inner meaning, and understands through beliefs and religion.

Lead

♑ *Capricorn the Goat.*   Cardinal, Feminine, Earth Sign   Tenth House

270°–300°   December 22 to January 20   Ruled by Saturn

Preservation; patience; reality; self-concentration. Perfected matter; ego objectives; organization; power; success; society; government. Capricorn is perfected matter, crystallizing the material into outer structures such as government and business, expressing the father principle of control and utility. Capricorn organizes and confines, defines and limits, suppresses, conserves, and shows integrity.

Chrome

♒ *Aquarius the Waterbearer*   Fixed, Masculine, Air Sign   Eleventh House

300°–330°   January 20 to February 19   Ruled by Saturn and Uranus

Waiting; fasting; Lent; observation; planning; abstraction. Social consciousness; humanitarian; collective; progressive; cold; altruism; utopian. Aquarius is universal yet detached relationship expressing social ideals in groups, organizations, and movements. Aquarius understands through wisdom, is eccentric in its understanding and use of knowledge, networks and propagandizes to further its worldviews.

Pisces the Fishes	Mutable, Feminine, Water Sign	Twelfth House
330°–360°	February 19 to March 21	Ruled by Jupiter and Neptune

Swelling seed; purifying rain; serenity; potential. Sensitivity; receptivity; self-sacrifice; psychic; karma; seclusion; hospital; dreaming. Pisces is the dissolution of boundaries, dependent emotional attachments, compassionate and passive to the will of others, subservient to fate. Pisces decays and brings chaos, resolves inner issues through meditation and spirituality, is self-sacrificial and unbound by structures.

Six of the signs are single signs and six are double signs. The single signs are Aries, Taurus, Leo, Virgo, Scorpio, and Capricorn, whose images are centralized, strong, singular, and refer to specific unambiguous traits. Aries the Ram is initiatory and single-minded. Taurus the Bull is stable and secure. Leo the Lion is strong, powerful, and dominant. Virgo the Virgin is naive, critical, and discriminatory. Scorpio the Scorpion is self-contained, potent, and secretive. Capricorn the Goat is tenacious, tough, and independent.

The double signs are Gemini, Cancer, Libra, Sagittarius, Aquarius, and Pisces. They are dualistic in their images, qualities, and personifications. They usually describe multiple personifications or dualistic concepts, and occasionally both. For example, when the Moon is in a double sign we tend to have two mothers, or there may be a duality between our mother and grandmother or an adoption, in which there is a "real" mother and an adoptive mother. Their symbols reflect their dynamics. Gemini the Twins is a mirror-image left–right split around the vertical axis, which is imitative, reflective, and indicative of sibling relationships, yet connected above and below. Cancer is two emotional values—a conscious feeling above an unconscious feeling—and the claws spiral or rotate and show changing emotions. Libra the Scales is a weighing and reciprocation of left to right, relating self with others, with the scales as an intermediary mechanism, indicative of the counterbalancing in ideological relationships. Sagittarius the Centaur is a split or reconciliation of a lower, horse-like influence that is athletic, outdoor, sensual, and materialistic, and the upper archer who directs us to higher philosophical, religious, or psychological matters. Aquarius the Waterbearer is two snakes swimming in parallel but opposite directions, one above the other, and is unconscious thoughts that counterpoint unconscious words and acts, and vice versa. Pisces the Fishes are two emotions swimming in opposite directions, yet tethered together at the tail, describing conflicting but interconnected feelings: One feeling seeks consciousness above, while the opposing tendency is to seek secrecy and dive deeper within. In three of these double signs the halves are attached to each other, and Cancer, Libra and Aquarius have separate halves. Often such elementary clues hidden in the form of the zodiac symbols contain interpretive data of great use. It helps to know that Aquarians are often thinking the exact opposite of what they say or that Cancers often harbor the opposite feelings to those they express outwardly.

The valuable understanding of the zodiac signs that we already possess can be a useful starting point to learn astrology as a guide for self-development.

To traditional astrologers the horoscope is an imprint of our life that comes into being, fully formed, at the birth moment. Although the Sun, Moon, and other eight planets each reside in one of the twelve numbered houses representing archetypal ways of being and personality types, astrologers rarely use this sequence for interpretation. Indeed, some virtually ignore the houses as interpretive qualities. They assume that all our traits come into being at birth, which is clearly not the case, because we gradually unfold, change, evolve, and are affected by our environment.

The houses in the daily cycle correspond to the zodiac signs in the yearly cycle, although they are not associated with specific times in life. Although they are numbered, they are seen as abstract or even mythic principles correlated with the signs rather than as a sequence of stages.

The new vision is that we order our life as we live it—in a sequence of development stages from conception through birth, childhood, and maturity and on to old age and death. The sequence of the twelve houses organizes our life pattern. By dating the time periods of the houses, the sequence of developmental stages correspond to the original meanings of the houses. The house times in childhood correspond to the stages of childhood development described by French developmental psychologist Jean Piaget.

Our *time scale* grades the sequence of unfolding around the periphery of the horoscope from conception to old age (Figure 1.5). When we include the planets, they show us when in life each planet (and its personifications) comes into being, beginning with our mother and father coming together to conceive us. The house divisions unfold in a logarithmic sequence that correlates to our perception of the passage of time. Our time sense changes throughout life, accelerating as we age.

This time scale corresponds to the numbered houses in the Natural Zodiac. We use our own horoscope to identify the sequence of life events that forms us, see which planets carry the influences, and determine how they influence us.[3] This is a

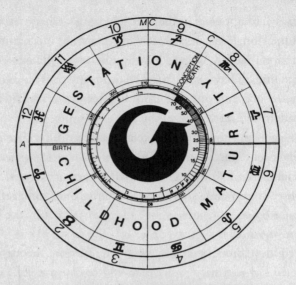

FIGURE 1.5: THE TIME SCALE AND THE NATURAL ZODIAC

We live our life around the wheel. At the upper right is conception, and at the left is birth. We move from conception around the circle counterclockwise to old age. The innermost ring shows dates in life: in gestation in months; in childhood in months, then years; and in maturity in years and decades. The positions of the planets show critical events in life, dated at specific ages. The twelve signs correspond to the houses numbered one through twelve in the Natural Zodiac.

sequential and cyclical model for creating and modifying the stories that compose our life in time. The horoscope shows the sequence of events of our entire life. After birth, the Sun, the Moon, and the planets continue their cycles around the horoscope, triggering off life events and their memories, again and again. We have many opportunities to work with our past patterns; by using the time scale we can know when they are likely to happen again.

The dating system is unique, easy to understand, and straightforward to use. If we cannot determine the astrological influence when a given planet registered, as a learning "trigger" we can try to remember what happened at that age and who transmitted the influence. One thing we can be sure of is that both mechanism and carrier are a part of us. We will track and clarify each stage of our astrological life process with case histories and stories, together with personal observations and unfolding insights that lead us to a deeper understanding of ourselves.

As we age, our time sense changes dramatically, accelerating faster and faster. This phenomenon is "biological time," and it is an essential part of knowing who we are and how we develop through life. It also allows us to date events in our life, reflecting more accurately their relative value and their places in the hierarchy of our life.

The eight planets, the Sun, and the Moon are our *cast of characters* in life and within the psyche (see chapter 6). The Sun is our father, male partners, and the masculine principle within; the Moon is our mother, female partners, and the feminine principle within. The five personal planets Mercury, Venus, Mars, Jupiter, and Saturn are those close to us, brothers and sisters, children and friends, teachers, relatives, and those with whom we form close bonds. The outer planets Uranus, Neptune, and Pluto, which move slowly through the zodiac signs (in approximately seven, twelve, and twenty-two years, respectively), characterize our relationship to our generation's consciousness. The astrological signs in which planets fall qualifies their influence as though they are lenses that affect our vision of the planet. For example, Venus in Aries may be our self-assertive sister, while Saturn in Virgo could be our critical or discriminative grandmother. Each planet corresponds with one or more significant people in our life, beginning with mother and father, helping us to recognize their role in our life, and then to find their influence within us. Even when parental figures are absent, the same symbols describe their surrogates. In this way, we begin to understand the formative influences through which we bring our life into being.

Once we learn with whom the planets correlate and the qualities they express in us, we can begin to see how the signs modify each of the planets in our horoscope and reflect their character. If the Moon at our birth is in the reserved, controlling, and perfectionist sign of Capricorn, then women permeate our emotional life with inhibition and controlling principles or critical insight and ambition that define how we feel about ourselves.

The planets signify influences that form our attitudes and beliefs and that unfold throughout our life process, and we gradually internalize them as we develop and age. They are what form us and frame what we are and who we become. It is possible through them to discover the origins of the mechanisms of our relationships with others, our ability to love and be loved, our potential and how to enable it to unfold, and the qualities we carry within that will provide us with a solid core of meaning and being in life.

The *aspect pattern* in the center of the horoscope connects planets to each other in a web of dynamic relationships that are either harmonious or tense (see chapter 7). They also link events at various stages of our life together to form constellations of meaning that define more complex patterns. The aspects link events that take place at different times and connect components of the self together in quite specific ways.

The geometric relationship between the Sun and the Moon in our horoscope reflects the relationship between our father and our mother. The understanding that ensues from attempting to reconstruct and understand our parents' relationship guides us from within, in resonance with our deepest self. The patterns and dynamics of conception and gestation from our parents' viewpoints describe our sexuality and relationships, as well as their higher octave in our creativity. When we can combine the male and female aspects of our own nature, despite their differences and tensions, our creative life is also nurtured. We must learn to include both sides into a whole that works, just as our parents were able to create us, whatever the difficulties in relationship they may have had. We must learn to see our patterns as they were created by the past and then let them go in being in the present.

TWO

SYMBOLS, MEMORY, AND MEANING

When I first learned astrology I found myself asking: Where in the horoscope do we see our family and the other important people in our life: our parents, teachers, partners, and children? Second, how can we explore the early events of conception and gestation, the essential prenatal time of life, not included in traditional astrology, when our parents' responsibility for conceiving us has a profound impact upon our sexuality, gender-awareness, and relationships throughout life? Which of our parents was responsible for our conception, and why? How did our mother feel with us within her, which reflects how we perceive our own body, and how does the nature of our birth process continue to affect us? Third, we continually change in life and are not the same when we are five as when we are twenty or forty. How does the horoscope describe this changing pattern? How do we unfold and develop in life? Last, modern astrology is primarily psychological: Surely, we must integrate our biology, our attitude to our body and health, into our being. Biology and psychology are interdependent, and both are critically important to us.

These questions led me to reframe astrology. The result is a synthesis of astrology with modern developmental psychology, the concept of biological time, and the Eastern philosophy of karma.

We use a time scale that dates events in our life from conception to old age, based on the ancient perennial philosophy, and provides us with a model that can describe and allow us to work with our life in time.

The horoscope is a graphic representation of our life pattern from conception to death. Movement through the horoscope follows our life and *is* our story—a tale involving everything essential in our life. Since birth, we have grown up hearing our parents' stories about themselves and about our early life. Then we start telling our own stories. We tell, retell, alter, modify, exaggerate, remember, and even forget these stories in the course of our lives. What we tell our partner, children, friends, associates, doctors, therapists, and ourselves are variations of our stories. Every time we tell our stories, we alter them minutely to suit the audience and the occasion. Indeed, we carry everything we know about anyone we have known in the form of a story. Of course, the stories we tell about our past, our family, our parents, and ourselves are true. Everyone else is subject to elaboration, to bending the truth to improve content, interest, and intelligence, but we ourselves are not. However, of course we do! Without informed feedback about our lives through therapy, inner work, counseling, or the astrological information in our horoscope, we are left with a narrow view of our lives that can lead to mechanical living without reflection.

The distortions of our own memory are a powerful area of change. We often perpetuate patterns that are not in our best interests, just because they are there. We do not realize how powerful they are, and only in identifying with them and releasing them can we be truly free to be ourselves. My father was a highly decorated World War II hero (indicated by my Sun in Leo and the Ninth House) who died three months before I was born. In my early childhood, my mother and grandparents always lauded him as perfect and a complete hero, almost as a god. It took me years to realize the more human qualities that lay behind his idealized image, which in turn released me to accept the imperfections in myself.

Much of what we remember before the age of five are vague scenes seen from cradles, reminiscences of parents and relatives, images triggered by photographs in family scrapbooks, or even vaguer recollections. If we remember events at all, they tend to be superficial in respect to our real being. Yet psychologists demonstrate daily that we possess clearly demarcated characteristics formed during the critical first years of our lives. We know even less about our gestation because we have to rely upon the memories of aged parents. How do we know that what we remember or what our parents tell us is true? Simply, we do not. They also alter their stories through many years of retelling them to verify their roles as responsible parents and to play down their own shortcomings. The more culpable they might have been, the more likely they are to have forgotten or modified their stories. When they remember and retell stories about our early life, they redefine their role in our life and extensively redefine our reality as a result.

To see and understand ourselves clearly, we must recognize our habitual ways of remembering, and go back to the beginning and reconstruct our lives. Reconstruction is integral to psychotherapy because therapy starts at the present and works backward into the past. We gradually recover the past through recall, dream analysis, free association, memory stimulation, psychodrama, or hypnosis, and as the analysis goes deeper, the importance of the emerging contents increases. Gaps in early life are often the subject of years of probing, and much of the confusion derives from what we "know" about early events. Is what we know true?

Astrology requires a unique skill that many of us naturally possess, but our education and experience of the world often minimalizes or denies it: We must learn to recognize and interpret

FIGURE 2.1: THE ZODIAC

The zodiac as drawn by Albrecht Dürer shows the constellations surrounding the Pole Star and the circle of the twelve signs. The symbols of the zodiac are animals, humans (Aquarius and Virgo), and objects (Libra), yet they represent qualities we express.

symbols. We must learn to read symbols, which have many layers of meaning, in intuitive ways, and to identify their layers of correspondences and manifestations in our lives, in the psychological, mythic, spiritual, literal, and healing senses.[4] In distinction from signs like the IBM logo, which have very specific meanings, symbols are active; they are continually changing, dynamic, and elusive, like the symbols presented to us in dreams. A tree is such a symbol. We can take it literally as a tree, but it can symbolize to one person his aspiration to higher goals, while to another its roots penetrate deep into the ground and indicate grounding. To some it signifies the structure of families.

Astrological symbols are broad and deep because their origins stretch back to the earliest expressions of the human mind, which

give them an archetypal quality that makes them relevant to all individuals at all times. The process of discovering how to use these
ancient symbols and their underlying mythologies brings a new
clarity and language to our lives. As we become familiar with them
our understanding grows, we see more and more connections, and
we understand the dynamics of our relationships more clearly.

An important distinction is: Which influences are within us
and which are outside of us? Most influences happen in a synchro-
nistic[5] way: The elements of our inner developments attract people
and influences that correspond to them. Indeed, in astrology and
in psychology inner and outer influences reflect, compensate for,
and potentially integrate with each other. If we have a controlling
mother whom we resist in early life, we might naturally resist expressing the controlling mother image within us and discover that
our own feelings are out of control. We will be sure to attract surrogate mothers or partners who carry this controlling feeling to us.
It may be our actual mother but could also be a teacher at school,
a close female friend, a grandmother or sister, or a husband. When
masculine characters reside in the feminine earth and water signs,
their role is often feminine.

If we do not recognize and express the qualities we carry within,
they will come to us through others. We attract or evoke what we
cannot express. This is especially true if it is a quality that we do
not particularly like about ourselves, which in psychology are
called a *shadow quality*. We usually dislike and resist expressing
such shadow qualities and refuse to relate to them, so they appear
through others that we attract.

Psychologists call this process *projection*. If we do not express an
inner quality ourselves, we project it onto others and keep attracting the quality until we understand and integrate it. Our projections are the parts of us that want to be "wanted," even though we
may resist them like crazy. They may reflect a part of us that might

not feel wanted by others. Each part of us has a purpose in the larger scheme of things, and it is up to us to identify, learn to utilize, and integrate each of those qualities in their right places and times, whether or not we like them.

As an example, if we lose a parent early in life through events beyond our control, we might be angry at the fates for having visited this situation upon us. How can we express this anger? If we cannot, or just simply do not feel that we have such anger, we are almost certainly suppressing it. Therefore, in order for that part of us to find a means of expression, we will attract angry people: perhaps a boss, child, husband, or wife. In time, these projections activate the same principles in us. Eventually we get angry at the person who carries the projection and, in the process, withdraw it and express it ourselves. In this way we *introject,* or take back into ourselves, the qualities we formerly projected onto others. Until we learn to identify the traits that we carry yet cannot express ourselves and learn to activate them on a higher level, we are not whole.

Molly B. has a group of planets—Pluto, Mars, and Saturn—in the sign Leo, which registered when she was under two years old. Pluto is transformative experiences that lead to change; Mars signifies energy and anger; and Saturn shows seriousness and inhibition originating in an older person (relative to a child). We can determine the source of these powerful influences by the fact that the Sun in Scorpio, representing Molly's passionate and secretive father, is in a square aspect to all three planets. This shows the effect of a violent or abusive parent at an age before she could remember such an incident. In addition, the asteroid Chiron is near the Sun, an influence that identifies the event as a "wound" for her and targets it for potential healing. When I presented Molly with this dynamic, so central to her being, her first reaction was to deny it, particu-

larly as her father was sixty at the time, instead of thirty-three,
his age when the incident originally happened. In addition, she
had later had a child with a foreign man who became abusive
to their child. She was an uncomprehending victim of these
events. Upon further questioning, I learned that her job was
working with children from broken or abusive families in the
slums of a northern English city. The children felt she naturally
understood them, and she did. Her profession was her way of
working through this traumatic childhood event that was re-
peated in adulthood, without her ever becoming aware of it
until the reading.

For our efforts at self-work to be helpful, it is essential to eliminate spurious stories and discover the real motivations of our past.
Our new vision of astrology provides a unique vantage point for
our life because we reverse the order in psychotherapy—instead of
regressing backward into life from the present, we recreate our life
from the beginning, in the order in which we lived it.

Our intention is to recreate the sequence of events in our life
that determined how we are. These in turn provide us with patterns of behavior that we repeat in many different guises. We can
see how various minor patterns of behavior join to interweave our
life in time. When we can begin to understand our life as a process,
we can liberate ourselves from the need to be mechanical and begin
to act from our inherent wholeness.

An important factor is that of contradiction. We are ambiguous
and always changing. As we age, we continually reinvent ourselves.
Despite wanting things to be different, we often simply reinforce
existing patterns that have defined us in the past, yet we always
have the opportunity to work with these patterns in more satisfying and spiritual ways. Ironically, we must learn to play ourselves
perfectly before we can begin to consider freedom.

This original and profound system allows us to convert our understanding of sun-sign astrology into a fuller and more realistic language for describing the entire rich range of human sensations, emotions, ideas, and spiritual aspirations, but without worrying about the technicalities or mathematics of astrology. We can explore our own horoscope and its meanings by studying our own life, our parental legacy, and the qualities we pass on to our children and to posterity.

An illustration of how these techniques work came about in an unusual way. In the early 1980s I was invited to appear on a television program in England that was investigating astrology. In the filmed segment I was able to demonstrate how an astrologer could discover crucial early events and psychological patterns from the horoscope, knowing nothing of the individual involved. There was also a live studio panel discussion, and the host of the program was notorious for being a skeptic, as was the BBC network itself. My only condition for appearing was that I wanted to have the horoscope of the host and give him a brief reading just before we went on the air. At first, he was openly hostile, but his hostility turned to disbelief and then support within the first minutes of the reading. I was able to show him that he was illegitimate and that he had repeated this pattern in his adult life. His horoscope (Figure 2.2) shows how I came to these conclusions. (As in many horoscopes in the book, for the sake of simplicity I have omitted planets that are not relevant to the issue being explored.)

We started the reading by reconstructing how he was conceived. We first found the Ninth House cusp ❶, the conception point. In this case we went back in a counterclockwise direction until we came to the Moon in Aries in the Second House ❷. His mother was a very independent, self-sufficient, and impulsively emotional woman (Aries qualities), probably inhibited in relationships due to the trine aspect to Saturn in the Seventh House of partnerships ❸. She was also idealistic and very open to seduction, as indicated by the opposition to ❹ Neptune in Libra, the sign of partnerships.

What was her relationship to his father, indicated by the position of the Sun? We see that the Sun ❺ is in Capricorn and conjunct Mars in the Twelfth House, which shows a conservative and stable man who feels trapped in an unhappy life, but who has hidden desires to change, is highly fated, and is also open to seductive situations, shown by its square to Neptune. Both the Moon and the Sun are aspected to the idealistic Neptune, and the Sun and Neptune are in the Twelfth and Eighth Houses, both of which are hidden and secretive. I came to the conclusion that their relationship was initiated by his mother, and that his father was already married and wanted it to be a secret. Although the Moon, his

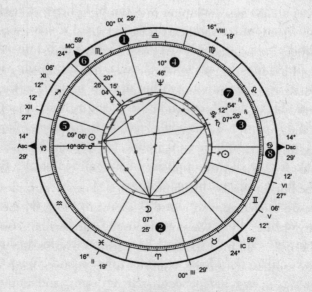

FIGURE 2.2: STRANGE RELATIONSHIPS

The numbers in circles correspond to the interpretation in the text.

mother, is below the horizon, showing that she is quite self-centered and unconscious in her actions, it is not in one of the "hidden" houses.

How did his conception happen? The conception point itself ❶ is in the sign Scorpio, which shows separation, deep and powerful passions, and a secretive nature. With Neptune just before the conception point, they could have been inebriated when the conception happened, as Neptune also governs alcohol, drugs, fantasy, dreams, and altered states. It may have been a combination of these factors. Mother brought Father to her and the conception occurred.

The Midheaven, which is the beginning of the Tenth House at the top of the horoscope ❻, shows the moment when his mother realized she was pregnant. This is also in the separate and hidden sign Scorpio and only aspected by the two planets on either side of it, Jupiter and Venus. As Jupiter in gestation is often a doctor and Venus is friends of the mother, I reasoned that his mother was isolated when she realized she was pregnant and kept it a secret. If there had been an aspect to the Sun from the Midheaven time, I would have thought she would have told the father, but she didn't.

By my reading of the situation, the father discovered he had fathered the child only five weeks before the birth, at the Sun ❺ in the Twelfth House. It was undoubtedly a confrontation due to the difficult and tense square aspect to the Moon. Because Mars follows the Sun in the Twelfth House, often shows action motivated by a desire to change, and is also in aspect to Pluto ❼, the transformative planet, in the Seventh House of partnership, I assumed that the father decided to leave his existing relationship and go with the mother of his child. And this is exactly what happened in the weeks before the child was born.

The look on the host's face confirmed the accuracy of the reading, even though it was highly compacted and distinctly not ther-

apeutic, like my usual approach. In short, he was instantly con-
verted from a skeptic to an advocate of my methods, although I
also think he was petrified that I would mention something of this
adventure on live television some moments later!

The final implication that turned him toward me was that I
wanted to bring his history up to date in his life. Because such early
events often form patterns that we repeat without realizing it, I
looked for a time when a similar dynamic existed in his more recent life. I therefore stated that at the exact opposite time of his
Capricorn Sun in the Twelfth House—just below the Descendant
on the right side of the horoscope—at the age of twenty-one ❽ he
was in a relationship and conceived a child with another woman.
When I said this, his face contorted in an incredible way as he
mutely confirmed my analysis. I had uncovered not one, but two
potent family secrets.

When we went onto live network television moments later, he
suddenly became an advocate of astrology and its accuracy, to the
extent that the BBC criticized his handling of what was supposed
to be a program denigrating astrology and astrologers.

I include this story not to show that astrology holds power, but
that the accuracy of reconstructing a life can bring up influences
that are not common knowledge, despite our resistance. This is
even more the case when events happen in our early life that our
parents either refuse to tell us or have kept as family secrets. Ironically, we must understand the power of our past in order to live in
the present.

THREE

THE NEW ASTROLOGICAL COSMOLOGY

Astrology *(astro-logos)* means "knowledge of the stars." However, what does this mean? Newspaper astrology simply correlates each zodiac sign with birth dates during the year. Astrology translates the earth's movement relative to the stars into a system of timings that determine the unfolding of events. But we understand little of the mechanism, dynamics, or realities of time, which is at the root of how we perceive our lives.

I discovered a revealing symbolic key to the mystery of time in the frontispiece of a book by the astrologer and mystic Robert Fludd, first published in 1617 (Figure 3.1). *The History of the Macrocosm* illustrates an essential principle of astrology: "As above, so below," or "The microcosm is the macrocosm." In the image, a man crosses a circle labeled the "Microcosm," which means the "small world" or the "inner world."[6] To the right and left of his head are the Sun and Moon upon concentric circles of the seven ancient planets and the four elements (fire, air, earth, and water); at the periphery are the twelve signs of the zodiac. The zodiac and the planets are a miniature solar system that we carry within us.

The outer circle, labeled the "Macrocosm," is the "large world" or simply "the universe." Outside is a circle of the fixed stars of the zodiac belt. Within are the Sun and Moon and the concentric cir-

FIGURE 3.1: MACROCOSM AND MICROCOSM

This seventeenth-century frontispiece shows a human as reflecting the microcosm within and the macrocosm outside.

cles of the planets and the elements. They constitute the solar system that contains us. The inner world of the microcosm and the outer world of the macrocosm reflect and mirror each other. This relationship symbolizes our idea of astrology. However, it is not only a metaphor for our relationship with the world, but also a literal description of it.

The key to Fludd's image is the angel in the upper-right corner. He carries symbols of the planet Saturn, the planet that governs time. He has goat feet (associated with the zodiac sign Capricorn, ruled by Saturn), a sand clock (time as Kronos) surmounted by a medieval version of the Saturn symbol as a crown. He is an emissary of time who tells us that time is the key that connects the microcosm to the macrocosm. The rope he pulls expresses this metaphor: It is a spiraling cord that encircles the macrocosm and microcosm four times. *This spiral cord binds the microcosm to the macrocosm, and is symbolic of the movement of the solar system and the DNA molecule.*

THE SPIRALS OF LIFE

When we imagine what the solar system looks like, what do we see? We probably picture the Sun sitting in space with planets orbiting around it in their regular cycles. In this classical image, Earth encircles the Sun and returns to its original place, marking a year. In reality, this image of the solar system is not the case: The Sun does not just sit motionless in space, but moves through space and time at a phenomenal velocity.

The Sun orbits around the galactic center (currently in the direction of 29° Sagittarius) within one of the spiral arms of the Milky Way galaxy, about three-quarters of the way from the center (Figure 3.2). The Sun travels approximately half a million miles every day, at a velocity of more than 20,000 miles an hour, dragging its entire planetary system along with it. We move very rapidly through space and time.

Rather than the planets making elliptical orbits around the Sun, they trace spiral paths around its central filament as they move through time and space. This spiral movement of the solar system is "the long body of the solar system." Its complex spiral looks like a step-down transformer, converting cosmic energy and information from the galactic center to the coiled cycles of the planets. In Figure 3.3, Mercury is the closest planet to the Sun,

Our Solar System is here

FIGURE 3.2: SOLAR SYSTEM IN THE MILKY WAY

Our sun is in one of the spiral arms of the Milky Way galaxy, three-quarters of the way out from the galactic center.

then Venus, and then Earth—each corkscrew cycle it makes around the Sun measures one year along the Sun's path. Between Mars and Jupiter is the asteroid belt of random bodies, surrounded by the sweeping motion of the outer planets Saturn, Uranus, Neptune, and Pluto.

Einstein transformed our awareness by stating that the universe is not three-dimensional but has a fourth dimension: time. Previously, the relativity of space and time was the province of mystics.

The DNA molecule is a spiraling double helix that makes a pattern similar to the movement of the solar system through time. This

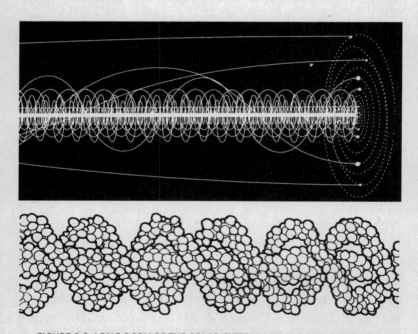

FIGURE 3.3: LONG BODY OF THE SOLAR SYSTEM AND THE DNA MOLECULE

The solar system (above) makes a spiral in time. This shows thirty years. A horoscope is a slice through this spiraling pattern at the moment of birth, its angle reflecting the exact place and time. The DNA molecule (below) is a double-helix spiraling around a central core, very much like the outer planets wandering around the tighter spiral of the inner planets.

early model of the helix shows a central core surrounded by twin he-lixes, which reminds us of the inner planets Mercury through Jupiter, which are separated by the asteroid belt from the outer planets. The parallel is further supported because the DNA molecule—made up of twelve components, four acid bases in three different forms—is similar to the zodiacal language of four elements in three modes.

The spiral cord evokes both these images that inform our new worldview: It is the spiraling solar system in time, the planets mak-ing their spiral orbits around the central filament of the Sun, and it is the spiral DNA molecule in every living cell. By a process called *resonance,* oscillating systems with similar frequencies con-tinuously exchange information instantaneously. The spiral solar system moving through time exchanges information with the DNA molecule within every living cell, tapping us into cosmic consciousness. We carry a miniature solar system within us that provides us with a link to the cosmos.

When we honor what is within us, our true essential self, we re-ceive information from the cosmos and act upon it—we are in tune with the world. When we withdraw from or lose our inner connectedness—through the demands of our society, urban habits, a distorted sense of self or relationship, ignorance of the natural world, or other reasons—we lose this essential contact and are out of tune with the world. Indeed, the word *disease* means a lack of ease with the world. We are sensitive to the cosmic forces around us, and mystics throughout history have felt this guidance. Physi-cist and astronomer Dr. Percy Seymour believes that "changes in the Earth's magnetic field have a direct and immediate effect on the birth process and our subsequent lives."[7]

Our horoscope is a plane that slices through the spiraling solar system at the time of our birth, tilted to reflect where and when we were born. This is the datum plane of our entrance into the world. The spiral movement of the Sun and planets moves backward into the past to our conception and even before that into the ovum's existence within the mother's life. It moves forward into our life, creating experiences until we reach the present time, the moving edge of the solar system, and the "surface of consciousness." This is where we create reality at this moment. To interpret later events, astrologers compare the birth horoscope to slices taken at subsequent times. We can see that our lifetime occupies a section of the spiraling movement. *Our life is a process in time,* measured by the spiraling solar system and its planetary cycles.

At conception, our soul enters the space-time continuum of the material world and for the duration of our lifetime we are subject to the laws and conditions of Earth incarnation, until we leave the body at death and our soul is liberated and returns to eternity. Astrology is a study of the sequence of events and influences that happen throughout this temporal process. Our new vision of astrology is unique in understanding life as a spiraling process in time, rather than the traditional view of the horoscope as a static symbol of our life. This transforms our relationship to time and space.

When I first read about astrology, I had to ask the question: Do all of our traits and patterns come into being at birth? They are there in potential, but they unfold throughout our life process. We will learn to interpret the planets, signs, and houses in a similar way to traditional astrology, but we will order the events of our life in time. This crucial difference makes our vision unique and revolutionary, and more in accord with the most provocative visions of psychotherapy, which are called "process work." Since we remember the events of our lives chronologically rather than randomly, it makes sense to see our astrology this way. The question I would ask is not: Do you express Virgo traits? Rather, *when* in your life do the Virgo characteristics that are a part of you come into being?

Our being in time unfolds from its essence, contained in the birth horoscope, through the spiraling solar system, synchronized

FIGURE 3.4: HOROSCOPE AND THE HORIZON

The Rising Sign, or Ascendant (ASC), is on the left side. The horizontal line across the center is the horizon. Above the horizon is heaven (consciousness), below is earth (the unconscious). The houses are numbered counterclockwise from the ASC.

by the planets as they continue their movements around the moving Sun.

OUR HOROSCOPE ORIENTATION

The distribution of the planets around the horoscope wheel gives us a sense of our potential for growth. The horoscope shows the ground rules of his incarnation, what we came into the world carrying as a karmic and hereditary burden. The distribution helps us see when the stories and information that constitute the life process are originated and when they will recur. The more conscious we are, the more likely we are to value understanding our lives, while the more unconscious we are, the more likely we are to just live our lives. That is not a value judgment about these issues, but simply a statement about them.

It is important to understand the orientation of the horoscope in time and space. The degree of the zodiac on the eastern horizon that rises above the horizon at our birth is called the *Ascendant* or *Rising Sign.* In the horoscope it is always shown on the left. The Ascendant symbolizes our birth, appearance, and personality, and is our orientation to the counterclockwise zodiac ring. The houses of the horoscope are divisions of the circle numbered from One to Twelve in a counterclockwise direction, starting from the Ascendant at the left. The sign opposite our Ascendant is on the cusp (beginning) of the Seventh House to the right—and is the Descendant, where the sun sets in the evening.

In the Northern Hemisphere, the path of the Sun passes through the southern sky against the direction of the zodiac signs. If we look to the south, the Sun rises in the east to the left, arcs up into the sky to the south straight ahead, culminates at noon, and then wends its way downward to the west to the right. This path is the *ecliptic,* along which we measure the positions of the Moon and the planets. When we tilt our horoscope so that it corresponds to the plane of the Sun's daily path, the horizontal line across the chart from left to right is the horizon. Planets above the horizon are *conscious, direct, objective, external, and collective* influences. Planets below the horizon are *unconscious, indirect, subjective, internal, and personal* influences. The distribution of planets above and below shows the conscious/unconscious, objective/subjective, external/internal, and collective/personal balances in our life.

The upper half is the conscious domain. The topmost point is the position of the Sun at noon, when it is brightest and shines vertically through Earth's atmosphere. This is the Midheaven (abbreviated as MC, from the Latin *medium coeli,* which means "middle of the heavens"). The Midheaven as the ego is the center of consciousness and the organizing center of the conscious realm. Its opposite point at the bottom is the Bottom of the Heavens (abbreviated as IC, from the Latin *immum coeli*), the center of the unconscious domain.

There are two contrary movements in the horoscope diagram, like two wheels with a common center rotating in opposite directions. The planets move counterclockwise through the zodiac measuring wheel, sign by sign. The Ascendant and the houses are our daily diurnal movement, reflecting Earth's clockwise rotation. The Ascendant shows the relative orientation of the two wheels. It is like the combination of a safe: Our exact orientation at birth helps unlock our psyche and our life.

FOUR

BIOLOGICAL TIME AND MEMORY

Time moves at different rates for each of us. It is that simple.

ALBERT EINSTEIN

W e know that our life is a linear process from birth to death and from cause to effect, but we remember our past randomly. This random temporal dynamic creates emotional eddies in our life that we need to work with. *We live and we also reflect upon living.* We are often so immersed in the day-to-day flow of our lives that we do not see the longer and broader canvas of our life as a whole.

To see our life pattern clarifies the relationship between our elusive past and our uncertain future. Although our past has already happened, we can always learn to understand or take advantage of it. We are always changing, because our perspective on life is always changing. This is not an option; we change whether or not we want to. It is not desirable to hold onto the past, and we are capable of using whatever its qualities were to grow and see. It is only when we crystallize and see our past as immutable that we stop changing and therefore stop living. Change is life.

I was fortunate to have read Rodney Collin's *The Theory of Celestial Influence* before I learned astrology. A central theme is the concept of biological time. This idea resonated with me because even then, in my late twenties, I felt that time was accelerating, and I could not understand why. I noticed that my time sense changed when I took in alcohol or stimulants, or experienced sad or exciting emotional events. Even sports stars talk about time slowing down in their peak moments of competition. Time seemed to have an elasticity that I had never heard explained.

Biological time is an essential yet almost unknown principle: Our metabolism governs our perception of the passage of time. Have you noticed that time passes faster as you age? Do you remember days at primary school that lasted forever? Do you remember when a day seemed to last an eternity? Are you now aware of how much faster time seems to be accelerating as you age? Have you experienced time distortions? There are reasons why we all experience these states of mind.

Clocks measure "objective" time in seconds, minutes, hours, and days. We say objective, meaning that while all clocks measure the passage of time at the same rate, they agree only with each other, not with us. We have inner biological and psychological clocks that have their own perceptions of the passage of time and deliver those perceptions to us. We constantly compare our inner perceptions of the passage of time with clocks, but our time sense is always changing. It sometimes seems that time is running away from us as we age. The way we perceive time profoundly affects how we live our lives.

As we age, our metabolism slows down, modulated in local rises and falls. Our metabolism slows down from conception to death, modulated locally and temporarily by our eating habits, our biological functions, our psychological perspective, and other factors. When we eat, digestion slows our entire body down. When we exercise, our metabolism speeds up. Cigarettes temporarily accelerate our metabolism. A faster metabolism is concomitant to early life, so stimulants make us temporarily feel that we are younger than we are. This may be why it is so easy to become addicted to tobacco, caffeine, and other stimulants.

We are subject to rapid changes within the womb during gestation. After birth, we are subject to longer growth cycles through adolescence and then a gradual crystallizing of life into the longer decades of adulthood. According to our biological clocks, our time sense is inversely proportional to our metabolism. When in early life our metabolism is fast, time passes slowly; as we age and our metabolism slows down, our time sense accelerates and compacts more and more until in middle age it is flying and in old age is passing by faster than we can keep track of it.

Among the many psychological implications of the acceleration of time is that the early stages of our life occupy proportionally greater importance in the whole. Because our metabolism is so fast and our time sense elongates in childhood, early events carry more energy, appear to last longer, and have a relatively greater importance in our psychological and emotional lives than do later events. Ironically, very few of us remember anything before the age of four or five, yet those earliest events carry the most powerful psychological changes.

When we divide an average lifetime of approximately seventy-seven years into three perceptually equal parts reflecting biological time, they are gestation, childhood, and maturity; we will call them *octaves*. Our time perception compacts logarithmically, so that the sequence of 1, 10, 100, and 1000 is equal to the arithmetic scale 1, 2, 3, and 4. Log scales are used to describe progressions that mul-

28 days	280 days	2,800 days	28,000 days
1LM	10LM	100LM	1000LM
Conception	Birth	7 years	77 years
	GESTATION	*CHILDHOOD*	*MATURITY*

FIGURE 4.1: THE LOGARITHMIC PROGRESSION OF LIFE

The three stages of life in perceptual time: gestation, childhood, and maturity. Each octave is ten times longer than the preceding one.

tiply radically in time, like population, the accelerated usage of energy, the number of cars, etc. We grade our accelerating life process according to the scale of 1, 10, 100, and 1000 lunar months. Figure 4.1 shows our perception of time throughout life.

One lunar month after conception our fertilized embryo has attached itself to the uterine wall and our cellular body develops. We create a physical body within our mother during the ten lunar months (nine calendar months) of the octave of gestation. We create our personality, which is an emotional body, within our home and family system, during the 100 lunar months or seven years of the octave of childhood. We create our mental body during the octave of maturity, which lasts from the end of childhood until death, whenever it occurs.

To apply biological time scale to astrology, we take the linear time scale of life and wrap it around the horoscope circle. Our starting point is the Ascendant on the eastern horizon at birth, which is the birth moment. Indeed the Ascendant is a clock pointer that stops at the birth moment, determining the orientation of the twelve houses of the horoscope to the zodiac wheel of signs. When we apply the three octaves of our time scale around the horoscope in a counterclockwise direction, we associate the first octave of childhood with the first four houses, which are associated in turn with the signs Aries, Taurus, Gemini, and Cancer. The second octave of maturity corresponds to the second four houses and their associated signs: Leo, Virgo, Libra, and Scorpio. At the end of the Scorpio time is the death point in the time scale. The octave of gestation happens before birth, and therefore we must go back from the Ascendant point clockwise one-third of the way around the horoscope circle. Gestation is the Ninth through the Twelfth Houses, associated with the signs Sagittarius, Capricorn, Aquarius, and Pisces.

What is fascinating is that the death point is at the end of Scorpio, the astrological sign associated with death and dying, while the beginning of Sagittarius is the astrological sign associated with rebirth. When I began studying astrology, this fact made great sense, because I had wondered why the sign Scorpio seemed to refer to death and the end of life, while it was only two-thirds of the way through the signs. An organization using the biological time scale answers this question nicely. The cusp of the Ninth House is therefore the death and conception point.

This image (Figure 4.2) is intriguing because the conception point (at the upper right) at the beginning meets the death point at the end of the life process. Are conception and death related to

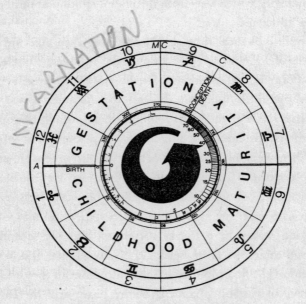

FIGURE 4.2: THE TIME SCALE OF LIFE

This figure shows the logarithmic time scale wrapped around the horoscope. Conception is at the upper right, birth at the left, and childhood and adolescence below the horizon. The Descendant at the right is about twenty-three years old, and we return to the Ninth House cusp, which is the archetypal death point. Planets in the horoscope can be dated using this wheel.

each other? They are, and in profound ways, even to the extent that a French paraphrase for an orgasm is the "little death."[8] At the moment of conception and fertilization of the ovum a pattern comes into being in time that expresses the future of our life. Apart from the genetic implications, this pattern in time also functions on spiritual, soul, and etheric levels.[9] At that moment our life is all potential. It is known that many people who have come close to experiencing their death have seen their life pass before their eyes in an instant. This is a dramatic replay of our life that has already finished, a "last judgment."[10] When we die our life has finished, all our potential has been used, and it is all actual. In our analogy, the life process moving around the horoscope circle of houses from conception to death is making our potential into our actual reality. So the death and conception point are the flip sides of the same phenomenon, outside of time. This image of a circle linking conception and death is like the mystical, alchemical figure of the ouroboros snake biting its tail.

When we superimpose the three octaves of the biological time scale over the astrological horoscope, we must grade the four houses that occupy each of the three octaves logarithmically. When we do this, we can determine an approximate or average time when each house *registers,* or comes into being. It is in the nature of a logarithmic scale that each house from conception to death is longer than the previous houses. In this way, as we move around the circle, each house takes almost as long as the entire preceding journey back to conception. In each house we get to recapitulate all previous development before we move on to the next developmental stage. Since our early biological development is extremely rapid and we slow down as we age, taking longer and longer to experience each stage of life, this sequence makes sense. And as we move through life, the stages of being get longer and longer, but due to the compaction of perceptual time, we seem to fly through life.

Since the houses in the horoscope are rarely equal due to the elliptical shape of Earth and our birth location, these dates are general, particularly the end point. Since it is a logarithmic scale we can continue spiraling around the wheel. We all live through the same developmental stages, but at different rates.

Psychologists agree that the importance of childhood emotional events warrants that we spend much therapeutic time attempting to reconstruct and remember that time. It is when our critical sensual, emotional, mental, and energetic patterns come into being before we are aware of them.[11] These primal patterns largely determine the way we are in the world. The integration of biological time and its implications for astrology opens a much more vivid and essential way of seeing our life in time that reflects the way we perceive time passing, and it restores the primacy of early events.

There are many conclusions we can draw from the application of biological time to astrology. In the early part of life, time seems to crawl by; it passes very slowly but is very intense. The shorter, early stages of life contain crucial perceptions that affect us in important ways. We exaggerate the importance and intensity of life events that happen then, yet we bury these memories in time. Since we remember little before the age of five years old, we tend not to know those very influences that have such a deep effect upon us. The hidden traumas and realities of childhood are the central subject matter of psychoanalysis and most psychotherapy. The deeper levels of gestation go further, deeper, and even more centrally into our core being, into what Jung called the collective unconscious.

The dynamics of the compaction of time affect the nature of life, how we live it, and how we remember it. Our time sense determines our life's passage and stores our dramatic moments in successive layers, stepping back through gestation to conception. Occasionally these deeper layers become available to us, but mainly we are subject to the seemingly random evocation of them in the context of later life events. In crisis, whether we want to or not, we revert to the awareness and psychology of certain earlier stages of our life, seemingly at random. Such events can even evoke the energy level of earlier years. Raising our children sometimes evokes the inner child in us and reveals our own hidden childlike energies. Understanding these mechanisms and dynamics of time reveals a mystery we benefit from knowing.

The three octaves of life represent levels of being in the sense that they are densest in the beginning and then gradually less dense as we age. It is like a three-act play in which we, as the central character, do not even appear until the curtain of the second act rises, at birth. In gestation, while our physical body is created, we have virtually no say in what happens to us; it is all in the hands, emotions, and psyches of our parents. The influences that register here in the form of planets in that part of our horoscope indicate people who affected our mother while she carried us, the events that ensued from those interactions, and the implications of this upon our being. As we do not yet have a personality, which comes into being at birth, these patterns are stored within our body. In computer language, it is the hard-wiring of our life, the etched passages that energy and emotional patterns take within us. We consider these influences our instincts or deepest urges. For example, if our mother is embarrassed to be pregnant and hides throughout the gestation, we would naturally be embarrassed about our body and find that we tend to hide our creative urges. This tendency would be amplified if the Moon, which is our mother, is near the planet Saturn, which tends to inhibit and make more serious anything it touches. The resultant shyness and reserve would thus be deeply rooted in our being and function like an instinct. When pressed, we would withdraw from physical encounters.

I noticed the implications of such influences when my own daughter's gestation coincided with my learning astrology. It was a dynamic and changeable time, with the need for continual clarifications of relationship. It is therefore not surprising that she now considers relationship as an area that requires constant emotional reevaluation.

The physical body created in gestation is the densest body, the most tangible, the one over which we have the least control. Our emotional body, which we call the personality and create during childhood, is less dense. Our emotions can change more easily than our physical being, shape, or appearance, and are therefore more flexible and less tangible. And being a higher body, our emotions can control our physical body. The mental body that we create during maturity is less dense than our emotional body because our ideas can change even more easily and more flexibly than our emotions. Even when we believe that we have our emotions "under control," something happens that shows us that we do not. Conversely, our mind is capable of controlling both our emotions and our physical body. As we go from denser to finer bodies, we also find they are more and more powerful and pervasive.

Our new vision of astrology entails going down to the beginning and recreating our life process from conception (and before). We reconstruct our life from the events leading up to our parents' relationship at conception and then into our life. We recreate our life in the same sequence in which it is lived, although because of the geometrical relationships within the circle, there are various harmonies and discordances between events in our life and their equivalent times. We discover not only the sequential process of our life, but also the resonances and harmonies inherent in it.

THE THREE OCTAVES

The three perceptually equal octaves are *gestation*, from conception to birth, *childhood*, from birth to seven years old, and *maturity*, from seven years old to death.

Gestation

Gestation is the development of our cellular body within our mother. Our father and mother make love at conception to create us. The sperm travels along its path to the womb, where it encounters the egg. After fertilization, which is typically from twenty-four to forty-eight hours after the act of conception, the fertilized ovum travels up the fallopian tube and embeds itself in the wall of the mother's uterus. In the early stages of gestation, we pass rapidly through many primitive stages of evolution, repeating the entire evolutionary process in the womb. The genetic code directs the development of our cellular body, while our mother surrounds us and simultaneously affects us. We absorb everything she thinks, feels, intuits, and senses while she carries us. Of course, we also have a reciprocal effect upon her. Gestation has four stages:

- How our mother conceives us and realizes that she is pregnant (*in the Ninth House, related to Sagittarius,* and from conception to seven weeks after conception);

- How she becomes conscious of the process, how others (such as our father) react to her pregnancy, and our parents' ability to organize things in the physical world (*in the Tenth House, related to Capricorn,* and from seven weeks after conception until thirteen weeks after conception);

- Our mother's ideals, wishes, and aspirations that affect us within her (*in the Eleventh House, related to Aquarius,* and from thirteen weeks after conception until twenty-three weeks after conception);

- Our mother's ability to accept her fate, to express her inner life, the psychic contact between mother and child, and our sensitivity to outer situations in the world (*in the Twelfth House, related to Pisces,* and from twenty-three weeks after conception until birth).

Each house of gestation also represents a biological phase of development and its associated higher function. Since this is the creation of our physical body, all the events of gestation are stored in our body as instinctive patterns or ways of being. This is the deepest and most powerful level of being within us and also the one over which we have the least memory or control.

Birth and Childhood

At birth, we come out of our mother into the world. Birth corresponds to the Ascendant, or Rising Sign, which rises on the eastern horizon with the Sun in the morning. This corresponds to the persona, the mask or face we present to the world. The personality also includes the mechanism by which we express ourselves in the world, based on our appearance, our way of acting, how we feel about others, and the environment that we either attract or create. The birth process corresponds to the dynamic mechanism of our personality. The zodiac sign on the Ascendant is the environment into which we are born, and any planets that are either near the Ascendant or in geometric aspect to it qualify it. The more planets we have in connection to the Ascendant, the more complex our personality.

Childhood typically lasts until we are about seven years old, during which time we create our personality within the structure of our home and family system. As the events during gestation affect and are embedded in our physical body, so the events during childhood affect and are mechanisms of our emotional body. This is an accumulation of four stages.

- How we bond with our mother (*in the First House, related to Aries,* and from birth until seven months old);

- How we come into contact with the physical world when we begin crawling (*in the Second House, related to Taurus,* and from seven months old until one year and eight months old);

- How we learn to walk, talk, communicate, and express ourselves instinctively (*in the Third House, related to Gemini,* and from one year eight months old until three years and four months old);

- How we begin to discover and either identify with or rebel against our family structure (*in the Fourth House, related to Cancer,* and from three years and four months old until seven years old).

Throughout childhood, we learn the nature of the emotional patterns that define our family system and the effects these have on our personality, our degree of self-esteem, and how we relate to our parents. This octave typically ends not when we enter school, but when we begin to make relationships outside of the family.

Maturity

In maturity, we gradually leave the family system. In the
early stages we go to school to learn about ourselves and
our society. We combine our instinctual ways of being
of the physical body in gestation with our developing emotional
personality from the childhood octave. Here we combine them
with a mental body, attempt to integrate the three bodies into a
whole, and work out our various possibilities in the world up to
our death. We create this mental body in the world, with which we
create a worldview, an occupation, family, and other interests, and
live our life. The four stages of maturity are:

- We leave home for our primary-school education and
  learn to play games, to exteriorize ourselves, and to express our intentions (*in the Fifth House, related to Leo*, and
  from seven years old until thirteen years old);

- We go to secondary school, develop an attitude to our
  body and sexuality at puberty, experience college and our
  first jobs (*in the Sixth House, related to Virgo*, and from
  thirteen years old until twenty-three years five months
  old);

- We form permanent relationships in our occupation and
  intimate contracts such as marriage, have family, and
  focus upon career (*in the Seventh House, related to Libra*,
  and from twenty-three years and five months old until
  forty-two years old);

- From midlife, we gradually detach from life, work with
  the metaphysical, disengage from the world through the
  diminishing of our senses in old age, and prepare for the
  end of life (*in the Eighth House, related to Scorpio*, and
  from forty-two years old until death).

The end of the octave of maturity is our death. It is appropriate that we return to the conception moment at death, symbolically. As conception is our entrance into the world, so our death is an exit from it. During the interim time we are subject to the laws of the physical world.

The three octaves describe our life in the world. In psychological terms, our gestation is a pre-personal realm of collective qualities—as Carl Jung called it, the "collective unconscious." Indeed the evolutionary process that we experience as our body evolves is similar to that of all other humans. As we create a personality based upon our appearance, our relationship to our parents, and the circumstances of our birth, our childhood is personal and self-conscious. Maturity presents opportunities for extending ourselves in the world and is the super-conscious.

Transcendence

There is a fourth octave beyond the first three. If we have the urge, opportunity, or instinct to go beyond ourselves, we enter the transcendent octave. In order to gain access to this realm we must metaphorically die or at least experience going beyond our body. This may be through a religious experience, a transcendent experience via hallucinogenic plants or drugs, a near-death experience, or an accident or near-fatal injury, or it can happen through meditation, enlightenment, or realization. The transition is what we used to call an initiation into the higher realms. Indeed, the influences in transcendence are the higher octave of the gestation influences. The pattern of influences of our mother carrying us within her reactivates itself on a higher level. It is as though we expand the metaphor of her carrying us inside her to include our own reality of carrying a potential higher self within, one that we must birth into the world. It is also a sym-

bol and metaphor for our creativity. We create as we were created.
If our mother resisted being pregnant when she carried us, we tend
to resist birthing our inner expectations and creativity. What is fascinating is that the events of our earliest time resonate so strongly
with the events that transcend time itself.

The pattern of the transcendent octave is as follows:

- We access the higher conception point as our initiation
  into higher realms *(in the higher Ninth House of Sagittarius)*.

- We communicate and express our higher goals and objectives of ego consciousness *(in the higher Tenth House of
  Capricorn)*.

- We join groups of like-minded people, organize, and
  share our realizations with our world *(in the higher
  Eleventh House of Aquarius)*.

- We finally withdraw from the outer world into a more
  meditative and solitary life of reflection *(in the higher
  Twelfth House of Pisces)*.

Conception and death are the boundaries of our life
in time, and it is ironic and symbolically critical that we
see them as being connected. At conception, our reality
is potential—we have not yet realized any of our potential. We activate an incarnation code of our astrological life in time that corresponds to the awakening of the genetic code that engineers the
creation and maintenance of our physical body. The two are parallel and resonate with each other, one in the material and one in the
immaterial realm. At death, many individuals experience a highly
condensed version of their entire life passing before their eyes. This
is what has been described as the near-death experience by people
who have almost died and returned, and may be what ancient cul-

tures was called the "last judgment." At the death moment, we have realized all of our potential: We have lived our life. Any moment during life is a translation of our potential into our actual reality. It is as though we are transforming our potential life into consciousness through living. A new vision of astrology takes this view as axiomatic and central, like the ouroboros snake biting its tail. Life is cyclical, circular, and eternal, and the image reflects all of these simultaneous realities.

A good way to understand this involves seeing the two-dimensional horoscope circle as it functions in three dimensions. If we extend the horoscope circle along its axis in time, it becomes the cylinder of life. As Figure 4.3 shows, the cylinder starts at conception at the bottom, and as we move around the horoscope circle in a counterclockwise direction, so we spiral up and around the cylin-

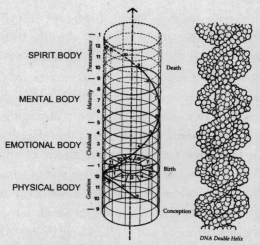

FIGURE 4.3: CYLINDER OF LIFE AND THE DNA MOLECULE

When the horoscope is tilted horizontally and projected into a cylinder, it forms the Cylinder of Life. From the birth layer one-quarter of the way up we go down to conception at the bottom. As we age, the cylinder fills with memories. Our present experience is the surface of the memories. The planets continue their journey spiraling up the cylinder as we age, resembling the DNA molecule shown on the right.

der of life. As we age, we spiral around the cylinder and stack our experiences as new layers. Our memories exist within us as layers, the lowest being also the deepest memories from conception. The slice that corresponds to our current age is the surface of the cylinder and the surface of consciousness. Our past lies beneath the present moment.

I liken the cylinder of an unexamined life to a transparent fish tank containing murky and unclear water. The further down to the bottom, the denser the body and the more opaque the waters. When we start to explore ourselves, we immediately look into our past to discover the source of our own behavior. Working with ourselves by delving deeply back into our life, we dredge up parts of our past, bring them into consciousness, and in the process clarify them. Eventually we can see the clear foundation of our entire life process in time.

Psychotherapy postulates dipping down into the cylinder to retrieve memories and then bringing them up to the surface of consciousness as we process them. We start with recent memories that are close to the surface and bring them up into the light of day. As we continue, we go deeper and deeper, further and further back, to our earliest memories. Once we have gone as far back as we can in remembering actual memories, we enter a domain of our parents' stories, what I call the "foundation mythology" of our life. Such myths, as Jung understood, often resonate with the myths of all humanity. We can learn about the deepest levels of our own psyche by studying the myths of all cultures, and astrologers have developed mythological astrology to a sophisticated degree.[12] It is not accidental that this part of the horoscope, the gestation time, is unique to our new vision of astrology, and corresponds to Jung's collective unconscious, the common inheritance of all humanity.

The way the planets are arranged in our chart gives rise to the density of each octave, the general distribution of qualities within the life phases, and the equivalent bodies that dominate us. For example, many planets in gestation means we tend to prefer the formative and creative phase of activities, while childhood influences imply a more emotional nature. In maturity we are more mentally identified and rely more upon our relationships with others. The distribution of planets in octaves also shows us when in life our primary influences take place. We may be an early developer with many planets in gestation and early childhood, or a late developer with most planets in the maturity octave. Well-balanced individuals have some planets in every octave.

The gestation octave does double duty as the prototype of the octave of transcendence. Therefore we might explore the dynamics of that time more deeply. Having many planets in gestation implies that we come into the world with strong influences acting within us, and since gestation planets are stored physically and we tend to perceive them as instincts, they lie very deeply within us. Since gestation is when we are physically created, it is also the case that often people with many planets are very creative individuals and tend to have many children themselves; there is sometimes a compulsion to create that is characteristic of such people. On the other hand, when so many planets manifest so early, there may be few planets in childhood or maturity. This may help explain why many creative people lack adequate emotional skills or experience, or even the mental capacities necessary for technical or office work.

An abundance of planets in the earliest gestation octave also implies that there is a similar importance or impact of the spiritual or transcendent qualities of the higher potential of that time. We therefore find that many gestation planets show those for whom the spiritual life is paramount, even outweighing their life "in the world." Of course, it depends upon which planets are in that area and what they really mean.

FIVE

OUR HOUSE ORIENTATION

As we age our vantage point changes. We gestate within our mother, and she is our relative vantage point during that time, up to birth. She and our father may be twenty-three years old and at the beginning of their lives. As children we are embedded in our family, with its particular structure and set of values. We become adults, and our perspective is reversed when we become parents. This dramatically affects how we relate to our parents and to the parental principles within us.

We carry memories of all of these stages but often choose to see others and ourselves in ways that may or may not be in our best interests. We may be affected by traumatic events or relationships, dramatic times when certain traits were dominant. Such life influences often constitute blockages of energy from which we do not recover. If our father threatened us in early childhood, we could regard all authority figures and all men as threats to our safety; without realizing it, we could terrorize our partners or children, completing a strange loop. Our perspective changes, and we often do not recognize the origin of our own patterns. This is how we trap ourselves in life, yet understanding this fact provides us with the possibility of freedom.

Our life process defines us, while our experiences, stories, and texts provide the fabric we continuously weave. The three-act drama of our life opens with our conception, a seminal moment between our parents that affects our own relationships profoundly. During gestation we are within and totally subject to the feelings and inner attitudes of our mother. She even qualifies the role of our father: It isn't who he is during gestation that matters to us, but who she thinks and feels he is. At birth, we arrive on the stage to play our role. The manner of our birth entrance, the way our parents acknowledge and accept us, are crucial factors in determining our specific role in the family system. We may be wanted or not, loved or not, attended and nurtured or not. We create a personality, a way of being that is either supported by our family system or not, and start immediately to prepare to leave the system. In the third act of maturity, we leave the family system by going to school, experience higher education and the choices that attend adolescence and early adulthood, and then make the binding choices of our occupation, partnerships, and worldview that will define us for the remainder of the drama.

What is important to know about this drama is that we have successively more flexible options about how to be and how to understand the context, if we can only first see and then go beyond our early conditioning. Many of us simply repeat the same early patterns that trapped us in childhood. Sometimes we live our lives without understanding the plot at all; indeed, we may feel subject to the plotting of others. Some of us are stifled by the role we have chosen to play, or feel it has been imposed upon us; others learn to play their parts so well that they transcend the part and become more universal. Still others become directors affecting the lives of those around them, or producers, taking charge of larger aspects of the drama, penetrating its mysteries and participating well beyond their individual personalities. The choice is up to us.

The houses are the context of the stories we tell about ourselves as a way to identify who we are. It is how we carry our history. Maybe our memory is who we are. Astrology is the language of our life history, its characters and their unfolding through time. If we are archetypal, we have Aries on the Ascendant at birth, Taurus qualities in the Second House, Gemini qualities in the Third House, etc. In reality only one in twelve people have Aries rising. Our personality as indicated by the Ascendant sign determines our specific relationship of the signs in the houses. In the following section we will see the qualities of each Ascendant sign in turn and how the signs affect the sequence of houses. We will use our own horoscope to explore our house orientation.

Our birth horoscope remains the same throughout our life, but our vantage point changes. We see the same circle from a succession of different angles. I consider this our *age point* in life. Although we are a certain age at this moment, in understanding ourselves we must learn to adopt the perspective of previous ages and times in our life, and indeed future ages and times. As we age from conception, this moving age point starts at conception on the beginning cusp of the Ninth House and moves in a counterclockwise direction through the twelve houses. See, for example, Figure 5.1: At birth our age point is on the Capricorn Ascendant, at seven years old it is on the Fifth House cusp in the sign Gemini, and at twenty-three or so it is on the Seventh House cusp opposite the Ascendant in the sign Cancer, etc. The angle of our perspective is always changing. We see the same horoscope pattern from a succession of relative points of view.

As our age point moves around the circle, our viewpoint changes, and ultimately we see the horoscope and the planets embedded in it from every possible viewpoint as we complete the entire journey through life. This is activated throughout shorter cycles because after our birth all the planets continue moving

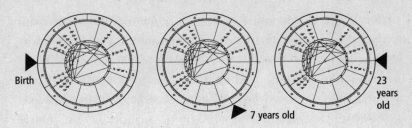

Birth   23
                                                         years
                                          ▶ 7 years old   old

FIGURE 5.1: RELATIVE VIEWPOINTS AROUND THE HOROSCOPE

At birth we see the horoscope from the Capricorn Ascendant at the left, at seven
years old from the Gemini sign at the lower right, and at twenty-three years old from
the Cancer quality at the right. We see and have the same horoscope, but see it from
different angles or sign perspectives as we age.

around the zodiac. The Moon makes a complete revolution every
lunar month and activates every viewpoint in our entire life from
an emotional view in that time, but the lunar months pass
quickly. Similarly, the Sun revolves every year, and we have the
opportunity to intellectually understand our process as it passes
through every sign, house, and planet around the horoscope
wheel. Each planet moves around the horoscope in its unique
cycle as *transits,* reactivating the events of our life. The web of
planets and their sensitive aspect points around the circle are activated in turn. We are always experiencing our entire life compacted into shorter cycles. We get to play them out many times
until we have learned our life lessons and connected with our
dharma.[13]

The duration of each house in the sequence changes, as they occupy successively more time. The houses in gestation last weeks; in
childhood they last years; and in maturity they last decades. Life is
cumulative, and as we age, memories of all our past experiences accumulate within our psyche, whether we are able to recall them or
not. In interpreting our horoscope we must bear this in mind. We
build the experience of each house upon a foundation of our expe-

riences from all previous houses. We remember earlier developments and incorporate them into new understanding, house by house. We never discard the old, as it becomes transformed as the foundation of the new. If we ignore our past, we risk building our reality upon an insecure foundation. The same is true for an interpretation.

THE ARCHETYPAL AGES OF THE HOUSES

Gestation: Physical Body within Our Mother

Ninth House (from conception to + 7 wks; 240°–270° from Ascendant)

After conception our mother gradually comes to realize that she is pregnant. Biologically our brain is created; we pass through early evolutionary stages until we become a fetus. Self-realization; higher mind; increased perception; religion and philosophy; wider relationships.

Tenth House (from + 7 wks to + 12 wks; 270°–300° from Ascendant)

Our mother has realized that she is pregnant and announces it to our father. Then our parents organize our coming into the world. Biologically our skeletal and organ systems develop. Structure; father; aspirations and success in the world; confronting reality.

Eleventh House (from + 12 wks to + 22 wks; 300°–330° from Ascendant)

We quicken, and our mother feels movement within; she is idealistic, and our parents project our future identity. Biologically our sympathetic and parasympathetic nervous systems are created. Stabilized reality; ideals, hopes, and aspirations; friends, groups, and idealistic relationships.

Twelfth House (from + 22 wks to birth; 330°–360° from Ascendant)

Mother gains weight, becomes isolated, and sacrifices herself for her child, preparing for birth. Biologically we gain water weight and our lymphatic system develops. Fulfilling dreams; fantasies; loneliness and isolation; fated relationships; weaknesses and dependency on others; sensitivity and frustration.

Childhood: Emotional Body within Our Family

First House (from birth to 7 mos; 0°–30° from Ascendant)

We are born, bond with our mother, and assert our personality in the family environment. We are breast fed and finally weaned. Self-assertion; personality; physical appearance and mannerisms; outward attitude.

Second House (from 7 mos to 1 yr 8 mos; 30°–60° from Ascendant)

We eat solid food, crawl, experience our senses, and explore the physical world, within which we are an object among other objects. Resources; our body; attitudes to possessions, property, money, security.

Third House (from 1 yr 8 mos to 3 yrs 6 mos; 60°–90° from Ascendant)

We begin walking and talking, gain mobility, and learn to communicate within the family. Brothers and sisters; instinctive mind and communication; immediate environment; relatives; short journeys; drawing.

Fourth House (from 3 yrs 6 mos to 7 yrs; 90°–120° from Ascendant)

We identify with parents, are aware of our home and family emotional system, our heredity and security. Parents; emotional set; deeper family relationships; grounding at home; life conditions.

Maturity: Mental Body within Our World

Fifth House (from 7 yrs to 13 yrs; 120°–150° from Ascendant)

We go to primary school, learn rules and games, play to exteriorize our self, identify with others outside the family. Children; teachers; education; games; pleasures, hobbies, and pursuing pleasures; entertainment and pets.

Sixth House (from 13 yrs to 23 yrs 5 mos; 150°–180° from Ascendant)

We go to secondary school and higher education, learn to control our bodies at puberty, discriminate, establish our health and work relationships. Service; craftsmanship; discrimination; health; work; illness.

Seventh House (from 23 yrs 5 mos to 42 yrs; 180°–210° from Ascendant)

We go out into the world to form career, partnerships, and family to establish our standing among the wider public. Harmony and integration; sublimation and partnership; marriage and children; enemies and protagonists.

Eighth House (from 42 yrs to death; 210°–240° from Ascendant)

We experience midlife crisis; children leave home; our twilight years; separation and the metaphysical. Old age and death; emotional and physical separation; others' resources; regeneration; losses, magic, and secrecy.

The *Ascendant* defines the relationship of the eastern horizon at birth to the zodiac. The rotation of house ages and twelve-sign qualities shows the permutations of viewpoints available to us. If we have Aries on the Ascendant at birth, we experience the sequence of houses synchronized with the traditional signs, as 0° Aries is on the Ascendant at sunrise on the Spring Equinox, but usually we have a unique Ascendant degree and sign. The archetypal arrangement of signs and houses aligning exactly we call the Natural Zodiac.[14] In this arrangement, we show Aries in the First House, Taurus in the Second House, Gemini in the Third House, etc. (See Figure 5.2.)

The twelve houses define our archetypal path from conception to death, although our individual qualities along that path change and are what define us as unique. The sequence of houses is the origin of the meanings of the twelve zodiac signs—both are a personal recapitulation of human history. Astrology mirrors this process in the yearly cycle in the twelve zodiac signs and houses. We will list, date, and explore the twelve houses and reveal their qualities.

The correlations are:

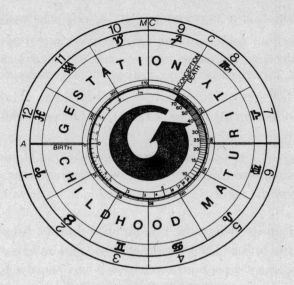

FIGURE 5.2: THE NATURAL ZODIAC

This shows the wheel of the houses from conception to birth and through child-hood to death. The signs are shown in their archetypal arrangement corresponding to the house locations. Inside the center is the dating wheel that shows when houses begin and end and that also can be used to date planetary positions within our life.

♈	Aries	First House
♉	Taurus	Second House
♊	Gemini	Third House
♋	Cancer	Fourth House
♌	Leo	Fifth House
♍	Virgo	Sixth House
♎	Libra	Seventh House
♏	Scorpio	Eighth House
♐	Sagittarius	Ninth House
♑	Capricorn	Tenth House
♒	Aquarius	Eleventh House
♓	Pisces	Twelfth House

In the following descriptions of the interpretation sequence of the twelve houses, we must realize that everyone experiences variations of the same sequence. We all experience the same set of cyclical house qualities that are phases of life, but at slightly different times in our lives and for slightly different durations, qualified by different signs of the zodiac. The Ascendant determines which signs correspond with which houses. In Figure 5.3, we can see that with Virgo on the Ascendant, Libra is in the Second House, Scorpio is in the Third House, etc., all the way around the horoscope. The sizes of the houses show us the dense and less dense times in life.

The signs that occupy each house are a primary influence on our character. Their quality provides the background framework of the development stages, into which we will later plug the ten planets. For a start, we will see the twelve Ascendant signs and the sequence of qualities on the twelve cusps for each type. In the example we are using, Virgo is the Ascendant. When we see the list of the house cusps and the sign cusps we notice that they alternate, and that we can see the ages at which each house and sign begin.

See the first page of your NewVisionAstrology printout, which looks just like the example in Figure 5.3. Scroll down the list until you come to the Ascendant. Following this is the month and year of your birth, and then the degrees and minutes and sign of your Ascendant. This is your Rising Sign. Following is a description of all twelve houses relative to each of the Rising Signs. To find your correct Ascendant in the list, refer to the printout, which will date the month and year when you entered each house. The sign immediately above it will correspond to those in the list.

Chapters 8, 9, and 10 provide more detailed descriptions of each of the twelve houses, their astrological meanings, and the significance of each sign in each house. Following each house description is a series of paragraphs that can identify how the signs

***0	**CUSP 9**	**MAY**	**1951**	**21.33**	**TAU**
***0	GEMINI	JUN	1951	00.00	GEM
***0	MC	JUL	1951	22.16	GEM
***0	CANCER	JUL	1951	00.00	CAN
***0	CUSP 11	AUG	1951	22.43	CAN
***0	LEO	AUG	1951	00.00	LEO
***0	CUSP 12	OCT	1951	22.55	LEO
***0	VIRGO	NOV	1951	00.00	VIR
***0	**ASCENDANT**	**FEB**	**1952**	**22.09**	**VIR**
***0	LIBRA	APR	1952	00.00	LIB
***0	CUSP 2	SEP	1952	21.02	LIB
***0	SCORPIO	DEC	1952	00.00	SCO
***0	CUSP 3	OCT	1953	21.33	SCO
***0	SAGITTA	MAR	1954	00.00	SAG
***0	CUSP 4	SEP	1955	22.16	SAG
***0	CAPRICO	MAY	1956	00.00	CAP
***0	**CUSP 5**	**FEB**	**1959**	**22.43**	**CAP**
***0	AQUARIUS	APR	1960	00.00	AQU
***0	CUSP 6	MAR	1965	22.55	AQU
***0	PISCES	MAR	1967	00.00	PIS
***0	CUSP 7	AUG	1975	22.09	PIS
***0	ARIES	JUL	1979	00.00	ARI
***0	CUSP 8	JUL	1993	21.02	ARI
***0	TAURUS	JUN	2001	00.00	TAU
***0	**CUSP 9**	**FEB**	**2027**	**21.33**	**TAU**
***0	GEMINI	JUN	2040	00.00	GEM

FIGURE 5.3: LIST OF HOUSE AND SIGN CUSPS

This list shows the house cusps from the conception point at the top. The Midheaven is in Gemini, the Eleventh House cusp in Cancer, the Twelfth House cusp in Leo, and the Ascendant in Virgo. Their dates are given by month and year. In the interpretation section in the text, read the zodiac sign qualities associated with each house cusp and see the duration of their influences. For example, in the Sixth House the time from March 1965 to March 1967 is Pisces, and the time from March 1967 to August 1975 is Aries.

modify the influence of the house. According to the sign on the cusp of the house or resident in the house, its planetary ruler or rulers refer us to other houses in refining their influences in a kind of cross-referencing that is characteristic of astrology. We are always linking different times in our life as a way to discover our energy life flow.

SIX

OUR CAST OF CHARACTERS

The sun signs are a series of types that underlie our behavior. We can know our type based on our time of birth. In this way astrology is a language that we can use to describe and explain behavior in a kind of shorthand. Once we know the language and share it with friends or family, the more we can express a wide range of qualities by talking about the "Gemini traits" someone is exhibiting. We come to know that Taureans are solid, material types, while Leos are gregarious, self-centered extroverts. The planets are also a typology. They describe ways of being, all of which everyone has. We all have a lunar dynamic that expresses our emotions and feelings, whether or not we have a close relationship with our mother or other women. If no women are present, we either project those emotional qualities on others, or discover them within.

The planets are the cast of characters in our life, and we experience them inside as well as outside. The Sun is our father and corresponds to the patriarchal, conscious, and objective part of us. The Moon is our mother and our emotional, unconscious, and subjective reality. The characters are parents, siblings, relatives, doctors, neighbors, friends, lovers, enemies, associates, partners, children, and everyone else of importance. Each character enters our life and plays his or her role, at a time corresponding to an equivalent planet's position in the horoscope.

Some roles are permanent, some elusive, some sporadic, but most are played by a succession of characters. The Sun is originally our father, and then might be one or both of our grandfathers; then he becomes a teacher or an employer, and then we become a father ourselves. Or, if you are a woman, you may marry the father of your children. All characters influence our whole being and play their part in forming our character. A key to the discovery of our essential nature is to identify and understand all the characters, their various guises, their times of appearance, and their meaning as they enter and leave our life. Each of the ten planets registers at a specific time, manifests through an outer event or an inner realization, and is carried by one or more characters. The event, the character, and their interaction are reflections of our being. All the planets are crucial parts of us.

In the following chapters you will see how the planets change their roles throughout your life. The Sun might be your father in gestation, grandfather or doctor in childhood, teacher or professor in adolescence, your husband or guru in maturity, and your son in old age. Shut your eyes, go inside in a meditative state, and visualize the people who have been most important in your life. Who are they?

Each important person in our life is reflected within us. We have an outer father, who raised us, but he also is reflected in our inner father. The father images reflect each other and affect our choice of male friends or partners, the nature of our conscious reality, and our objectivity. If we reject our father, we are rejecting the masculine and possibly the conscious side of our nature. If we are angry at our father, there is an inner anger that can affect our life profoundly, especially our dealings with authority or any value we perceive as masculine, and that anger is ultimately directed back into our self.

Our mother affects and is associated with our feelings, nurturing, and values in life, and our choice of female friends or partners. To the extent that we were nurtured and loved, we are able to express our own nurturing and love for others. If we feel detached from our mother, it often implies a detachment from our feeling nature.

When we relate to someone, we create an image of them within that reflects the way we see and feel them. Through time they and we change, mutual attitudes change, and our internal reflection of them changes. A central development in life is the balance of the way people really are as opposed to our attitude toward them. This mechanism is the origin of the work with the "inner child," for example. We all carry an inner child who often needs to be allowed out in order to express the freedom he or she signifies.

The planets are personality types or "subpersonalities."[15] They are inner or ideal models of the world that influence us and our perceptions. As Piero Ferrucci says, "For each of them we develop a corresponding self-image and set of body postures and gestures, feelings, behaviors, words, habits, and beliefs."[16] When our subpersonalities are active we stand differently, act differently, and behave according to their patterns. In astrology the eight planets, the Sun, and the Moon represent qualities we express in our life, as well as their equivalent subpersonalities. But, of course, they are always represented by the people in our lives, the "cast of characters." We learn about masculinity and male qualities through our relationship with our father, our grandfathers, and other men in our early life. Similarly, we learn about emotions and feeling from our mother, grandmothers, sisters, or other feeling relationships we have in life.

Indeed, in early years we project these qualities out of ourselves onto these crucial people. As we grow up, the way we see our father or mother is the way we see the principles of father or mother within our self, however distorted they may be. As we develop and mature, we gradually withdraw these projections back into ourselves, in a way taking our power back from our parents. We have then interiorized the qualities of "father" in the inner father in us, and we have taken the qualities of "mother" back into the inner, nurturing mother in us. This is why it is essential that, even if we have problems with a parent or even hate or blame a parent, we nonetheless maintain a relationship with our parents.

Some of the most powerful work we can do on ourselves is to first recognize and identify our various subpersonalities, their ways of being and their needs, and then learn to disidentify from them, which means to choose to not let them dominate our total self. We have ten planetary subpersonality mechanisms, and they naturally compete with each other to determine which one is dominant. This will result in a person who is perceived as being fatherly (Sun dominating), nurturing (Moon), angry (Mars), dominating (Pluto), loving (Venus), living in their head (Mercury), controlling (Saturn), eccentric or flaky (Uranus), sensitive (Neptune), religious and philosophical (Jupiter), or collaborative (North Node of the Moon), although these are simplifications.

It is useful to imagine a dinner table around which sit our subpersonalities. Father and mother, grandparents, siblings, friends, mates, children, doctors, therapists—they are all there together. They argue, discuss, negotiate, and bully each other continually. Our higher self is a higher organizing center that sits above the table, looking down onto the other personality mechanisms. The higher self is capable of choosing which subpersonality to allow to be dominant in the appropriate situations. When we need to think about things, it is appropriate to allow the Mercurial qualities to dominate, or when we need to defend ourselves to allow Mars to express its aggression, etc. This ability to act through choice rather than allow the mechanical, competitive nature of the subpersonality to dominate brings a new vision and integration into our life.

Since our life begins at conception, some of the central characters—our parents, family, and their friends—precede us onto the stage of life. Initially, they do not realize our potential existence and therefore play their parts uninfluenced by us. We have no control at all over those who determine the earliest and deepest levels of our identity—our parents—although there is a case to be made that we karmically choose our parents. A primary paradox of life is that by the time we think to question those who have affected our gestation and childhood, their influence is already past. It is a law that our parents and the events surrounding conception and gestation cannot be changed. Only our understanding of them and our attitude toward them can change. Our primary task is to put our past into perspective by determining who was present in our early life, how and why they behaved as they did, and what it all means.

Astrology provides us with a tool to reconstruct our story of these early times, but it is essential to realize that the therapeutic effect is in the process rather than in the answers. Knowing exactly what happened can pale in significance to understanding why it happened as it did, because these past events are essentially programming our behavior now. And we cannot be afraid of being wrong, especially in the beginning. Fortunately, I realized early on that in order to explore our lives in this way it was necessary to pose possible scenarios, to create probable stories, to model lives as best I could in order to be able to alter correct, modify, and edit them. We are trying to come to an experience of the life event, to be compassionate to the participants, whomever they are, and to pass through life without holding back or in. Sometimes being wrong can allow us to release powerful energies that would otherwise be tied up in being right. As I have come to see in relationships: Would you rather be right, or in a relationship?

The planets function as *archetypes* in a Jungian sense. Jung defined archetypes as patterning structures that carry and transform psychic energy, and symbolically express instinctive processes like love, hate, fear, flight, nurturing, and repulsion. We inherit these essential ways of being from all humanity, and they link us back (*religio,* in Latin) to humanity in expressing them in our lives. Instincts are channeled through each planet as an archetype. Each planetary archetype contains both positive and negative characteristics. Venus is loving, lovers, and the desire to integrate and be one with another but is also a rejection of relationship when it is badly aspected. Venus may also generate its opposite martial qualities in frustrated love, leading to anger and withdrawal.

The planets are associated with signs with which they are sympathetic. The planets rule signs and remain connected to them by similarity of quality. The Sun rules Leo, and both take on qualities of extroversion, energy, consciousness, optimism, and positivity. The Moon rules Cancer, as both are emotional and concern feelings, nurturing, and the feminine essence. Saturn is at home in Capricorn, as both are paternal, conservative, inward-looking, material, and restrained. The planets signify types of behavior that have even percolated into our language. We talk about people being martial, lunatic, saturnine, mercurial, plutonian, and so on. The planets combined with the signs make more specific traits clear and show us the finer points of our behavior. Each planet is in one of the twelve signs, each time modifying its action either by amplification or suppression.

These cartoon figures show general planetary correspon-

FIGURE 6.1: PLANET SUBPERSONALITIES

The planets are our subpersonalities, initially our family members and later aspects of us. These are archetypal images of the planets. *Drawings by John Astrop.*

Sun=Father   Moon=Mother   Mercury=Child
Venus=Sister Mars=Brother   Jupiter=Elder   Saturn=Elder
Uranus=Change   Neptune=Dreams   Pluto=Strife   Node-Group

dences within the family. The Sun is father; Moon, mother; Mercury, baby; Venus, sister; Mars, brother; Jupiter and Saturn, grandparents. The outer planets show generational influences: Uranus is explosive events; Neptune, sensitive situations; Pluto, forceful circumstances; and the Node, groups, including the whole family.

As we age and move through life, our attitudes toward our parents, friends, siblings, and others change as the people themselves change. Our movement through the succession of twelve houses is affected by their developmental qualities and the signs that occupy them. A planet is modified as its character changes according to the quality of the sign occupying the house. Venus in the Twelfth House could be a midwife or mother's friend in the time just before birth; Venus on the Ascendant could be a nurse or mother's helper; Venus in the Second House could be a favorite doll or toy; Venus in the Third House could be a sister or playmate; etc.

The house or residence changes the quality of events in addition to changing the character indicated by a planet. Since Venus is relationship, the house and age of Venus's registration qualifies the type of relationship in question. Venus in the Third House at two years old is communication with a sister or playmate, while

Venus in the Seventh House at thirty-two is a love relationship and a significator of our lover.

A planet's house position qualifies whoever carries its effect and the role it has to play within us. Early in life, events are most often caused by those around us; therefore, the planets are other people. Later in life, events are more likely to be a result of our own actions, if not directly caused by us, as well as being significators of the other participants. Mercury is our mental development but also those with whom we exchange ideas. Mars accidents would happen to us when the planet is in the Second House but would be caused by us in the Sixth House, and if we are injured, it can also be the instrument or person causing the injury. It is important to know whether we or others cause the critical events in life, even though we ultimately must take responsibility for them all. Our outer life always reflects and is echoed in our inner life.

The sign location of a planet qualifies its action and character. When the loving Venus is in Libra, the sign of partnership and balance, our relationships reflect that. But when Venus is in Aries, the sign of self-assertion and individuality, relationships are more difficult and we are often in conflict about whether or not our partner infringes on our freedom. The sign qualities further qualifies the house location of a planet.

Each planet rules a sign or signs and their equivalent house or houses. When a planet resides in the sign it rules, it functions at its purest and most archetypal. The Moon rules the sign Cancer and the Fourth House, both of which govern mother, home, family, and emotions. When we have the Moon in either of these positions, our maternal relationship is archetypal. Mercury rules the positive Gemini and the Third House of communication, walking, and talking, and the negative Virgo and the Sixth House of discrimination, criticism, and decision-making to define our position in the world.

Sign	Ruler	Detriment
♈ Aries	♂ Mars	♀ Venus
♉ Taurus	♀ Venus	♂ Mars and ♀ Pluto
♊ Gemini	☿ Mercury	♃ Jupiter
♋ Cancer	☽ Moon	♄ Saturn
♌ Leo	☉ Sun	♄ Saturn and ♅ Uranus
♍ Virgo	☿ Mercury	♃ Jupiter and ♆ Neptune
♎ Libra	♀ Venus	♂ Mars
♏ Scorpio	♂ Mars and ♀ Pluto	♀ Venus
♐ Sagittarius	♃ Jupiter	☿ Mercury
♑ Capricorn	♄ Saturn	☽ Moon
♒ Aquarius	♄ Saturn and ♅ Uranus	☉ Sun
♓ Pisces	♃ Jupiter and ♆ Neptune	☿ Mercury

When a planet is in the sign or house opposite to the one it rules, like Venus in Scorpio or in the Eighth House, it is "in detriment" and does not express itself as easily or effectively.

Planets located above the horizon in a horoscope are conscious, and those below the horizon are unconscious. Venus represents a relationship, so Venus above the horizon is a conscious relationship, and Venus below the horizon is an unconscious relationship. When the naturally objective, active, and vital Sun is below the horizon, it may still carry conscious qualities, but we could be unaware of them. When the naturally subjective and receptive Moon is above the horizon, our maternal side is prominent and we tend to be very conscious of our feelings and emotional life.

Look at your horoscope. Find the planets that are above the horizon. Is your Sun/father there in the conscious domain? Find the planets below the horizon. What is the balance between conscious and unconscious planets: Are you mainly conscious or unconscious? Does the distribution feel right?

Planets located in the left, eastern half of a horoscope are bound up with our self-identification, and planets in the right, western half are bound up with our orientation to the world. Jupiter as the indicator of our life philosophy would be exclusive and self-oriented when in the left side, and inclusive and collective when in the right side of the horoscope. Planets near the Ascendant in a horoscope affect our personality, and planets near the Midheaven affect our objectives and aims in life.

When planets occupy a double sign like Gemini, Cancer, Libra, Sagittarius, Aquarius, or Pisces, there is often more than one individual carrying the planetary influence, and a duality results in the equivalent influence. If the planet is the Moon it might be our mother and grandmother, while if it is Jupiter it could be two grandparents. This also means a duality within us that must be understood and worked with—it may manifest as an ambiguity or as a polarization; for example, we might love one grandparent and despise the other. This always identifies to us polarized parts of our own nature. We can easily be canceling out mutually valuable aspects of our nature, or even countering the advantages of having two different views of a given issue by forcing ourselves to choose one or the other. The healthier practice is to acknowledge both halves, to allow each divergent opinion its own leeway and attitude, and learn to take advantage of both parts.

The planets are considered masculine, feminine, or neuter, although these values are usually modified by the signs, the houses they inhabit, or by the aspects they make. They are ways of being rather than gender designations. Since fire and air signs are considered masculine, and earth and water are feminine, when a masculine planet like Mars is in a feminine sign like Taurus, it will tend to produce a person, male or female, who loves cooking or gardening as a way of nurturing their family and others. It is obvious and natural that all women and men are composed of both masculine and feminine qualities, and the overall balance of masculine and feminine varies dramatically through life. We fluctuate from one pole of our being to another, and back again. Women may exhibit as much objectivity, consciousness, and vitality as men, in the same way that men may exhibit as much subjectivity, unconsciousness, and passivity as women.

When planets aspect others they may affect their natural traits considerably. If the Sun has close aspects to Neptune or is in the sign Pisces, it softens, dilutes, weakens, and brings illusory qualities to the archetypal masculine nature. Similarly, when the Moon is in a sign like Aries or has aspects to Mars, it hardens, strengthens, and makes more virile the archetypal feminine nature.

> *A client, Mr. A., has Neptune in Libra in the Tenth House opposite the Moon in Aries in the Fourth House. The Tenth House is typically the domain of Capricorn and is the father and the patriarchal, while the opposite Fourth House is typically the domain of Cancer and is the mother and matriarchal influences. Mr. A lost his father early in life (Neptune in the Tenth), and therefore his mother, signified by the Moon, had to be more aggressive and assertive in the sign Aries.*

If feminine planets are dominant by sign and house position in your horoscope, feminine qualities predominate whether or not you are biologically male or female. The planets are paired in masculine–feminine dyads that depend upon each other for wholeness. When the following pairs of planets are also in aspect with each other, especially when they are either conjunct or in opposition, it exaggerates their polarity in us.

The Sun is the principle of integration and understanding that leads to consciousness and objectivity. The Moon is feelings and emotions that form the foundation of our value system. The geometrical aspect between the Sun and Moon in our horoscope describes the nature of our parents' relationship, as well as forming a pattern for our own relationships and the masculine–feminine balance within us.

Mercury is communication in all of its forms and determines our intelligence and creativity. It is neutral. In classical mythology Mercury was a masculine god but was also known to be hermaphroditic, which means that it is affected by all the gender signals around.

Venus and Mars are the feminine–masculine polarity manifest in the physical and sexual realms. Venus is passive sexuality and is the urge to become the other, to merge with the object of its affections, or to be possessed. Mars is active sexuality and believes that it alters the object of its affection, wants to change others, and is angry if these desires cannot be met.

Jupiter is a masculine expansion of horizons, and Saturn is the feminine contraction of concentration. Their polarity is that of philosophy, religion, and psychology versus materialism, pragmatism, and science. Jupiter expands, opens up, and is manic, while Saturn contracts, closes down, and is depressive. Jupiter allows; Saturn controls.

The three outer planets are far from the Earth and the Sun, and pass through the zodiac signs in such long periods of time that they signify transpersonal and generational mechanisms within us. Uranus takes almost seven years to pass through each sign and eighty-four years to circulate the zodiac, about an entire lifetime; Neptune takes about fourteen years and has a cycle of 165 years; and Pluto takes about twenty-two years and has an extremely long cycle of 265 years. One reason so many people are saying that the events of September 11 have such a powerful impact is that the opposition of Saturn and Pluto, which occurred at that time, happens only every forty years.

We experience a complete cycle of our inner planets (the Sun, the Moon, Mercury, Venus, Mars, Jupiter, and Saturn) through all twelve signs by the age of twenty-nine years and six months, when Saturn has completed its cycle. The planets from the Sun to Saturn are the personal characteristics everyone shares. The three outer planets show influences that affect the masses and the equivalent inner understanding of collective values some people possess.

THE SUN, THE MOON, AND THE INNER PLANETS

The Sun (Rules Leo; in Detriment in Aquarius)

The Sun describes our relationship to the masculine, conscious, and vital forces of life, as shown by our attitude toward our father. It is will, creativity, personal power, self-expression, leadership skills, individuality, nobility, and also egotism. The Sun is Apollo.

Our first contact with our father starts before birth, indeed before conception, and is a component of our reality from that time on. It determines our life energy, our level of consciousness, and our masculine qualities. The masculine principle becomes most evident when we begin to focus light clearly at about eighty days after birth, and it remains the symbol of our objectivity, rationality, and ability to detach, based on how our father related to us. Although the Sun is often considered the most important planet in a horoscope (or as the only planet in "sun-sign astrology"), this is of course not the case. Many of us have weak, absent, or multiple fathers. When the Sun is opposite the Ascendant, which is the birth moment, it implies that our father is not present when we were born and therefore remains separate from us; when the Sun is on the Ascendant, it shows our father was there and identifies with us.

If the Sun has no direct aspect to the Ascendant, our father was not present when we were born, due either to absence or not being present emotionally. The Sun as our father, although central to our life, is also a component of the whole.

We gradually come to realize that our father is not the only man in the world; there are other men stronger, more intelligent, more objective, and more masculine. This signals the transformation of the Sun's influence beyond that attached to our actual father. The solar image and our vitality depend upon finding ever-higher forms upon which to project our life focus. Sexual energy, libido, psychic energy, or kundalini metamorphoses into purer channels as we age. The energy of sucking in the First House transforms into chewing in the Second, talking in the Third, emotional give and take in the Fourth, game-playing in the Fifth, competition in the Sixth, and sexuality in the Seventh. When energy is blocked from transforming itself into the next-higher level, symbolized by the next house position of the Sun (or any other planet), it regresses. When we cannot find the next gradient of energy, it moves back to a previous house. When there is no outlet for sexual energies, we must return to games to express them. The Sun symbolizes the gradual process of becoming conscious of self, energy, and life.

In early life, the Sun is carried by those who organize or control our environment. This may include, in addition to the father, masculine qualities of the mother, grandparents, housekeepers, uncles, doctors, priests, and those who exert influence upon the mother. Early paternal projections transfer to teachers, heroes, actors, athletes, politicians, ideologues, celebrities, royalty, impresarios, the wealthy, and anyone in authority. From the beginning of maturity, at about seven years old, until the Descendant point, at twenty-three years and five months, these projections happen often and are natural. Past the Descendant it is time to begin repossessing these paternal projections: We must become fathers ourselves. The quality, variety, and number of paternal projections made in early life define our own masculine nature. Our father and his surrogates provide models of consciousness, and the degree of awareness depends upon understanding this relationship, whether we are male or female. We can and must be aware of our father and his role, even when he is unsympathetic, absent, unconscious, or instinctive.

The Sun in a horoscope is vitality, objectivity, consciousness, organization, decisiveness, and spiritual focus.

☾ The Moon (Rules Cancer; in Detriment in Capricorn)

The moon in a horoscope is our ability to value, feel, and reflect emotions. The structure and intensity of our instinctive value systems is derived and influenced by the way in which we relate to our mother. The Moon is our inner illumination, subconscious forces in us, instincts and habits, hereditary qualities (from the maternal line), our feelings, emotions, imagination, and receptivity, and our domestic and nurturing traits. The Moon is sensitive, receptive, and empathetic, while negatively she can be cautious, depressed, closed, changeable, and inconstant in her feelings, and moody or secretive.

She carries us within her during gestation and bonds to us at birth. From that time on we begin to differentiate ourselves from her. Feelings about our mother are continually in flux, like the changeable but repetitive lunar phases each month. The time of the Moon's registration in a horoscope shows the time when we relate to her most strongly. In early life she is an extension of our own reality, but with age she occupies a relative position in our affections.

Early maternal projections surround us within the womb yet are also transmitted by grandmothers, aunts, midwives, female doctors, emotional people, women in general, and the feminine component in our father. From birth the Moon signifies everyone who protects, nurtures, and feels toward us, including nannies, medical people, and males within our environment. From school age, lunar projections are displaced by teachers or girlfriends, just as home and family are displaced by school and classmates. Beginning at the Descendant, the Moon becomes a pattern for feelings about partnership, sexuality, mating, raising children, and the world. Ultimately, we must integrate maternal feelings into our whole being. When the traditional child-raising function is rejected, variants emerge to take its place, like finding others to protect or being protected emotionally, or an instinctive return to sports, nature, or the land.

The Moon moves rapidly and functions as a connecting agent and catalyst in our horoscope. She reflects and values the other planets and establishes the tone of emotional life through events that bring out our feminine nature.

☿ Mercury (Rules Gemini and Virgo; in Detriment in ♓ Sagittarius and Pisces)

Mercury is our ability to communicate with and mediate between mother and father outwardly, and our feminine and masculine natures inwardly. Mercury is flexible to the point of being elusive, interprets and analyzes, and governs self-expression, reasoning skills, language ability, and work with facts. It is mobile, spontaneous, and imitative.

Our intellect, intelligence, and mental and nervous processes are determined by the fluidity of our communication. As communication requires the acquisition of visual and audio skills, it is essentially imitative. We communicate as we observe and hear others around us communicate. Our mind interweaves masculine and feminine by the connecting bridge between the left-brain hemisphere, which has domain over logical, analytical, mathematical, and verbal functions associated with masculine, linear qualities, and the right-brain hemisphere, which has domain over holistic, mental, artistic, and spatial functions associated with feminine, simultaneous qualities. When Mercury registers it shows at which age mental development is most critical. Mercury in the Third House is an adaptable, communicative mind, while Mercury in the Seventh House is comparative, balancing, and team thinking.

During gestation Mercury is an indicator of our mother's expression of her changing mental state, and may represent her brothers or sisters, friends, or confidants, or our own siblings. In childhood Mercury connotes other children and teachers, those after whom our own communication methods are patterned. Mercurial influence is also carried by books and the media, especially by television in the present world. Later manifestations include business sense, criticism, scientific work, and individual self-expression.

Mercury is a gauge of our breadth of communication as formed in early childhood, which is modulated by our parental relationships. Even when parental attitudes openly conflict they must combine within us. Mercury ranges from quick wit and easy superficiality to scathing criticism and serious scientific logic. Mercurial events are adaptations, changes of mind, perceptive insights, and the learning and teaching phases of life.

♀ Venus (Rules Taurus and Libra; in Detriment in Scorpio and Aries)

Venus represents beauty, relationships, harmony, love, and personal aesthetics as determined by an ability to accept physical situations in life and to make them work, whether furnishing a room, adorning oneself, choosing a partner, or making love. Venus is integration and physical attraction, clothes, decorations, pleasure, enhancement, luxury, and warm sympathy.

During gestation Venus shows a mother's relatedness to herself and others. Venus may be older sisters, friends of our mother, or any women who guide her through gestation and birth, such as midwives, those who teach or espouse natural childbirth, and those who write about these subjects. In childhood Venus indicates other children, aunts, friends of our mother, or even our mother herself. In maturity Venus describes woman friends, lovers, artists, mates, anyone attractive physically, or those involved with beauty, art, clothes, and appearances.

Venus indicates relationship to the physical world as amplified by the character of our sexual contact. Relationships with others mirror our understanding of the feminine reality within and the ways of projecting it outside in associations, artistic involvement, and indulgence.

♂ Mars (Rules Aries and Scorpio; in Detriment in Libra and Taurus)

Mars represents the masculine sexual reality and physical situations that we cannot accept and that we desire to change. Mars is never satisfied with what is, only with what can be altered to suit its affections. Mars resists absorption and is assertive, initiatory, passionate, energetic and conflicting, aggressive, intense, and desiring. Sexual energy can be channeled into the physical world, but if no outlet is available Mars is violent, overbearing, and ruthless.

During gestation Mars indicates doctors, medical examinations, men in general, aggressive midwives, and our parents' sexual contact. At birth Mars is often the doctor in his role as surgeon and intervening agent. In childhood Mars is active children, men, athletes, medical people, brothers, uncles, or craftsmen. In maturity it is the acceptance of any of the former occupations or roles and those who change the world. On the sexual level Mars is men to whom we are sexually attracted and the masculine aspect of women that attracts us.

Mars is an active desire to change the physical world into our own image, to produce progeny, and to assert our own will. The degree of competitiveness in our persona mirrors the strength and nature of inner masculine reality. Mars events are accidents, creative moments, changes, alterations of attitude or situation, transactions we initiate, crises, resoluteness, and enterprising moves. When Mars has no viable channel it becomes violent, angry, and self-destructive.

♃ Jupiter (Rules Sagittarius and Pisces; in Detriment in Gemini and Virgo)

Jupiter represents expansive influences that are optimistic, positive, generous, enthusiastic, cohesive, philosophical, psychological, or religious. Jupiter is wisdom, higher mind, and consciousness; it is experienced, benevolent, rich, outgoing, and spontaneous. Even in negative connections, although it is indulgent and lazy, Jupiter is our life view and those who provide patterns for optimism.

During gestation Jupiter indicates religious influences, grandparents, socialites, prominent people, spiritual or psychological advisers, and beneficial midwives or doctors. When registering at birth Jupiter represents anyone who enlivens or is wise. In childhood it indicates surrogate parents, nannies, aunts or uncles, grandparents, early teachers, religious trainers, or merchants. A registration of Jupiter in maturity shows those people who determine our worldview, psychologists and therapists, advisers, successful or notable people, politicians, and those associated with education.

Jupiter indicates expansiveness, openness to new influences, and a willingness to adopt educational, religious, or psychological standpoints in life. We grow toward the goals we set for ourselves; the higher the goals, the greater the possibilities. Jupiter events are expansion in work or philosophy, the advent of wealth and the appearance of people who help us. It is the ability to accept higher tasks that transcend our material appetites.

♄ Saturn (Rules Capricorn and Aquarius; in Detriment in Cancer and Leo)

Saturn is a self-regulative counterbalance to Jupiter and tests, limits, concentrates, structures, orders, focuses, crystallizes, contracts, and conserves. Saturn is accept- ance of material and unavoidable restrictions of life, the maker of tests, hard, disciplined, structured, stable, enduring, sustaining, and the process of aging. When we resist life's responsibilities, restrictions increase, while the willingness to confront reality enables us to focus and center.

During gestation Saturn is restrictive grandparents, serious doctors, pessimists, the authorities, and those who inhibit our mother. When registering at birth Saturn shows over-regulators of the birth process, emotionally restricting people who are present, and the seriousness of the atmosphere. In maturity Saturn represents teachers, employers, elders, bank managers, authorities, and those who seek to form and crystallize our reality. Saturn symbolizes those older, more depressive, more concentrated, and more restricted than us.

Saturn is the acceptance and perfection of life through discipline, tests of strength, seriousness, confrontation, and resolution of the problems of aging. Saturnine events are inhibited crossroads, paralyzing circumstances, illnesses, troubles, and difficulties resulting from changes.

THE OUTER PLANETS

Uranus (Rules Aquarius; in Detriment in Leo)

Uranus is the ability to step beyond the purely personal characteristics of the seven inner planets. Uranus represents originality, eccentricity, uniqueness, intensity, inspiration, inventiveness, and rhythm, which allow you to integrate diverse influences that initially seem divisive, unusual, or disconnected. It is the part of you that wants to be unique and free of the fetters of physicality.

During gestation Uranus indicates anyone who responds in an original way to a mother's pregnancy, including medical practitioners, midwives, childbirth instructors, other women, or those who disrupt her natural rhythms or introduce new rhythms, such as breathing exercises. When Uranus registers at birth or in aspect to the Ascendant it indicates medical technicians, doctors, and anyone who changes existing patterns and acts independently. In childhood Uranus shows rebels, eccentric playmates, independent friends, and ambitious people. During maturity Uranus represents eccentrics, independent people, reformers, inventors, dancers, technicians, inspired people, and fringe medical practitioners. Uranus symbolizes anyone who breaks down our established life patterns in unexpected ways and provides prototypes for our own independence.

Emotional and mental rhythms condition material rigidity, and Uranus is the potential to integrate and balance new output.

Uranus events are sudden, traumatic, unusual, and eccentric, and often happen in rhythmic phases.

ψ Neptune (Rules Pisces; in Detriment in Virgo)

Neptune represents our psychic, sensitive, imaginative, mediumistic, and intuitive nature derived from the finer levels of reality and mirrored in dreams, fantasies, ideal- ism, utopian projections, and imagination. Neptune shows our sensitivity and receptivity to the spiritual impulse as well as our illusions; it is the domain of drugs, psychic experiences, ESP, and dream states. These are mechanisms that allow existing but hidden principles to rise to the surface of consciousness.

During gestation Neptune is those near our mother who sense that she is pregnant or act as mediums for her, as often others divine our innermost psychic states before we ourselves do. Psychic friends, dreamers, mystics, gurus, dieticians, drug dealers, and anyone who exerts psychic influence upon our mother are also covered by Neptune. At birth Neptune is anesthetists, hospital nursing staff, the watery medium of birth itself, or sensitive participants. An amusing parallel is that the Neptune influence attracted in induced or anesthetic births is similar to when babies are born into pools of water, as is done in one modern practice. Neptune registering in childhood indicates dreamers, idealists, doctors treating childhood illnesses, fantasy characters, dream images, and invented roles, as well as the omnipresent teddy bear or doll. In maturity Neptune represents those who live in fantasy, illusion, dreams, or sickness, or sensitives, mediums, tricksters, psychics, astrologers, or mystics, in addition to those who are sensitive and who dispense drugs.

Neptune symbolizes those who make us aware that the higher and finer levels of consciousness and reality are available and who teach us how to gain access to them. Neptune events are particularly difficult to describe as they are vague, internal, dreamy, psychosomatic, or spiritual.

 Pluto (Rules Scorpio; in Detriment in Taurus)

Pluto is contact with the masses and transformation, which involves the destruction of existing behavior patterns and environments as a necessary prerequisite for regeneration. Often Pluto refers to world events that disrupt people and society—world wars, economic collapses, mass movements, and super-power politics. Pluto is the effect upon us of the world in which we live and, specifically, historical transformations. Most of us are affected by mass events without understanding what they are. Pluto shows our relationship to the influences that affect entire generations, as well as our own parallel, internal changes. Changes of residence, school, attitude, partnership, and other dramatic alterations of importance are governed by Pluto.

Pluto in gestation shows world events affecting a mother's pregnancy, her contact with public figures such as medical specialists, authorities on childbirth, and even indirect contact with public influences through books or media. Being born during a world war, being raised according to Dr. Spock, and being delivered by the LeBoyer technique are examples of such influences. At birth Pluto is people who exert influence, take charge of, or transform us. Pluto in childhood is bossy people, parents, or teachers. In maturity Pluto indicates figures who carry generational influences, such as politicians, musicians, actors, propagandists, and all those who affect us through public opinion or those who change our world.

Pluto is the part of us that responds to the challenges and trials of the masses and participates in public events, either actually or as

a surrogate of mass movements for friendships or acquaintance-
ships. Pluto events are gradual but extreme, exceptionally powerful, and critical; they carry long-lasting influence.

☊ ☋ The Moon's North Node (Rules Gemini; in Detriment in Sagittarius)

The North Node of the Moon is a point symbolizing
how our individual feelings, symbolized by the Moon
in our horoscope, intersect with our collective feelings
about the family or other structures. It shows how we are able to
integrate with others and be part of a group. In Hindu Vedic astrology the nodes are very important and signify our fate in and
fortune in life. Because the Nodes are essentially an axis through
the zodiac ring, there are really two Nodes directly opposite each
other. The nodal axis moves backward through the zodiac in a cycle
of eighteen years. In our horoscope, the North Node is our adaptability, associations, family, and groups of all varieties of which we
are a part. The opposite South Node is our inability to adapt to
others and our resistance to family heritage and groups of which we
are a part. In Hindu astrology the North Node is our material, he-
donistic nature and the South Node describes our spiritual
potential.

The Node in gestation shows the influence of groups upon a
mother, particularly her family. At birth it is the influence of everyone present. Natural childbirth or women's groups often reflect the
Node. In childhood the Node is other children and our family, or
playschool; in maturity the Node is our family, clubs, social or political organizations, friends, circles of associates, and all other
groups of people.

The Node is collective influences in life, and its events are com-
ings together with others and a desire to link with groups.

PLANETARY TIMING

The date when each planet registers is called its age point. The age point indicates the time in our life when a planet makes its most significant impact. It is not necessarily the most dramatic, but it is an archetypal time in that it fully characterizes the nature of the planet. For example, we might remember a specific event when our mother told us something about herself that defined her in our eyes. This would be when the Moon registers its age point.

We can discover the age points in a number of ways. One of the easiest ways to visualize the dating of the planets is by using a dating disk, a model of which appears on page 312. To use it, take the book to a photocopy store and have some copies made on clear acetate. Simply align the dating with the horoscope so that the 0 (the birth moment) in the inner ring is on the Ascendant at the left of the horoscope. Dates during gestation (the Ninth, Tenth, Eleventh, and Twelfth Houses) are graded in months before birth. Dates immediately after birth, during the first year of life, are graded in months, and then the scale is graded in years. When a house cusp falls between two years, estimate the date in between. In most horoscopes the conception/death point does not correspond to that shown on the dating disk. The conception point is the actual location of the Ninth House cusp in the horoscope, not the point on the disk! This reflects the fact that most gestations are either shorter or longer than the exact full term.

Included in the package of horoscopes you have downloaded from the website www.newvisionastrology.com is a list of age points in your life from conception to the age of ninety-nine. This list starts with the Ninth House, which is the conception point, and extends around the horoscope circle. The planets are shown in **boldface** in the sample list in Figure 6.2. Each planet is followed by the date at which it registers in your life by month and year, and

***0	CUSP 9	Concept		15.55	ARI
*****0**	**MARS**	**JUL**	**1950**	**19.48**	**ARI**
*****0**	**MERCURY**	**JUL**	**1950**	**21.47**	**ARI**
***0	0 TAURUS	JUL	1950	00.00	TAU
*****0**	**VENUS**	**JUL**	**1950**	**07.46**	**TAU**
***0	MC	AUG	1950	18.58	TAU
***0	0 GEMINI	AUG	1950	00.00	GEM
***0	CUSP 11	SEP	1950	24.26	GEM
***0	0 CANCER	SEP	1950	00.00	CAN
*****0**	**URANUS**	**OCT**	**1950**	**05.28**	**CAN**
***0	CUSP 12	NOV	1950	27.22	CAN
***0	0 LEO	DEC	1950	00.00	LEO
*****0**	**PLUTO**	**FEB**	**1951**	**17.39**	**LEO**
*****0**	**ASCENDANT**	**MAR**	**1951**	**25.51**	**LEO**
***0	0 VIRGO	APR	1951	00.00	VIR
***0	CUSP 2	AUG	1951	18.17	VIR
*****0**	**SATURN**	**NOV**	**1951**	**28.24**	**VIR**
***0	0 LIBRA	DEC	1951	00.00	LIB
***0	CUSP 3	JUN	1952	15.55	LIB
*****0**	**NEPTUNE**	**JUL**	**1952**	**18.30**	**LIB**
***0	0 SCORPIO	FEB	1953	00.00	SCO
***0	CUSP 4	MAR	1954	18.58	SCO
***0	0 SAGITTA	FEB	1955	00.00	SAG
*****0**	**MOON**	**JUL**	**1955**	**04.13**	**SAG**
***0	CUSP 5	DEC	1957	24.25	SAG
***0	0 CAPRICO	OCT	1958	00.00	CAP
***0	CUSP 6	JUL	1964	27.22	CAP
***0	0 AQUARIU	MAR	1965	00.00	AQU
***0	CUSP 7	SEP	1974	25.51	AQU
***0	0 PISCES	SEP	1976	00.00	PIS
*****0**	**N NODE**	**SEP**	**1987**	**18.14**	**PIS**
***0	CUSP 8	OCT	1987	18.17	PIS
*****0**	**JUPITER**	**MAR**	**1992**	**24.12**	**PIS**
***0	0 ARIES	FEB	1997	00.00	ARI
*****0**	**SUN**	**MAR**	**2003**	**06.20**	**ARI**
***0	CUSP 9	OCT	2013	15.55	ARI
*****0**	**MARS**	**SEP**	**2018**	**19.48**	**ARI**
*****0**	**MERCURY**	**MAY**	**2021**	**21.47**	**ARI**

```
***0   0 TAURUS      JUN   2033   00.00   TAU
***0   VENUS         OCT   2046   07.46   TAU
```

FIGURE 6.2: PLANETS IN SIGNS AND HOUSES

The list shows life beginning at the cusp of the Ninth House, which is the conception point. As we come to each planet we can see its house by looking directly above it for "cusp" and a number. Farther along its line is the date it registers, followed by the degree and minute of the sign in which it resides. In the example: Mars is in the Ninth House in Aries; Mercury is in the Ninth House in Aries; Venus is in the Ninth House in Taurus; Uranus is in the Eleventh House in Cancer; Pluto is in the Twelfth House in Leo; Saturn is in the Second House in Virgo; Neptune is in the Third House in Libra; the Moon is in the Fourth House in Sagittarius; the Node is in the Seventh House in Pisces; Jupiter is in the Eighth House in Pisces; and the Sun is in the Eighth House in Aries. Due to the geometry of the houses, we can pass planets twice: once in early gestation and later in old age. Here we pass Mars, Mercury, and Venus again.

then by the degree and minute of its zodiac sign. By looking up the table to the closest cusp number, you can see in which house the planet resides.

It is also possible to calculate the dates of planets in the horoscope based on the number of degrees from the Ascendant point, but as this is technical, you can find it in Appendix 2. There is also a computer program available that creates the list shown above, which may be purchased from www.newvisionastrology.com.

SEVEN

ASPECTS OF RELATIONSHIP

The planets interact with each other in geometric relationships that we show as connecting lines in the center of the horoscope. They determine particular links between planets, personifications of those planets, the psychological mechanisms carried by the planets, and the glands and organs with which the planets correspond, and they connect events that occur at different stages of our life. They are casual connections in the sense that by tracking a linkage of planets back into our past, the earliest influence shows the origin of the dynamic that might play itself out throughout our entire life.

The houses, starting with the Ninth House cusp conception point and proceeding in a counterclockwise direction, describe a sequence of events in time. These "outer" events follow each other in their inexorable fashion, from cause to effect, throughout life. Our parents' relationship leads to our birth and its circumstances; their relationship conditions our childhood; and our childhood dynamics form the foundation of our schooling and early relationships out in the world, which in turn form the basis of our later relationships in the world. Influences follow each other but may seem to leap over gaps of time when they are not so obvious.

As the periphery of the horoscope exists *in time,* so the center

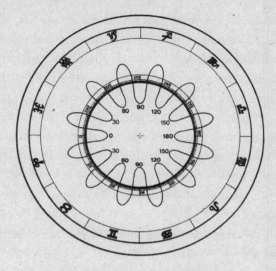

FIGURE 7.1: ASPECT STANDING WAVES

The aspect patterns are like standing waves around the circle. A planet at the 0 point manifests its energies around the circle at thirty-degree intervals. At each of these points there is a statistically greater chance their energies will manifest as an inner or outer event. This is a twelfth harmonic of the circle, which includes many of the common aspects. Eighth harmonic waves include squares, oppositions, sesqui-quadrates, and semisquares.

of the horoscope is outside of time or *timeless*. A sign and house defines every point on the periphery of the horoscope, the sign describing its qualities and the house its time of manifestation in our life. The center of the circle, the axis around which the planets revolve, is not subject to any of the sign qualities. The center is the core of our being, which is without or beyond qualities. The center is the combination of everything we are and simultaneously the still point within us. We might experience this point through meditation or through centering exercises.

If the center is timeless and the periphery is a sequence of events embedded in time, then the aspects mediate between the two. They connect events at different times in our life, outside of time, by their harmonics and meaning, like the internal dynamics of notes in a musical scale that has internal harmonies and dissonances. These connections qualify the nature of the planets they connect. Often they override the qualities of the planets they combine. For example, as aspect between Venus (love, harmony, and balance) and Jupiter (expansion and optimism) would seem to be totally positive, yet when they are in the opposition aspect, directly opposite each other around the circle, there is a conflict between our desire for harmony and our ability to expand. We can experience it as an "either-or" dilemma, or as two separate but somehow linked qualities. We might feel that being in love cannot combine with our natural optimism. It is also possible to integrate two qual-

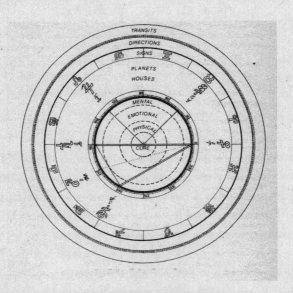

FIGURE 7.2: ASPECTS IN THE CENTER

The extent to which aspects penetrate into the center of the horoscope show how deeply their energies are felt. The sextiles and trines are peripheral, while squares and oppositions go through the center of the horoscope, into our core being.

ities by understanding that they need not necessarily be in conflict, which would require an overview of one's whole being. Such contrasts in value are critical to see and understand in terms of their dynamics within us.

Certain combinations of events in our lives may be either harmonious or dissonant, depending on the aspects that join pairs of planets. This is true of our parental relationship (the aspect between the Sun and the Moon shows this), of our sibling relationships (the aspects between Mercury, Venus, and Mars, and either the Sun or the Moon), and all others. Although tension or dissonant aspects do not necessarily require a negative outcome, because most of us are quite mechanical in the way we behave they often do manifest this way.

Complex events involve more than two planetary aspects and are a blend of the qualities included in the mix. Most often planets have a series of aspects with other planets that bring both harmony and dissonance into being at different times. For example, our parents' relationship may have created as many painful memories as blissful and protective ones for us.

It is the "web of relationships" shown by the aspects that determines many significant qualities about us. Complex patterns show complex individuals, relationships, and lives. The interconnectedness of the planets shows the relative tendency to integrate our various subpersonalities, selves, personas, and qualities. I like to lead my clients to understand this phenomenon by doing the following guided imagery.

Imagine you are in a room with a huge circular table at its center. Around the table are a number of chairs. Entering the room is a procession of all of the significant people in your life. Not only are they all there, but they are there at the age at which your primary contact with them happened. Although you can see them, they cannot see you. You are the reason they are there, but they do not know that you are there. You are floating around in space, moving yourself at will, like a free spirit. Imagine them taking their places at the table, as they choose. They may or may not know each other. If not, they will introduce themselves and talk about you and their relationship with you, and will remember you. Some of these people will get along well; others may strike up immediate dislikes to others. Still others could gravitate toward those who are unknown to them. Small groups emerge. You hover over the table and can overhear any conversations you choose. Try to notice which people gravitate toward one another. Notice their relationships. Is there a sense of integration at the table as a whole, or is there primarily discordant feeling about it? What feelings does this event evoke in you?

This guided imagery is fascinating, as it is a reflection of our inner dynamics. It is analogous to the horoscope wheel with planetary personifications around the periphery. Certain planets relate and integrate to others, while some are discordant and choose not to connect. It is this way within us. Yet all the relationships are an integral part of us if we allow them into the whole.

It is interesting to note how the aspects manifest these qualities. John Nelson of RCA did research in the 1960s that showed that the angular relationship between the other planets and Earth affects the quality of radio reception. When groups of planets are at 60° or 120° angles relative to Earth they produce disturbance-free fields and an absence of static, but when groups of planets are in 90° or 180° angles relative to Earth they produce disturbances in the form of static. This correlates with the meaning of these angles for experience and relationship.

In my book *Astrology and the Art of Healing,* I describe another

way in which planetary aspects can be seen and understood. I sub-
divide the central zone of the horoscope into concentric rings defined by certain types of aspect called Healing Zones.[17] Particularly
because the houses are associated with developmental times in our
life and have clear biological correlations, the aspect connections
between planets have not only event correlations, but also health
tendencies. As we move around the horoscope from the Ninth
House (conception) through gestation (our physical body), to
childhood (our emotional body), and on to maturity (our mental
body), we create successively less dense bodies, until we reach the
transcendent octave, where there is a luminous, light body, which
is beyond time. The aspects often connect a planet in one octave,
like gestation (signifying an inherited trait) with another, like
childhood (signifying a behavior pattern learned in the family sys-

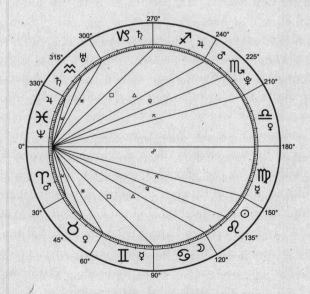

FIGURE 7.3: ASPECTS

The aspects are geometric divisions of the circle. The archetypal beginning of the zodiac is 0° Aries. This shows all the aspects relative to 0° Aries.

tem). Such an aspect would combine a physical pattern with an emotional pattern and would indicate a potential health issue. For example, if we feel inhibition in childhood because we cannot speak our minds, we may revert to the confinement of gestation, when our mother felt unable to speak to our father and withdrew from the world. In this way, we can often put health issues in the context of our life pattern and through this begin to work on our own health.

The geometric aspect between the Sun and the Moon in our horoscope shows the relationship between our father and mother. Each type of aspect (one-third of the circle is a trine, one-quarter is a square, half is an opposition, etc.) describes a particular type of relationship. Some are harmonious and fluid connections, while others create tension and external opposition. Both are ultimately necessary to both activate and balance us in our relationships.

Some pairs of planets have no aspects connecting them, which implies a lack of obvious connection and ensuing difficulties in communication between the personality types around and within us. A difficult relationship between your father and your sister can reflect a difficult aspect between the Sun and Venus in your horoscope.

Some aspects indicate superficial connections, while others show deeper and more central relationships that we experience as more stimulating and challenging. And since these relationships are also internalized, they provide us with guides and clues to the dynamics of our personality. Sometimes planets form complex aspect shapes like grand trines or squares that show powerful and compelling combinations of characteristics that either block us or prove useful in generating greater understanding of ourselves. Aspects are the inner dynamics and paths of movement that activate us in life.

Figure 7.3 shows the common aspect types around the horoscope circle. Notice that the various aspects penetrate into the center of the horoscope differently. One way to determine the depth and strength of an aspect is to see how deeply into the center it penetrates. The further in it goes, the more profound the effect of the aspect and the more significant it will be on our psyche.

In some charts, the aspects are differentiated by color: The fluid sextile and trine aspects are green, while the tension-related and blocking square and opposition aspects are red. This allows us to see at a glance the distribution and dominance of each type.

In portraying the aspects, it is important to understand the *orb of influence* we use in astrology. When planets are within anywhere from 3° to 8° apart, they are considered in aspect. Some planets, including the Sun and the Moon, have quite large aspect orbs because of their sheer size and their speed across the sky. The farther away and the smaller the planets, the narrower their orb. For example, the Moon moves more than 12° each day, while Pluto may take ten years to move that distance. The orbs are important as they show us how strong the mutual impact of pairs of planets is. Within the time scale this is critical because the later in life aspects happen, the longer the period of time they occupy. An aspect combination that takes days to happen in childhood may take years to manifest in our fifties.

The *conjunction* (♂ or CJN) is two planets within a few degrees of one another, a relationship of 0°, the aspect of unity. Conjunction designates influences that originate at approximately the same time in our life, blend their qualities with one another, and tend to activate their influences at the same time in later life. The closer they are, the more bonded they are and the more difficult they may be to differentiate. If a horoscope has a conjunction between Venus and Saturn, the restricting and serious qualities of Saturn modify the loving and attached quality of Venus. When they are very close to one another, we may see all love relationships as inhibiting.

Conjunction is two planets next to one another and enmeshed in the casual wheel of our life, firmly in time. We consider it the "outermost" of the aspects and therefore one of the easiest to identify and work with. It already exists on the surface of our life and is therefore rarely a deep connection, but rather an obvious one of synchronicity. Because conjunction is so much an outer influence it reflects health issues that are both obvious and latent.

The *sextile* aspect(✳ or SXT) is two planets 60° apart, one-sixth of the circle and two signs apart, and makes an inscribed hexagon within the circle. Because it penetrates only a sixth of the way into the center, it is a primarily peripheral aspect, indicating a mental or communicative connection between two events or personality types within us. Sextiles also connect to planets that are two signs away in each direction, usually fire to air or air to fire, and earth to water or water to earth. As the signs alternate masculine and feminine around the circle (we consider fire and air to be masculine, and earth and water to be feminine), sextiles connect masculine to masculine and feminine to feminine. They also tend to link qualities within an octave of the horoscope. Whatever the quality of the planets and signs joined, they tend to be quite superficial and temporary rather than deep and lasting. They define the mental zone of the horoscope and hold health issues that are triggered or caused by mental stress or imbalances.

The *trine* aspect (△ or TRI) is two planets 120° apart, one-third of the circle and four signs apart, and inscribes an equilateral triangle in the circle. As the triangle is the most stable shape in geometry, unable to collapse, trine aspects, which penetrate halfway into the center of the circle, are the foundation of our security and stability in life. They are fluid, balanced, easy, and smooth, the parts of us that mediate inner and outer, bringing what is inside of us out. Trines also connect planets in one octave with planets in another octave. They are therefore like an octave reach on a piano, and are in harmony and balance with each other, being simply higher octaves of the same influence. This defines the emotional zone in the circle and corresponds to psychosomatic illnesses and those with emotional causes.

The *square* aspect (□ or SQU) is two planets 90° apart, one-quarter of the circle and three signs apart. Although we show them as direct lines connecting planets at even quarters of the circle, we can imagine them as being connected by a right-angled line that must go all the way into the center of the horoscope before moving back out to the periphery. Thus squares activate our center and link periphery to center, which is often tense, difficult, and challenging, but can produce change capable of resolution. The astrologer Eileen Nauman says that squares are either stumbling blocks or building blocks.[18] They force us to go to our center (or find it in the first place) and then to change life direction in an area, depending on which planets are involved. Within the context of the life process, we must either go radically ahead or step back to resolve outstanding issues. The square aspect penetrates into our core and therefore is capable of bringing much energy up to consciousness in its process.

The *opposition* aspect (☍ or OPP) is two planets 180° apart, directly across the circle and six signs apart. The line connecting them goes directly through the center of our being and halves the circle, creating a striation that affects our core energies and self-constructs. This creates maximum tension and polarity, or even irreconcilable differences within us, yet also signals the attraction of opposites in relationships. We often attract partners whose horoscope activates our oppositions. We allow our partner to take one pole as we take the other, and in the process, we project half of our opposition upon the other person. In addition, opposition shows influences, critical individuals, and events that occur at opposite times of our lives.

For example, influences in the First House just after birth show our bonding with our mother as a reflection of our ability to get what we need from our environment. The opposite house (and time)—the Seventh House of partnership and relationship with the outside world (from twenty-three years old to about forty-two years old)—is when we must balance and equilibrate our early attention to self by relating to others and, by extension, to the outside world at large. The more attention and focus we receive in the First House, the more we must give away to others in the Seventh House in order to achieve balance in our lives.

MINOR ASPECTS

Minor aspects describe more subtle relationships. They are all harmonics of the major aspects, dividing the circle into smaller sections. They can be divided into two families, the first of which results when we divide the circle into eight parts. The *semisquare* aspect (∠ or SSQ) is two planets 45° apart, half of a square, and one-eighth of the circle. As the square and opposition are tension aspects creating movement and change, so the semisquare performs a mediating function in situations where there is a buildup of tension but not necessarily its release. The *sesquiquadrate* aspect (⬚ or SQQ) is two planets 135° apart, halfway between a square and an opposition, and at one of the eighth points around the circle. This very competitive aspect typically functions in situations where we form a relationship with someone on the assumption that they will change to conform to our vision of them. Of course, since the energy flows both ways, there is a mutual expectation of change. Often the signs involved, and especially comparing the modes (cardinal, fixed, or mutable sign) will determine which part of us will hold its ground and which part will yield. Both these aspects represent tensions that do not necessarily have the strength to produce an outcome, but rather activate and amplify such choices in our psyche.

The *semisextile* aspect (⊻ or SSX) is two planets 30° apart, half of a sextile and one sign apart, and one-twelfth of the circle. The sextile is a mental connection, and its half is an even more tenuous form of communication. The *quincunx,* or inconjunct, aspect (⊼ or QNX) is two planets 150° apart, halfway between a static trine and a voluble opposition, and five signs apart. This aspect signifies frustration and irrational differences between parts of us, or between others and us, as it passes closest to the center of the horoscope without really reaching it. It is also associated in medical astrology with the cause of chronic illnesses and emotional problems, issues that almost touch our center but rarely discharge their energy.

In this book we will use only the five major aspects and the two minor aspects, the semisextile and the quincunx. This will simplify the horoscope diagrams. When we are more comfortable with understanding the aspects we can introduce the semisquare and sesquiquadrate aspects.

The printout you receive from NewVisionAstrology.com has an aspect grid that shows aspects between all planets and the Ascendant and Midheaven angles in your horoscope.

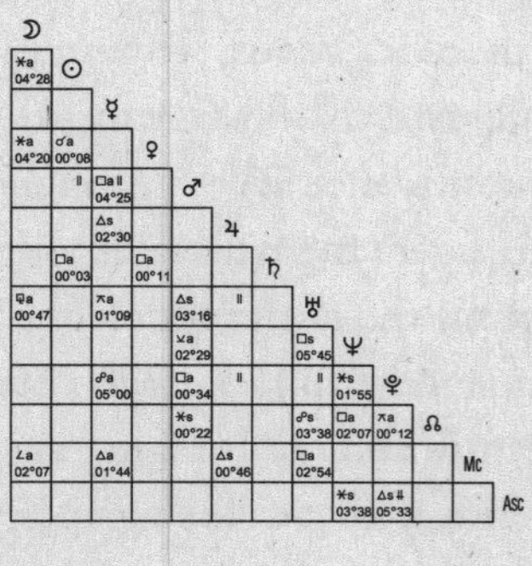

FIGURE 7.4: ASPECT GRID

The aspect grid on the lower left side of the horoscope form shows the aspects between planets and the Ascendant and Midheaven angles in the horoscope. For example, the planet Venus is in sextile to the Moon, in conjunction with the Sun, and in square with Saturn. The little "a" shows an aspect that is applying, moving closer to exact and getting stronger, while the "s" shows the aspect is already past and is getting weaker.

The sequence of the planets is important in all aspects. There are two ways to understand how planets work in sequence. One is to determine which planet is moving faster: Is planet A moving toward planet B or away from it? This, in turn, shows whether the planets are in the process of moving toward an exact and stronger aspect, or moving apart into a vaguer and weaker aspect. In general, the Moon is the fastest planet, the Sun second-fastest, Mercury third, etc., following the sequence of planets away from the Sun. While this is complicated to figure out, the aspect grid on your horoscope form shows this information. The little "a" next to an aspect shows that it is applying, moving closer to exact and getting stronger, while the "s" shows the aspect is already past and is getting weaker. This movement has to do with the apparent motion of the planets at and after your birth. The higher the number of degrees below the aspect symbol, the farther apart the planets are and the weaker the connection between them.

Another way of determining the sequence in which subsequent events will happen is by their position in the counterclockwise sequence of houses. The entire sequence of planets is dated in your printout. The earlier degrees determine which planet in an aspect happens first. For example, Venus and Saturn have two different possible dynamics depending on which planet happens first. If Venus is at 15° Gemini and precedes the square to Saturn at 17° Virgo, we fall in love first and then experience the restrictions or seriousness of the attachment. If Saturn precedes Venus, we tend to feel the restricting factors first and then create an attachment. Although both qualities act together, their sequence is very important. Because our birth horoscope is an underlying pattern in our lives, every month the Moon passes around the entire horoscope, emotionally triggering each planet in sequence. Similarly, each year the Sun follows the path around the entire zodiac, bringing the light of our consciousness into every aspect of our being. The

SQQ	ASCENDANT	AUG	1942	23.30	AQU
SQQ	MC	OCT	1942	24.24	AQU
***0	**SUN**	**OCT**	**1943**	**29.22**	**AQU**
***0	O PISCES	DEC	1943	00.00	PIS
SSQ	URANUS	MAR	1945	05.32	PIS
SQQ	PLUTO	JUL	1945	06.37	PIS
***0	**MERCURY**	**NOV**	**1945**	**07.53**	**PIS**
***0	**N NODE**	**DEC**	**1945**	**08.19**	**PIS**
QNX	ASCENDANT	DEC	1945	08.03	PIS
OPP	NEPTUNE	FEB	1946	09.04	PIS

FIGURE 7.5: PLANET SEQUENCE

The sequence of planets is shown in your printout. The Sun is at 29° Aquarius and Mercury is at 7° Pisces. The Sun therefore always happens just before Mercury, or exercising will occurs before thinking about it. This is from Yoko Ono Lennon's chart.

sequence of aspects is critical because every time a passing (transiting) planet activates an aspect, resonant events will happen in the same sequence.

Aspects exchange information and meaning. Each aspect type modifies the information carried by the two planets involved in a specific way. The trines and sextiles are a blending of meaning in distinction to the squares and oppositions, which represent either–or choices and exclusive meaning. The semisquares and sesquiquadrates are conditional in that there is an exchange subject to a particular condition. For example, "I will love you if you act according to my expectations of you," would be described by Venus and Saturn in a sesquiquadrate aspect.

The flow of information in aspects is much like the diagrams used to describe chaos theory. The diagram called *a strange attractor*, shown in Figure 7.6, is a flow of information around two centers. For example, if the planets Mercury and Neptune are in aspect, Mercury is a mental, logical, thinking way of being, while Neptune is receptive and psychic. When they come together in a

FIGURE 7.6: STRANGE ATTRACTOR

The strange attractor, first discovered by Lorenz, functions like aspects in that they are a flow of information.

trine, our thinking would be affected by our psychic nature in such a way that it would be difficult for us to separate the two; indeed, an individual may even believe that thinking *is* intuition. The tendency is for the information to localize around one of the planets and then shift to the other in regular rhythms. When the Mercury qualities dominate we are more logical, while when the Neptune qualities dominate we are more psychic. The diagram shows that aspects are the rhythmic flow of information.

CONSTELLATIONS

Aspect patterns that connect more than two planets become a constellation, which is a chain of planets joined by meaning. Sometimes the constellations are totally integrated and form a closed loop with energy circulating around it, while in other configurations a chain of planets may make a dead end that forces the energy to go to its end and then return by the same path in reverse. There may be one such major constellation in the horoscope, or even many independent constellations that do not easily join with each other.

Yoko Ono Lennon's horoscope is a fascinating example. Although her horoscope aspect pattern is very complex, there are two unusual constellations. One is the triangle formed by Uranus,

Pluto, and Jupiter, where all three planets are above the horizon in the conscious domain, implying that whatever dynamic they carry is a conscious and willful one. This signifies creativity in isolation (Jupiter in the Twelfth House) and fated partnerships with powerful people (Pluto in the Tenth), along with sextile Uranus in the Seventh, which is highly eccentric, idiosyncratic, and willful.

The other unusual position is that the Sun in Aquarius does not aspect any other planet; it is alone below the horizon, out of communication with the rest of the chart. As the Sun represents the father and also the husband, it obviously refers to her father when she

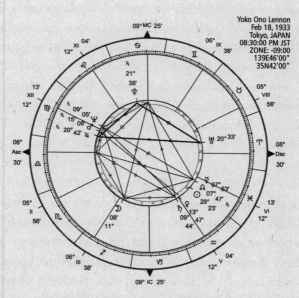

FIGURE 7.7: HOROSCOPE OF YOKO ONO LENNON

The triangle constellation containing Uranus, Pluto, and Jupiter is separate from the rest of the horoscope. The Sun in the Fifth House has no aspects at all. All the other planets are interconnected. In the sequence of their action we can see by the degrees which acts first. Uranus at 20° Aries 33' is first, then Jupiter at 20° Virgo 42', then Pluto at 21° Cancer 38'. All around the circle they manifest in the same sequence. Eccentric actions become a philosophy of life, then lead to major change.

was young, and then John Lennon when she was older. The Sun is in the fixed but eccentric air sign Aquarius, which brings an extreme idealism of men to her being, but also a profound kind of detachment. It is in the Fifth House of children, selfish love, and creativity. Indeed, this characterizes her impact on John, who although he once claimed the Beatles were more famous than Jesus, became more and more isolated from the world, ultimately becoming in his own words, a "house husband" in New York. This is in contrast to the constellation that contains all other planets in the horoscope.

Constellations or chains of planets are the webs of relationships that define us in life because they function like a psychological complex, a network of emotionally charged associations that create and discharge energy. We all have such natural structures in us, and they are a problem only when they are suppressed or not well integrated. Indeed, the presence of a planet like Saturn in a constellation can indicate when and where blockages are likely to be an issue.

Constellations of planets can compete with each other for control within us. They are like complex collections of inner voices that vie for dominance in our inner and outer life. Indeed, in psychology they are called complexes. We all know what they sound like, especially when they start making their presence known in sleepless nights or when we experience the dawn patrol. It is natural for one constellation to dominate the others, but when there are two equally developed constellations of planets, the energy switches from one to the other, often in frustrating and infuriating ways. Unless we learn to listen to both voices, satisfy both sets of needs, and learn to bring the two sides together, we experience inner distress.

Within constellations, energy and feelings tend to follow the path of least resistance. This means that if we have a complex shape of two planets in opposition connected by one planet sextile to one and trine to the other, the energy will often avoid the central route that involves tension and circuit around it through the third

planet. We can also see this in Yoko's horoscope. She has an opposition between Neptune (sensitivity and drugs) and the Moon's
North Node (family or associations) that is mediated by the sextile
and trine to the Midheaven (her ego-conscious goals and objectives). This little dynamic hits the core of her being through the
opposition and was a primary factor in the Ono-Lennon marriage.

We may avoid inner conflict at the expense of staying out of
our center. This is either superficiality or laziness, and when we act
this way continually, we end up "stuck" on the periphery of our
own life. The more we avoid dealing with issues that penetrate to
our psychological and emotional core (as indicated by opposition
and square aspects), the more difficult it becomes to work with
them and the more we lose our spirit and liveliness. When we work
with our most central issues, we learn that we can choose which
path to take in a given situation. This freedom to choose constitutes freedom from necessity.

When we look at a horoscope, we learn to identify how complex the individual is—whether there are clear constellations,
whether there is an energy flow, whether there are obvious blockages, where those blockages are, and when they came into being.

COMPLEX SHAPES

The major aspects derive from a few regular geometric shapes. The
grand trine is three planets mutually in trine (3 x 120°) with each
other, making an equilateral triangle in the horoscope. Unless any
of the planets are at the boundary of their signs all three planets are
in the same element. Similarly, they are planetary events and personifications that are in even harmony around the horoscope, one
in each octave. They signify a series of linked events that happen in
gestation, childhood, and maturity. It matters critically which
planets are involved in such shapes. Although a grand trine is typ-

ically a harmonious shape, if active and disruptive planets like Uranus, Pluto, Mars, or the suppressing Saturn are resident, it may exaggerate their influence and impact upon us.

There are fire, air, water, and earth grand trines. They represent stability and balance in that element. In a fire grand trine we have quite powerful but self-contained energies, which tend to make us extremely independent, self-centered, and reluctant to form partnerships unless we have a high degree of freedom, and we are often loners. In an air grand trine we have strong ideas that dominate and control our worldview and relationships, which are often so important to us that they supercede all other considerations. Since air signs are all double signs and since air is communication, we are defined by our partners, our ideas, or our interests in life. If the planets are harmonious we tend to look for agreement in others, but if they are inharmonious, we attract disagreements, even in our closest partners and friends. In a water grand trine our feelings form the central factor in our life, building us a strong and often conservative family life, a reverence for past patterns, and a tendency to seek emotionally stabilizing influences. In an earth grand trine we seek the physical in property and wealth, both of our body and possessions, and our relationship to nature is a defining quality. In all of these cases, the inner security of knowing who we are forms a solid core around which other traits are often secondary.

We usually consider the grand trine a very positive shape because of its stabilizing qualities, but it can often lead to a laxity or laziness because things in the area described by the trine planets tend to come very easily. In that sense, the center of our being is contained, and we might even feel trapped by the qualities carried by the grand trine.

The *grand cross* is two sets of planets in mutual opposition that are square to one another. In this dominant shape, which creates a high degree of tension and power, all four planets are usually in the same mode: cardinal, fixed, or mutable. It obviously exaggerates the qualities of the mode, making people extremely initiatory, fixed, or changeable. The fixed grand cross has planets in Taurus, Leo, Scorpio, and Aquarius, and none of these signs are flexible or easily changed, making us extremely bound to the qualities of the planets involved. We are passionate about our being and unwilling to change anything about it. Typically if the grand cross can be utilized and worked through it can manifest in very powerful ways, but equally it can be too much to handle the intensity and stress. It is almost a do-or-die shape and is quite rare.

The *T-square* is an opposition that has another planet at the middle of it that is square to both ends of the opposition. It defines half of the horoscope and half of our life, and therefore is a dominant shape. T-squares tend to be quite unstable and changeable shapes unless they are in the fixed signs, and indeed they are designated as either cardinal, fixed, or mutable T-squares.

The aspects form webs of relationships that bring together disparate traits in us and also connect events that register at different times in life. A trine aspect connecting a planet registering in the maturity octave at twenty-five years old might trigger an earlier event in the middle of gestation, indicating that a process is gestating at that time. In a woman's horoscope it could indicate a pregnancy as it evokes her own gestation time, but equally it could refer to a specific event while you were being carried by your mother. Since all gestation influences are seen from the mother's viewpoint, this might be an opportunity to nurture or be nurtured, or it may be a relationship like our parents' or something similar.

ORBS OF INFLUENCE

The aspects are strongest when they are exact, meaning that Jupiter at 15° Aries is exactly in a 120° trine relationship to the Sun at 15°

Leo, from fire sign to fire sign. However, this is rarely the case. The designation "orb" is the margin on either side of an exact aspect when it still functions. Medieval astrologers often used orbs of up to 15° between planets, which is considered very wide today; the usual distance is about 8° when two planets are conjunct and about 6° for all other aspects. The minor aspects are often smaller and can be as close as 3° apart to make their influences felt.

When two planets are within 10 degrees of each other and there is a third planet between them, that third planet mediates between the other two and all three are considered conjunct to each other. This is a constellation of planets that would be quite powerful in the horoscope and would also be events that happen in close succession in our life.

In traditional astrology the orb of degrees stretches before and after each planet, like a zone of influence. This has an important implication in the time scale. Because the degrees before and after a planet's registration at a specific time also reflect a period of time, we can see exactly how long it takes for a given combination of planets to start to form, become exact, and pass out of importance. This is a process of coming-into-being and is central to understanding how astrological influences work, both initially and in our daily life, because the planets' movements continue after our birth and pass around our birth horoscope again and again. The Moon passes around each month, the Sun each year, Saturn in 29.5 years, and so on. The planets and their aspects are activated in the same sequence each time. Because of the dynamic of the time scale it also matters which planet comes first in the sequence of the degrees.

SENSITIVE POINTS

Due to the inherent geometry of the circle, every planet has a series of exact aspect positions around the horoscope. In Figure 7.8, we can see that Jupiter registers at its sensitive points around the circle. The sensitive points show other times in our life when the Jupiter influence can be felt and experienced, qualified by the nature of the aspect. At the sensitive trines to Jupiter we would expect to experience an integration of our religious or philosophical views or to meet someone who is a guru or supports our viewpoint, while at sensitive squares to Jupiter we might meet influences or people who challenge our views, leading to changes in attitude. All of the sensitive points have dates around the circle of the horoscope.

The primary rhythm of your life is the placement of the eight planets, the Sun, and the Moon. Since there are twelve houses, it is impossible to have a planet in each house. The probability is that

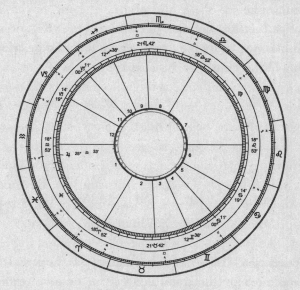

FIGURE 7.8: SENSITIVE POINTS

Jupiter is in the First House. The exact aspect points to Jupiter around the horoscope circle show other times in life when its influence will be felt. At the opposite point, its influences will naturally be opposed to its original place and meaning. In the example, Jupiter in the First House is a protective and optimistic grandparent. This grandparent died at the opposite point, twenty-four years later.

four or more houses do not have planets present. This does not mean that nothing happens at those times. The sensitive points enable you to discover what influences happen in any part of the horoscope and at any time in your life, using the dating wheel. The printout list of the houses, signs, planets, and sensitive points in your horoscope is therefore the texture that covers your entire life.

When you use the printout to discover the quality of an event that happened in your past, you must only find the nearest dates in the list and interpret the pair of planets that bracket that event as though they are in aspect to each other. In the example below, the individual was born in March 1951. In December 1980 she was thirty-nine and nine months old when the Venus sextile sensitive point registered. She is also nearing the end of the Seventh House of partnership and marriage in October 1987, and starting the Eighth House of midlife crisis, separation, and emotional detachment. This is clearly a transitional time.

SXT	VENUS	DEC	1980	07.46	PIS
QNX	PLUTO	APR	1987	17.39	PIS
***0	N NODE	SEP	1987	18.14	PIS
***0	CUSP 8	OCT	1987	18.17	PIS
QNX	NEPTUNE	NOV	1987	18.30	PIS
SXT	MC	MAR	1988	18.58	PIS

She experienced a breakdown of her marriage in the early and mid-1980s, indicated by the transition from a positive sextile from Venus to a difficult and frustrated quincunx from Pluto in 1987. Venus/Pluto is stressed love relationship, excessive desire, and the possibility of an affair. Indeed, her husband had an affair with another woman. The following transition from Pluto to the Node age point in September 1987 shows antisocial attitudes, being cramped by others, and the tragic consequences and destiny. She was forced to go public with her relationship difficulties, as the Node refers to family, neighbors, and her circle of friends. After separating from her husband in October 1987, she experienced a time of uncertainty, shown by the frustrated quincunx from Neptune the following month. By the time the sextile Midheaven sensitive point registered in March 1988, she had adopted new objectives and goals and started remaking her life.

We can examine any time period in the horoscope using the sensitive points around the circle, seeing the planet aspect combinations in the context of their house time and their sign qualities.

For the interest of more advanced readers I would recommend a resource book that is invaluable in interpreting such aspect combinations. *The Combination of Stellar Influences,*[19] written by the German astrologer Reinhold Ebertin in 1940, is renowned among serious astrologers as a profound interpretation guide. It is of great interest because it takes each of the aspect combinations and shows their principle positive and negative psychological correspondences, their biological correspondences, including body parts and medical indications, and their sociological corresondences, along with their probable positive and negative manifestations. Ebertin pioneered a school and technique of astrology called cosmobiology, and he uses midpoints, which are pairs of planets with a third planet at their apex. Using such triads of planets increases the specificity of interpretation at least tenfold. Instead of the seventy-eight aspect combination shown in the interpretation tables in our book, Ebertin explores 1,118 combinations. In the context of "a new vision," we would look at sequences of three planets in the printout. The first planet is a passing state, the middle planet is an existing situation fulcrum point, and the third planet is an outcome. These techniques combined make very specific and delicate distinctions for interpreting the horoscope.

EIGHT

INTERPRETATION TABLES

The interpretation tables list the range of possible meanings of each planet in each sign and house and in aspect with every other planet. Each planet is qualified in three ways:

By the sign (its quality as a division in space)

By the house (its developmental stage of life and exact time of release)

By its aspects to other planets (its connections to other planetary events at other times in life)

The interpretation tables describe a range of possible manifestations, usually ranging from the most positive to the more negative expressions. We evaluate the positive or negative expression on a few values. Each planet has a quality that can be naturally difficult or easy. The Sun, Venus, and Jupiter are considered positive in most circumstances, while Mars, Saturn, Uranus, and Pluto often show tension, negative energy, or difficult situations; and the Moon, Mercury, and Neptune are neutral and easily influenced by whether they are in congenial signs or houses and by which planets aspect them. The outer planets—Uranus, Neptune, and Pluto—are generational influences that everyone experiences according to how closely they connect with the more personal planets. Aspects between outer planets act for months or even years and therefore show generational dynamics that all born in their orb carry.

We consider the types of aspects that connect planets. Conjunctions are neutral aspects of unity. Sextiles and trines are connections that support other planets. Squares and oppositions create tense relationships that can change suddenly. Planets aspecting either the Midheaven or the Ascendant affect our worldview and personality, respectively.

The location of planets by octave conditions their interpretation. The general rule is that the further back toward conception they are located, the deeper and more ingrained their pattern in our being. Planets in gestation are deep, archetypal influences that have a primary effect from within our body; planets in childhood are emotional influences from our family system that we take personally; maturity planets are mental and affect our individual soul through our worldview and overall attitudes.

The old system of planetary rulerships shows strength or weakness in sign and house positions. For example, Venus rules the active sign Libra and the Seventh House, and the passive sign Taurus and the Second House, and it is weak in detriment in the active sign Aries and the First House, and the passive sign Scorpio and the Eighth House.

PLANETS IN SIGNS AND HOUSES

SUN PRINCIPLES
Spirit; mind; energy; wholeness; holism; ruling; individuality; life; vitality; organization; consciousness; libido; kundalini; objectivity; conscious life; sympathy.

Sign	Interpretation
Aries	Assertion; energy; boldness; leading; warlike; impatient; sporty; enterprising; egotism; pride.
Taurus	Perseverance; materialistic; practical; secure; physical; obstinate; possessive; jealous.
Gemini	Dexterity; articulate; educable; dual; identity crises; nervous; glib; superficial; moody; changeable; vivacious.
Cancer	Domesticity; shrewd; conservative; parental; comfortable; religious; psychological; feeling; deepness.
Leo\Rule	Confident; domineering; assured; rising in life; publishing; protection; speculative; teaching; bossy; arrogant.
Virgo	Efficient; detail oriented; orderly; attentive; critical; fault-finding; service; demanding; healer.
Libra	Balancing; relaxed; consistent; sociable; political; charming; amenable; unitary; unreliable; lazy; dominated; loyal mate.
Scorpio	Passionate; dependent; moody; vindictive; jealous; forceful; self-destructive; dynamic; tempered; magnetic; imperturbable.
Sagittarius	Aspiring; free; sloppy; imaginative; success; broad; undisciplined; open; realized; exploratory; hedonist; split.
Capricorn	Goal conscious; egocentric; inhibited; dutiful; hardworking; selfish; industrious; loyal; inflexible; noble; material.
Aquarius\Det	Abstract; humanitarian; knowledgeable; human nature; understanding; social; methodical; help from others; selfish.
Pisces	Compassionate; universal; loving; addictive; empathetic; poetic; deceitful; absorptive; negligent; restricted.

SUN PERSONIFICATIONS
Administration; ruler; governor; politician; leader; captain; speculation; public figure; father; grandparent; doctor; personality in media; official; famous people.

House	Interpretation
	Childhood
First	Attention; parental approval; strong will; vitality; awareness; recuperation; temper; selfishness; physical health; compulsive.
Second	Endurance; humor; enjoyment; gentle; constant; sensual; secure; withholding; stubborn; solid; possessive; indulgent; parents protect.
Third	Quick mind; verbal; curiosity; versatile; adaptable; learning; change; siblings; expression; inquisitive; charming.
Fourth	Secure family; emotional base; pride; parents; beautiful; possessive; domestic; natural; love of comfort; benevolent.
	Maturity
Fifth	Self-expression; self-conscious; boastful; domineering; leading; artistic; practical; fastidious; virginal; discriminating.
Sixth	Methodical; analytical; naive; simple; critical; fussy; studious; verbal; practical; fastidious; virginal; discriminating.
Seventh	Sublimination; partnership; adaptive; vain; worldly; constancy; associations important; popular; dependent; diplomatic; friendly.
Eighth	Separate; insular; intense; metaphysical; mysterious; secretive; obstinate; intense; suspicious; esoteric; fanatical; fearless.
	Gestation (Transcendence)
Ninth	Mobile; enthusiastic; changeable; dualistic; spiritual-religious; inspired; foreign; moral; positive; open; imaginative; unreliable.
Tenth	Pragmatic; paternal; practical; calculating; reserved; tight; depressed; self-concentrated; reversals; tenacious; clinging; hardness.
Eleventh	Idealistic; grouped; observative; detached; friendship; intuitive; planning; cranky; independent; reformative; erratic.
Twelfth	Sympathetic; impressionable; secretive; retiring; solitary; estranged; institutional; drugged; sacrificial; passive; reserved; odd.

MOON PRINCIPLES

The feminine; mother; feeling; emotion; home; family; reflection; rhythm; instinct; change; protective urges; catalytic action; child-raising; integration.

Sign	Interpretation
Aries	Volatile; restless; haste; rashness; power lust; primal; lusty; rebellious; spontaneous feeling; impatient.
Taurus	Constancy; art appreciation; enjoyment; firmness; caution; protection; stubborn; gardener; wealthy; lazy.
Gemini	Unpredictable; vacillation; talkative; multiple relations; sentimental; imitative; inconstant; instinctive.
Cancer\Rule	Related; secure; obsessive; clannish; indigestive; ulcerated; hypersensitive; restrained; inhibited; dissolute.
Leo	Gambler; fertile; childlike; amusing; luxurious; social; magnanimous; open; impressive; sporty; entertaining.
Virgo	Exacting; methodical; hardworking; neat; clean; retiring; emotionally critical; serving; perfectionist.
Libra	Reactive; close partnership; charm; elegance; need approval; public relations; dependent on others; social.
Scorpio	Death wish; licentiousness; control; bias; seriousness; extreme jealousy; revenge; domination; subtlety.
Sagittarius	Imaginative; foreign feelings; kind; hedonistic; jovial; lofty; traditional; travel; mobility; holier-than-thou.
Capricorn\Det	Austerity; unforthcoming; reserved; materialistic; ambitious; egotistic; personal bias; selfish; calculating.
Aquarius	Unable to be alone; civilized; humane; cold; inane; abstracted; detachment; political; frigid; unreliable.
Pisces	Yielding; restless; seductive; poetic; secretive; occult; sympathetic; vulnerable; lonely; mysterious; too open.

MOON PERSONIFICATIONS

Mother; women in general; midwife; grandmother; aunt; wife; emotional person; gynecologist; obstetrician; cook; collector; domestic; gardener.

House	Interpretation
	Childhood
First	Self-awareness; influenced; impressionable; impulsive; strong personality; susceptible; maternal strength; corpulence; irritable.
Second	Stable home; comfort; physical focus; food; deep emotional ties; beauty; firmness; stable; possessive; jealous; habitual; growth.
Third	Manifold emotional expression; mobile; change in mother; fantasy; dreaming; curious; fond of siblings; restless; contradictory; superficial.
Fourth	Familial; affectionate; impressionable; depth of feeling; domestic; unconscious; mediumistic; attached; sensitive; smothered; withdrawn.
	Maturity
Fifth	Speculative feeling; intuitive; confident; passionate; vain; impressive; romantic; imaginative; hedonistic; warm; popular.
Sixth	Head rules heart; psychosomatic; practical; careful; correct; naive; pedantic; coldness; reserved; modest; restrained; undemonstrative.
Seventh	Emotional dependence; compromising; evasive; irresponsible; fateful partners; vivid expression; sensitive; mother figure; fickle.
Eighth	Separation; destructive relations; intense; death of mother; possessive; reserved; deep; psychic sensitivity; resentful; dependent.
	Gestation (Transcendence)
Ninth	Vivid inner life; moody; striving; idealistic; changes; fullness; frank; free; restless; alert; emotional attachment; careless; offhand.
Tenth	Recognition; paternalism; repressed; patient; dutiful; sobriety; ungratified; depressed; cautious; reserved; loyal; possessive.
Eleventh	Friendly; little meaning; group activities; woman friends; idealism; influenced; opinionated; many plans; sympathetic; hoping; wishes.
Twelfth	Moody; insular feelings; isolation; sacrifice; psychic; mediumistic; druggy; induced; easily hurt; hypnotic; reluctant; susceptible; dreamy.

MERCURY PRINCIPLES
Mentality; intelligence; communication; understanding; mediation; neutrality; nervousness; balancing; business sense; criticism; scientific work; logic; self-expression; adaptable.

Sign	*Interpretation*
Aries	Quick thinking; repartee; creative; rash; mental overwork; decisive; argumentative; impulsive; temper; irritated.
Taurus	Logical; material; decisive; common sense; organized; businesslike; blind; secure; structured; obstinate; closed.
Gemini	Businesslike; contractual; writer; variety; rule changeable; inconstant; talented; alert; articulate; perfunctory.
Cancer	Psychological; intuitive; capricious; sentimental; parental ideas; slow mind; conservative; profound.
Leo	Willed; fixed ideas; prudence; planned; foresight; dignified; expansive; broadminded; intellectual; self-centered.
Virgo\Rule	Unholistic; nervous; collaborative; shrewd; patient; organized; sedentary; precise; scientific; psychosomatic.
Libra	Social; learns through others; vapid; eclectic; unoriginal; reasoned; boring; comparative.
Scorpio	Critical; fanatical; practical; skeptical; cunning; crafty; profound; crafty; sharp; investigative; piercing; acid.
Sagittarius\Det	Frank; versatile; foresight; unstable; thinking deeply; manifold interests; philosophical; just; conflicting views.
Capricorn	Organized; practical mind; capable; material ideas; goals conscious; realistic; humorless; crafty; shrewd.
Aquarius	Informed; collective; abstract; cold; inconstant; scattered; quick grasp; scientific; archetypal ideas; occult.
Pisces\Det	Receptive to others; imaginative; plans without energy; irrational; unconscious; karmic; feeling; psychic.

MERCURY PERSONIFICATIONS

Sibling; friend; intellect; thinker; mediator; teacher; writer; artisan; architect.

House	Interpretation

Childhood

First — Mental activity; observation; quickness; nervous; precocious; noisy; assertive; enthusiasm; awake; overactive; self-expressive.

Second — Patience; logic; possessive; deliberate; one-sided; talkative; ponderous; thick; sensible; slow; acquisitive; formal; endurance.

Third — Versatile; conversant; active; adaptable; imitative; siblings; naughty; facile; clever; friendly; gossipy; fluent; superficial.

Fourth — Perceptive; familial; thinking feelings; memory; immersed in reality; individual; homely; talk; disputative; irrational; retentive; narrow.

Maturity

Fifth — Enthusiastic; creative; extrovert; talkative; bossy; critical; mental competition; games; teachers; conceit; organized; dogmatic; rude.

Sixth — Specialized; skills; methodical; patient; alert; superior intellect; analytical; critical; sarcastic; naive; tidy; healthy.

Seventh — Sublimation; teamwork; just; balanced mind; thoughts of others; cooperative; public; intellectual; mediators; opinionated; charmed.

Eighth — Deep; occult; hidden; spiritualistic; deadly; intriguing; grudge holders; interest in the dead; penetrating; senile; suspicious.

Gestation (Transcendence)

Ninth — Deep mind; higher mind; rebirth; ethics; moral; curiosity; knowledgeable; religious; gurus; prophetic; scattered; evasive; free; learning.

Tenth — Ambition; egotistic thoughts; prestige; power; planning; career thoughts; concentration; patience; reserve; rational; serious; exact.

Eleventh — Interested; detached; progressive; groups; reform; invention; involved; utopian; planning; inquisitive; eccentric; contrary; work alone.

Twelfth — Influenced; sacrificial; reproductive; dreamy; imagination; retentive; mediumistic; poetic; impressionable; refined; influenced by others.

♀

VENUS PRINCIPLES
Relationship; harmony; love; aesthetics; physical affection; beauty; art; unity; integration; aberration; bad taste; sentimentality; indulgence; affection; affectation; illusion.

Sign	Interpretation
Aries\Det	Aggressive love; outgoing; passion; ardent; creative powers; attractive personality; erotic; self-centered.
Taurus\Rule	Love of luxury; taste; constancy; conservative; artistic; musical; loving; indolent; loyal; touching; innate value.
Gemini	Many loves; social; flirtatious; attractive; charming; accommodating; discuss ideas; superficial relations; romantic.
Cancer	Domestic; delicate; feminine; sentimental; indigestible; lush; tender; indulgent; exploited; affectionate; unselfish.
Leo	Premature relations; ardent; fixed affection; fiery relationships; garish taste; squandering; indulgent; pride.
Virgo\Fall	Repressed feeling; fastidious; polite; perfectionist; indecisive; shared work; hypercritical; cold exterior; beauty.
Libra\Rule	Lively; crafty; companionable; engagements; artistic skill; important affections; bonding; beauty; money; conformist; social.
Scorpio\Det	Intemperance; legacies; withholding love; deep feeling; immoral; secretive; serious relations; hatred; indifference; occult art.
Sagittarius	Spiritual love; frank; moodiness; many loves; demonstrative; objective relations; ethical; foreign aesthetics.
Capricorn	Materialistic; distrusting; jealous; maturity; attached; experienced; over-controlled; separate; proud; reserved.
Aquarius	Easy contact; free love; refined; amenable; indiscriminate; unconventional; gay; sponsorship; effervescent.
Pisces\Exalt	Longing for love; exploited; tender; gentility; sentimental; musical; romantic; religious; cosmic feeling; suffering.

VENUS PERSONIFICATIONS
Lover; maiden; woman; the beautiful; artist; musician; entertainer; clothier.

House	Interpretation
	Childhood
First	Beauty; personal grace; proportionate; happy; love; demonstrative; popular; love at first sight; social life; clothes; enhancement.
Second	Physical beauty; objects; needing love; good taste; grasping; deep feelings; personal attraction; possessive; faithful; plodding.
Third	Love of words; drawing; social; siblings; close relationships; variety; curiosity; friendly with everyone; flighty; fickle.
Fourth	Deep love; familial; appreciating home; love; dreamy; imaginative; posessive; loyal; tender; flattered; shy; deeply sensitive; stable.
	Maturity
Fifth	Love relations; games; pleasure; amusing; hedonistic; vivacious; creative; proud; jealous; romantic; popular; warmth; social.
Sixth	Work love; critical affections; naivete; friendly cooperation; moral; practical considerations; puritanical; refined; modest.
Seventh	Great love; affairs; infidelity; attractive; amorous; friendly; artistic; happy marriage; public; charming; gentle; lovable; frivolous.
Eighth	Strong attraction; love of separation; lust; fanatic love; passion; jealousy, wavering; licentious; sexual; magnetic; charming.
	Gestation (Transcendence)
Ninth	Love of art, religions, philosophy; wishing; romantic; responsive; scattered emotions; idealistic; imaginings; unstable; cultural.
Tenth	Social ambition; good relations; legal; cold emotion; faithful; constant; control; formal sense; loyal; undemonstrative.
Eleventh	Abstract love; frigidity; homosexuality; idealistic; progressive; social; kind friend; group activities; women's groups; protected.
Twelfth	Secretive; solitary; masturbater; artistic; impressionable; sensitive; soft; psychic love; sexual restraint; charitable.

MARS PRINCIPLES

Energy; aggression; will; activity; desire for change; conflict; intervention; adventure; impulse; competition; sexual drive; initiatory force; passion; violence; ruthlessness.

Sign	Interpretation
Aries\Rule	Fighting; spirit; ambition; temper; zeal; independent; irascible; brutal; headstrong; competitive; egotism.
Taurus\Det	Work capacity; practical; foresight; executive; acquisitive; industrious; material; skilled; aggressive; strong.
Gemini	Mobility; communicative; sarcastic; versatile gifts; agile; lively; ready; mental; debater; journalistic; rude.
Cancer\Fall	Instinctive actions; temper; lacks persistence; irritable; sensuous; tenacious; frustration; ulcers.
Leo	Confident; possessive; ardor; frank; domineering; creative; willed; leading; competitive; strong belief; strength.
Virgo	Scientific; orderly; irritable; astute; criticism; skilled; medicine; practical action; perfectionist; fussy; nervous.
Libra\Det	Social activities; public affairs; leading; teamwork; dependence on feeling; frank; ardent; idealistic; loving.
Scorpio\Rule	Magnetic sex; strong emotions; forceful; selfish; critical; revengeful; occult; sex magic; courage; jealousy.
Sagittarius	Explorative; enthusiastic; strong beliefs; religious; hedonistic; rude; unconventional; adventurous; spiritual.
Capricorn\Exalt	Authoritative; directed; independent; energetic; extremely materialistic; possessive; power mad; efficient; controlled.
Aquarius	Organized; inconstant; superficial; masculine groups; perverse; impatient; revolutionary; upsetting; methodical. *quick action rapid thought*
Pisces	Addictive; silent work; uncontrolled; overemotional; romantic; illusory men; seductive; vivid dreams; waiting.

MARS PERSONIFICATIONS

Fighter; soldier; surgeon; athlete; mechanic; craftsman; men in general; strong woman; engineer; metalworker; technician; builder; police.

House	Interpretation
	Childhood
First	Energetic; lively; self-willed; violence; muscular; robust; impulsive; strength of personality; action; impatience; injuries.
Second	Endurance; practical ability; obstinate; intractable; possessive; purposeful; desiring; tenacious; sensuous; persistence; intense.
Third	Witty; criticism; scattered; active mind; direct; writing; impulsive movement; anger; argumentative; nervous; talkative; hasty.
Fourth	Intense feelings; moody; impulsive; instinct; not persevering; domestic dominance; ecology; acquisitive; energetic; uncontrolled; working.
	Maturity
Fifth	Formative power; self-assurance; enterprise; gambler; player; athlete; audacious; sexual; artist; speculation; egotism; dictatorial. *creative, theatrical.*
Sixth	Detailed work; organizing; tidy; endurance; methodical; critical; skill; energy in work; surgeons; precision; ingenious; frustrated.
Seventh	Associative; sublimated; cordial manner; work partnership; impulsive; aggressive affairs; joint finance; entangled; passion.
Eighth	Survival instinct; courageous; sensuous; dissipated; sadistic; craving power; active corporate desire; violent death; illegality.
	Gestation (Transcendence)
Ninth	Sport; convincing others; adventurous; brave; travel lust; social causes; reform; inspired; experienced; extravagant; rude; sloppy.
Tenth	Famous; ambitious; self-reliant; hard work; realistic; sober; defiant; obstinate; heroic; irritable; cold; unfeeling; reversals; power.
Eleventh	Male friends; reforming; detached; asexual; deliberate; freedom; contradictory; revolutionary; superficial; progressive; perverse.
Twelfth	Energyless; drug desire; alcoholic; secretive; hidden emotions; sensuous; hoping; unconscious; desire; institutions; isolation; unreliable.

JUPITER PRINCIPLES

Expansion; optimism; positivity; generous; enthusiastic; philosophical; religious; psychological; travel; wise; justice; harmony; aspirations; amoral; indulgent; sloppy.

Sign	Interpretation
Aries	Leading; travel urge; noble; positive; generous; free; spiritual; extravagant; frank; innovative; faithful; foolish.
Taurus	Hedonist; good-hearted; indulgent; exploitative; financial interests; stewardship; productive; beneficent.
Gemini\Det	Obliging others; many relations; joy; crafty; sociable; free; mannered; empty; legal; curiosity; advanced; friendly.
Cancer\Exalt	Pleasure; prolific; deep feelings; charitable; intuitive; receptive; deep love; family important; secure.
Leo	Speculative; grandeur; openness; arts; great energy; positive in games; fond; generous; big hearted; noble; vain.
Virgo\Det	Morality; prudent; ambitious; honest; intellectual; conscientious; critical; perfectionist; overrated; serving; work.
Libra	The law; mildness; open partnerships; advantage through marriage; benign; unfulfilled commitments; psychology.
Scorpio	Metaphysical; passionate; shrewd; striving for possessions; craving pleasure; corporate affairs; mystical.
Sagittarius\Rule	Philosophy; religious; humanitarian; esoteric; nobility; foreign; jovial; liberal; psychological; superstition.
Capricorn\Fall	Acquisitive; wealthy; recognized; trusty; responsible; integrity; conservatism; austere; tight; materialist.
Aquarius	Impartial; sympathetic; fellowship; human nature; occult wisdom; social reform; intolerant; astrology; broad.
Pisces	Deep emotions; hidden life; drugs; modest circumstances; kind; unreliable; visionary; indolent; illusory; alcohol.

JUPITER PERSONIFICATIONS

Priest; philosopher; psychologist; psychiatrist; the wealthy; lawyer; banker; physician; official; publisher; guru; wise man or wise woman; fortune hunter.

House	Interpretation
	Childhood
First	Self-sufficient; optimistic; extrovert; fat; aspiring; imbalanced; sociable; well-liked; protection; indulgence; promises; vigor.
Second	Expansiveness; growth; reliable; wasteful; generous; enjoyment; insecure; trusteeship; liberal; open; exploitable; wealthy.
Third	Positive mind; optimism; religious influence; intelligent; flexible; versatile; changing; popular; travel; conceited; carefree; sweet.
Fourth	Receptive; attachment; contented; religious; psychology; family sense; impressionable; congenial; strong home; morality; fortunate.
	Maturity
Fifth	Creativity; artistic; self-confidence; lead; popularity; vanity; honor; achievements; dignified; intolerant; prestige; dominant.
Sixth	Ambition; learning; teaching; teamwork; carefree; service; healing; work ethic; morality; conscientious; organization; professional.
Seventh	Fortunate marriage or job; justice; popularity; temperance; charitable; social contacts; selfless relationships; judgment; spiritual.
Eighth	Religious; separated; legacies; funerals; sex values; overrated; proud; self-indulgent; peaceful death; materialistic; occult.
	Gestation (Transcendence)
Ninth	Religious; moral aspiration; foresight; plans; expansive feelings; speculative; foreign matters; inner development; justice; balance.
Tenth	Responsible; productive; material; practical; prominence; recognition; reliable; dignity; standing; domestic affairs; egotist; capable.
Eleventh	Humanitarian; prominent friends; groups; help from others; liberal; obliging; collective goals; invention; ulterior motives; sociable.
Twelfth	Altruism; contentment; solitude; generous; imaginative; inner life; compassionate; spiritual search; meditation; fantasy; crisis.

guardian angel at the right time.

ħ

SATURN PRINCIPLES
Contraction; pessimism; negativity; stingy; concentration; focus; seriousness; economy; inhibition; reserve; inadaptable; formative energy; discipline; limitation; suffering.

Sign	Interpretation
Aries	Selfishness; diligence; reserved; humorless; lonely; mechanical; autocratic; willful; strong character.
Taurus	Perseverance; method; constructive; money worries; ambition; hard work; father; elders; serious finances.
Gemini	Intellectual; scientific; businesslike; serious; difficult; abstract; inhibited; calculating; detached; systematic.
Cancer\Det	Sensitive; self-centered; elderly; paranoid; lonely; jealous; suspicious; estranged; respectful; unstable.
Leo\Det	Limited; authoritarian; leader; simple; loyalty; hard work; loss through children; ungratified; resentful; need recognition.
Virgo	Perfectionist; hard worker; serious; materialistic; acting alone; pedantic; detail-oriented; attentive; discreet.
Libra	Industrious; conscientious; impartial; austere; reliable; managerial; corporate; mediator; businesslike; legal; enemies.
Scorpio	Resourceful; restrained; melancholy; metaphysical seriousness; cautious; corporate; legal conflict; perfectionist.
Sagittarius	Moralizing; high-minded; religious; serious traveler; prudence; law; separation from home; doubts.
Capricorn\Rule	Paternal; advanced; suspicious; slow; patience; method; pessimism; diplomacy; materialistic; partial; strong; egotist.
Aquarius	Serious groups; collective; ambitious; organized; responsible; mental work; detached; selfish; domineering; games.
Pisces	Struggle; melancholy; restrained; older friends; retirement; deep meditation; spiritual; withdrawal; distrusting.

SATURN PERSONIFICATIONS

Doctor; banker; worker; farmer; worker with metals; scientist; grandparent; uncle and aunt; businesspeople; archaeologist; geologist; miner; computer programmer.

House	Interpretation
	Childhood
First	Ambitious; restrained; obstinacy; responsible; cold; unfriendly; limitation; hardship; lonely; older people; defiance; selfish; serious.
Second	Material; ordered; possessive; stability; endurance; inhibited; restricted movement; grasping; conservative; inertia; difficulty.
Third	Difficult siblings; zealous; thorough; not adaptable; shy; disciplined; practical; scientific; critical; mechanistic; clumsy; logic; serious.
Fourth	Reserved; ambitious; difficult family; love; independent; defensive; repressed; economy; responsible; isolated; secure; reclusive.
	Maturity
Fifth	Responsible; reliable; loyal; informal; shy; conservative; repressed; unsportsmanlike; strict; serious school; inhibited sexuality.
Sixth	Critical; correct; responsible; methodical; pedantic; scientific; serious study; detailed; sedentary; inhibited; asexual; misunderstood.
Seventh	Dutiful; older partner; serious relations; estrangement; impractical; loyal; inhibited; discontented; enduring; hard work; responsible.
Eighth	Partners' finances, emotions; lack capital; obstinate; transformations; strong; reserved; selfish; occult; concentrative; rebirth.
	Gestation (Transcendence)
Ninth	Aspirations; serious philosophers; separation; devotion; sincere; hurt; religious; stable; unsocial; achievement; status; morality.
Tenth	Patience; will power; restraint; ambitious; strong will; concentration; economy; partial; egocentric; cautious; karmic affairs; debts.
Eleventh	Responsible; planning; reliable partner; extravagant expectations; aspirations; false friends; faithful; detached; inhibited mate.
Twelfth	Reserved; lonely; restrained; secluded; nerves; timid; isolated; fear of failure; inferior; depressed; retiring; sacrificial; worrying.

♅
⊖

URANUS PRINCIPLES

Originality; eccentricity; independence; rhythm; inspiration; individuality; invention; rebelliousness; dancing; perception; excitable; obstinacy; operations; accidents; changes.

Sign	*Interpretation*
Aries	(1928–1934) Utopian; enthusiasm; unusual; peculiar; odd personality; free; unconventional; intuition; courage; daring; tempered.
Taurus\Fall	(1934–1942) Erratic; sudden changes; unstable finances; independent; ingenious; risk; speculative; premature; reform; original.
Gemini	(1942–1949) Mental energy; spontaneous; inquisitive; scientific; methodical; original methods; free thinker; bizarre; comprehension.
Cancer	(1949–1956) Erratic feelings; strange mother; impulsive; residence changes; rebel; freedom; excitement; psychic; sensitive.
Leo\Det	(1956–1962) Egomaniacal; peculiar love; children; individual; licentious; determined; organizing; unrestrained; sexually free.
Virgo	(1962–1969) Health professions; mechanical; free; subtle; original job; intellectual; revolutionary; ingenious; computers.
Libra	(1969–1975) New relationships; divorce; irritable; affairs; free love; magnetic; quick associations; imaginative; restless.
Scorpio\Exalt	(1975–1981) Regeneration; rapid change; destined struggles; violence; danger; ruthless; occult explosion; rebellious astrology.
Sagittarius	(1981–1988) Adventure; astrology; progressive education; reformed; unorthodox; utopian; excitable; spiritual; neurotic.
Capricorn	(1988–1996) Power; great aims; fanaticism; penetration; acquisitive; resolution; headstrong; strange career; radical.
Aquarius	(1996–2003) Detachment; trouble; magnification; penetration; spiritual energy; religious change; inventive talent; wayward.
Pisces	(2003–2011) Intuitive; peculiar methods; isolated; investigative; occult; mystical; self-willed; strange aspirations; idealism.

URANUS PERSONIFICATIONS
Eccentric; inventor; unusual person; technician; revolutionary; dancer and musician; astrologer; radio–TV; electrician; healer; feminist; rebel; surgeon.

House	Interpretation
	Childhood
First	Energetic; unusual; original; restless; odd; scientific influence; obstinacy; irrational electric; willful; abrupt; erratic; stubborn.
Second	Unusual objects; gains and losses; headstrong; determined; jealous; speculative; premature; unsettled; precocious; impractical; lively.
Third	Inventive; original; precocious; creative; desultory; quick understanding; restless; intuitive; scattered; sharp; witty.
Fourth	Strange family; peculiar emotions; intuition; wandering; odd associations; homelessness; estrangement; impatient; rebellious; changes.
	Maturity
Fifth	Enterprise; boldness; creative; originality; peculiar games; dramatic; sudden affections; gambling; adventurous; quick learning; arty.
Sixth	Peculiar work; individual learning; quick; scientific effort; genius; occult; original; reforming; detailed; foolish; critical.
Seventh	Eccentric relationship; drug experiences; rebellious; inspired; peculiar marriage view; many marriages; aesthetic; talented; rigid.
Eighth	Penetrating; investigating occultism; energy realized; danger; fearless; strength; tenacious; great change; rebirth; violence; super-physics.
	Gestation (Transcendence)
Ninth	Spiritual; enlightenment; prophecy; rebelling; religious reform; advanced ideas; progressive fanaticism; restless; unconventional; danger.
Tenth	Ambitious; shrewd; concentrated energy; resolute; technical ability; professional; radical ideas; sudden fall; affliction.
Eleventh	Scientific; profound; inspirational; organizing; magnification; progressive; intuitive friend; perversity; rebellious; peculiar ideas.
Twelfth	Mystical; reveling; intuition; estrangement; strange disease; visionary; secretive; being misunderstood; yoga; seek liberation; unreal.

♆   **NEPTUNE PRINCIPLES**
Sensitivity; psychic; impressionable; fantasy; imagination; dreams; illusion; drugs; mediumship; intuition; idealism; utopian projections; ESP; transcendental experiences.

Sign	Interpretation
Aries	(1861–1874) Inspiration; idealism; unselfish; highly sensitive; far distant; social welfare; confused; mad; insane; addicted.
Taurus	(1874–1888) Good taste; formal; unusual objects; idealistic finances; visionary; healing; natural beauty; alcoholism; addiction.
Gemini	(1888–1901) Nature love; mystical; magical; inspired; confusion; vagueness; scattered; poetic; quick perception; variety; worrying.
Cancer	(1901–1914) Intuition; psychic force; sensitive to home and mother; cherishing; inhibited; susceptible; unstable; suffering.
Leo\Exalt	(1914–1928) Passionate; easily stimulated; acting; leading; flattery; certain; love of pleasure; misdirected affection; waste.
Virgo\Det	(1928–1942) Fault-finding; hypercritical; work difficulty; psychic communication; chaos; chemical; drugged; preoccupied.
Libra	(1942–1956) Uncertain relations; divorce; sensitive partner; drug abuse; psychedelics; strange feelings; disappointed; receptive sex.
Scorpio	(1956–1970) Hidden emotions; mystery; sex urge; confusion; clairvoyance; occultism; sensationalism; depression; sickness.
Sagittarius	(1970–1984) Higher mind; religious regeneration; travel; foreign ideas; meditation; enlightenment; aimless; inspiration.
Capricorn	(1984–1998) Supernatural; meditation; strange objectives; deception; depression; parental sacrifice; mystic reality.
Aquarius	(1998–2012) Soul unions; noble aspirations; easy temptation; social theory; group stimuli; independence; intuitive.
Pisces	(2012–2026) Mysticism; inner life; mediumistic; neurotic; metaphysical; escapist; druggist; addictive; seductive.

NEPTUNE PERSONIFICATIONS

Psychic; sensitive person; dreamer; utopian; trickster; mystic; guru; dietician; drug dealer; anesthetist; chemist; inventor.

House	Interpretation

Childhood

First
Sensitive personality; intuition; dreamy; impressionable; delicate digestion; drugs; strange appearance; peculiar relationships.

Second
Sensitive to form; artistic; sensuous; beauty; soft; imaginative; addictive; moody; strange form; muddled; impractical; lazy; dependent.

Third
Duality; sensitivity; fantasy; confusion; unrealistic; inspiration; wrong ideas; weak memory; misunderstanding; nicknames; siblings.

Fourth
Great sensitivity; spiritual perception; deep feeling; inner union; discontent; anxiety; residence changes; addicted; sacrificial.

Maturity

Fifth
Beauty; peculiar pleasures; sexuality; acting; exaggerating; romantic; psychological problems; broken family; intuitions; waste.

Sixth
Psychosomatic; serving; healing power; gentle; deceitful; hypersensitive; addictive; easy; despondent; magnetic energy; inspiration.

Seventh
Receptive; idealistic relationships; platonic; seductive; artistic; impulsive; harmonious relationships; psychic connections; oddness.

Eighth
Psychic; spiritual; unconscious processes; mediumistic; depressive; secretive; drugged; wasting diseases; hospitals; disappointment.

Gestation (Transcendence)

Ninth
Presentiment; clairvoyance; idealism; overactive mind; dreams; unrealistic; wishes and plans; self-deception.

Tenth
Aspiration without application; deep ideas; uncertainty; lacking reality; family trouble; psychic experiences; scandal; mysterious.

Eleventh
Artistic; idealistic; strange attraction; hopes; wishes; mental change; insincerity; psychic experience; notoriety; theorizing.

Twelfth
Reserve; psychic communication; reverie; art, external influences; drugs; hospitals; ill; inducement; craving, alcohol; pessimism.

PLUTO PRINCIPLES
The masses; transformation; revolution; destruction; major forces; power; magic; willpower; propaganda; coercion; media; major changes; regeneration; passages.

Sign	Interpretation
Aries	(1823–1852) Self-assertion in the world; power-lust; new ideas; revolutionary person; potential; courageous; dauntless; free.
Taurus\Det	(1852–1884) Possessiveness; materialist; endurance; utilitarian; genius with materials; art; depending on finances; productive.
Gemini	(1884–1914) Inventive; mobility; comprehension; intellectual assertion; science; adventures; ruthless behavior.
Cancer	(1914–1939) Intense personal feelings; familial restraint; compulsive; paternalism; transformed family; liberated woman.
Leo	(1939–1957) Revolution in self-expression; change of attitude; exteriorization; outburst of consciousness; creativity; talent.
Virgo	(1957–1972) Health revolution; mental disease; psychosomatic; holistic medicine; workers; reactionaries; punks; birth control.
Libra	(1972–1984) Liberation; homosexuality; changes in partnership; social justice; regenerated civilization; arbitration; delicate balance.
Scorpio\Rule	(1984–2000) Death and rebirth; regeneration; force; fanaticism; atomic warfare; world war; daemonic forces; transformation; rage.
Sagittarius	(2000–2011) Prophecy; sagacity; exploration; travel; strive for wisdom; philosophical change; psychoanalysis; utopian aims; religious fundamentalism; profound revolution.
Capricorn	(2011–2023) New ideas; practical revolutions; great ambition; corporate; executive; inventive; obsessed; materialistic.
Aquarius	(2023–2042) Democracy; mental change; scientific; advancement through friends; psychological; synthetic ideas; intellectual.
Pisces	(1799–1823) Profundity; apocalyptic; universal; compassionate; Christian fanaticism; born again; mystical; astrological.

PLUTO PERSONIFICATIONS

Revolutionary; mass media person; politician; dictator; propagandist; actor or actress; public speaker; atomic scientist; outlaw; prostitute.

House	Interpretation
	Childhood
First	Power drive; extraordinary energy; assertions; rage; powerful will; hardships; robust; strong parental changes; advanced; rapid growth.
Second	Great ambition; acquisitive; great gains or losses; dependence on money; insatiable; change material situations; stewardship.
Third	Ingenious; specialized learning; rapid speech; penetrating mind; resourceful; secretive; strong opinions; strange siblings; gossip.
Fourth	Strong heredity; unusual task; solitary; deep feelings; magnetic; magic; domination at home; nature love; ecology; occult; secrets.
	Maturity
Fifth	Dynamic emotions; authority; self-awareness; powerful will; force; dramatic expression; great achievements; creative power; talent.
Sixth	Healing; psychosomatic diseases; working with others; inquisitive; collecting; scientific; energetic; great criticism; fanaticism; zeal.
Seventh	Fateful partnerships; fame; strong unions; divorces; multiple partners; personal magnetism; dramatic changes; domineering; intuitive.
Eighth	Fanaticism; tragic events; record achievements; search for meaning; transforming; public death; influential; tenacious; occult; secrets.
	Gestation (Transcendence)
Ninth	Higher knowledge; spiritual regeneration; pioneering; the unattainable; travel; reform; social change; religious fantaticism; atheism. or Hydrotheism.
Tenth	Dictatorship; struggle for recognition; practical problems; independence; danger; isolation; plans; dramatic change; willpower.
Eleventh	Communal; utopian communities; reforming; friendship important; sudden death; changes of attitude; exaggerated hopes; popularity.
Twelfth	Isolation; universal; revelatory; destructive; metaphysical; secretive; tempted; suppressed emotions; strange illness; retirement; occult.

NODE PRINCIPLES
Associations; alliances; sociability; communal sense; sublimation; fostering; collective influences.

Sign	Interpretation
Aries	Cultivating friendships; honors; wealth; associative urge; extrovert; social; ardent; enthusiastic.
Taurus	Gain through property; sharing resources; debt; gain by learning and property.
Gemini\Exalt	Good mind; language facility; gains from siblings; publishing; writing; words create anxiety.
Cancer	Close parents; soul associations; gain by property; obliging at home.
Leo	Speculative with others; large circle of friends; sporting; clubs; society affairs; wasteful; pompous; love affairs.
Virgo	Scientific associations; teaching; institutional; research; nagging; critical of others; sensitive health.
Libra	Unable to be alone; gregarious; dependent on others; contention; communal sense; social meetings; business success.
Scorpio	Deceptive; secretive associations; esoteric organizations; sexual relations; subversive affairs.
Sagittarius\Fall	Legal teamwork; administrative; orderly; communal; mental quality; prophetic dreams; psychoanalysis.
Capricorn	Responsible to others; exploitation; practical groups; unions; professional groups; authorities; social climbing.
Aquarius	Stimulating friends; many friends; social life; inseparable; grasping; helping others communally.
Pisces	Beliefs; religious communities; collectives; institutions; isolation within groups; gaining possessions.

NODE PERSONIFICATIONS
Associations; groups; clubs; political parties; labor unions; organizations.

House	Interpretation
	Childhood
First	Self-expression; desiring to rule; recognition; social life; personal associations.
Second	Permanent bonding; alliances; money from others; devoted people; reliable; loyalty; legacy.
Third	Many associations; ideas from others; important contacts; superficial association; nursery school; short relationships.
Fourth	Family ties; prominent parental contact; confused ancestry; soul unions; dependent; attached.
	Maturity
Fifth	Popularity; game-playing; large schools; many loves; affectionate with family; organized; team sports.
Sixth	Teaching associations; science; health interests; love of animals; serving others; work relationships; honest employees.
Seventh	Love affairs; teams; public affairs; profit through others; gain through women and partnership; making friends easily; social.
Eighth	Occult organizations; associations; cooperative effort; socialism; old age home; secret relations; gifts; legacies; violent policies.
	Gestation (Transcendence)
Ninth	Utopian ideas; idealistic groups; legal affairs; educational interests; dreams; water journeys; political idealism.
Tenth	Honor; credit; great achievements; business organizations; corporate affairs; deception; material objectives.
Eleventh	Many friendships; support family; ideal plans; complex relationships; compulsive joining; social life prominent; helpful.
Twelfth	Secret associations; rest homes; hospitals; nursing staff; teams of doctors; restraint from others; philosophical interests.

AS

AS PRINCIPLES
Environment; personality; birth circumstances; people present at birth; reaction to the world; mask; way of acting; personal attitude; surroundings.

Sign	Birth Circumstances and Environment
Aries	Restlessness; energy; self-assertive; aggressive; impatient; surgery; forceps delivery; hurrying; ruthlessness.
Taurus	Stable conditions; security; quiet; beautiful surroundings; women present; midwife; home; domesticity; practical.
Gemini	Changes; quick birth; talking; many people present; siblings present; nerves; observers; moving around; adaptation.
Cancer	Moody; home; family contact; humid; caring; feminine; protected; simplicity; sensitivity; anesthetics; women.
Leo	Authoritarian; confident; extrovert; active; joyous; open; prominent doctor; purposeful; bold; luxurious environs.
Virgo	Critical; hospital; doctors; nurses; naivete; first births; virginal; nervous; stable; painstaking; hygienic; observant.
Libra	Harmonious place; balanced; teamwork; physically easy; obliging; social; talkative; craving approval; women; nurses.
Scorpio	Disharmonious; humid; hot-headed; brutal; surgical; forceps; violence; force; tragic; caesarean; circumcision; cautious; angry.
Sagittarius	Enthusiastic; athletic; joyous; good humor; natural; easy; active; messy; lively; expansive; foreign; recognized.
Capricorn	Concentration; inhibition; restriction; long labor; serious; restraint; older doctor, reserved; anxious; methodical.
Aquarius	Communal; detached; serious; idealistic; restrained; cold; progressive; friendly; abstract; mechanical; unorthodox; rhythmic.
Pisces	Self-sacrificial; drugged; governed by externals; unconfident; anesthetics; induced; isolated; psychic; dreamy; vague.

ASPECT INTERPRETATION TABLES

The Aspect Tables show each planetary pair with their keywords; negative keywords are given in parentheses. Each entry concludes with personifications that carry the aspect.

 SUN ASPECTS

SU/SU The will to live; power; the physical body; health and energy; bodily and spiritual harmony. (Lack of incentive; illness; weakness; changes in direction; being without focus.) The body; father and son; grandfather to son; colleague; man to man.

SU/MO Conscious and unconscious; relationship; inner balance; public life; success. (Inner discontent; conflict; unrelated; inner tension; struggle.) Man and wife; father and mother; marriage partner; friend.

SU/ME Common sense; understanding; thoughts; practical mind; businesslike; organizational. (Unclear; confusion; aimlessness; nervousness.) Youngster; intellectual; businesspeople.

SU/VE Physical love; beauty; popularity; social life; aesthetics; romantic. (Frigidity; ugliness; unpopular; antisocial; tasteless; cold; indulgence.) Artist; beloved man or woman.

SU/MA Vitality; vigor; advancement; vocational success; endurance; impulsiveness. (Dissidence; violence; headstrong; contentious; daring.) Fighter; soldier; doctor; husband; quarreler.

SU/JU Health; recognition; religious; expansive; happy; successful; creative. (Materialistic; indulgent; arrogant; illegal, lazy.) Wealthy; healthy; prominent; socialite.

SU/SA Separate; concentrated; absorbed; serious; hard worker; ambitious; dedicated. (Selfish; inhibited; suppressive; pessimistic; inferior; anxious; weak, negative.) Serious person; elderly; sick; inhibited; cruel father; weak father; missing father.

SU/UR Progressive; eccentric; technological; original; free; changeable; dynamic; individual. (Obstinate; self-destructive; rebellious; tense; irritable.) Innovator; reformer; rebel; technician; troublemaker.

SU/NE Sensitive; delicate; imaginative; uncertain; refined; inspired; visionary; psychic. (Insecure; weak; sick; deceptive; seducible; tasteless.) Medium; romantic; dreamer; psychic; sensitive; drug addict; seducer; weak father.

SU/PL Power; attainment; conscious objectives; leading; growing; autocratic; ruthless. (Ruthless; arrogant; forced; brutal; fanatical; destructive.) Leader; fighter; revolutionary; transformer; martyr; strong father.

SU/NO Physical associations; public; adaptive; sociable; popular; educational. (Anti-social; disharmonious; inadaptable; unrelated; isolated.) Associate; fellow; colleague; witness; relative; dignitary; police.

SU/AS Personal relations; physical relations; confidence; advancement; esteem; recognizable. (Pushy; disharmonious; disliked; self-seeking; shy; quarrelsome; dependent.) Men in the environment; contact; husband.

SU/MC Individual; objective; self-knowledge; success; missionary; authority; famous. (Egocentric; unclear, arrogant; conceited; uninteresting; misguided.) Body and Soul; "I"; one's own ego.

☾ MOON ASPECTS

MO/MO Emotional life; feminine relations; changeable things; pleasant moods; motherliness. (Emotional suppression; moodiness; separation from mother; unemotional; tension.) The feelings; the Soul; mother and daughter.

MO/ME Emotional thoughts; perception; judgment; valuation; feminine ideas; discretion. (Changeable; lying; gossip; criticism; calumny; ingenious; highly strung.) Intellectual women; girl; authoress; psychologist; traveler.

MO/VE Love; devotion; art; conception; romantic; cultured; marriage; graceful. (Moody; shy; tasteless; sterile; irritable; loveless.) Lover; expectant mother; mother; artist; woman; actor.

MO/MA Excitement; intense emotion; frankness; candid; sincere; feeling will; industrious. (Impulsiveness; rash; fighting; intolerant; rebellious; irritable.) Wife; woman colleague; hard worker; housewife; businesswoman.

MO/JU   Happy; religious; social conscience; travel; faithful; recognition; positive feeling. (Indifferent; negligent; rebellious; unpopular; illegal; marital problems; sloppy.) Successful; generous; happy woman; female; bride; expectant mother, official women.

MO/SA   Self-control; duty; care; attentive; circumspect; lonely; ascetic; critical; ambitious. (Depressive; separated; widowed; inferior; melancholy; anxious; estranged.) Inhibited person; sad; widow; single parent; female grandparent.

MO/UR   Subconscious forces; instinct; sudden events; occult; intellectual specialization. (Schizophrenia; emotional tension; overstrain; abrupt; exaggeration; anxiety.) Restless woman; ambitious; reformist; schizophrenic.

MO/NE   Refined; inner vision; imagination; inspiration; relaxation; romantic; idealistic. (Frail; self-deception; unreality; weakness; addicted; seductive; supernatural.) Sensitive; medium; impressionable person; card-reader; psychic; indolent; weak person.

MO/PL   Extreme emotion; one-sided fanaticism; overzealous; devouring; dynamic; insatiable. (Fanatic; sadistic; obsessed; shocking; jealous; demanding; insane demands; upheavals.) Emotional persons; public relations persons; publicists; schizophrenic; revolutionary.

MO/NO   Spiritual union; inner relationships; alliances (between women); family ties; devoted. (Estrangement; multiple relationships; inadaptable; frustrated; not housebroken; insular.) Woman alliances; blood union; associate.

MO/AS   Emotional relations; obliging; feminine; adaptable; personal ties; subjective ties. (Hypersensitivity; disagreements; moody; changeable; overreactive; annoyed.) Feminine environment; mother; alcoholic; drug addict; lover; personality.

MO/MC   Emotional objectives; sentiment; home; family; soul-ties; intuitive understanding. (Difficult women; unprofessional; vacillation; unreliable; sentimental; wavering.) Woman; feeling and emotional person; governess; mother; soul person.

MERCURY ASPECTS

ME/ME   Movement; thinking; mind; news; opinions; perception; good comprehension; understanding; easy. (Static states; subjectivity; dullness; lacking objectivity; lying; no communication.) Active person; friend; confidant; mediator; intellect; teacher; sibling; young person.

ME/VE   Love thoughts; beauty sense; design; feeling intellect; hilarity; art success; writing. (Vanity; conceit; hypersensitive; irresolute; squandering; luxury.) Lover; author; writer; beauty salesperson; art dealer; aesthete; artist; female friend.

ME/MA   Thought power; realized plans; resolution; repartee; enterprise; debate; settling affair. (Criticism; nagging; malice; hasty action; speech difficulty; obstinate; cynical.) Critic; quarreler; debater; writer.

ME/JU   Constructive mind; erudition; literature; business sense; common sense; science; fluent. (Negligence; fraud; unreliable; exaggerating; conflict; indiscreet.) Speaker authority; negotiator; businessperson; publisher; traveler; philanthropist.

ME/SA   Mental work; concentration; deep thought; logic; organization; experience; industry (Dullness; reserve; shyness; estrangement; difficulty; hard infancy; distrust.) Philosopher; intellectual; scientist; crook; logician.

ME/UR   Intuition; astuteness; flexibility; independence; influence; mathematics; original mind. (Scattered; madness; nerves; erratic; eccentric; contradictory.) Mathematician; scientist; technician; musician; astrologer; lively person.

ME/NE   Imagination; fantasy; deep perception; vision; presentiments; poetic; idealistic; clear. (Faulty judgment; paralysis; deception; fraud; dissipated; foolish.) Actor; fantasizer; dreamer, saint; liar; faith healer; psychic.

ME/PL   Persuasion; understanding; cunning; diplomacy; influence; wit; slyness. (Breakdown; hasty expression; excessive opposition; overeager; impatience; crudeness.) Speaker; politician; fascist; critic; tyrant; propagandist.

ME/NO   Joint plans; exchanging ideas; social-business meeting; correspondence; relationship. (Unsociable; unpopularity; closed; blocked; disloyalty.) Joiner; groupie; writer; organizer; negotiator; networker.

ME/AS   Personal ideas; definition; verbal communication; meetings; intelligence; talkative. (Gossip; misjudgment; anxiety; superficial; flighty.) Thinker; gossip; organizer; friend; administrator; diplomat.

ME/MC   Intellectual objectives; observation; self-knowledge; meditation; own aims; clarity. (Aimlessness; unselfconscious; changeable; vacillation; dishonest.) Expressive person; talker; media person; MC; job counselor.

♀ VENUS ASPECTS

VE/VE   Peace; goodwill; love; desire; feeling love; humor; beauty sense; art. (Unrelated; listless; tasteless; aberration; carelessness.) Lover; aesthete; beauty; model; girl; actor; artist; musician; clothier; nurse.

VE/MA   Sexual love; artistry; passion; creativity; lively expression; intimacy; prolific. (Asexuality; seduction; unsatisfied; infidelity; irritable; sexual disease.) Lover; sexist; seducer; polygamist; active lover.

VE/JU   Joyous love; happiness; popularity; form sense; marriage; bliss; comfort; gay; hedonism. (Laziness; lacking feeling; indolence; arrogance; legal conflict; indulgence.) Artist; film star; model; socialite; expansive lover.

VE/SA   Dutiful emotion; soberness; loyalty; inhibition; sacrifice; fidelity; economy; reserve. (Jealousy; torment; deprivation; lonely; depressed; mother separation.) Lonely person; widow(er); illegitimate children; older lover.

VE/UR   Arousal; eccentricity; impulse; talent; music; sentimentality; refinement. (Repressed sexuality; inconstancy; estrangement; unconventional; loose.) Musician; artist; eccentric lover.

VE/NE   Rapture; eroticism; mysticism; idealism; platonic affairs; travel; refinement. (Seducible; tasteless; infatuation; dreaming; illusion; escapist.) Artist; musician; dreamer; visionary; romantic; drug dealer; addict; weak lover.

VE/PL   Fanatic love; sensuality; gifted; attractive; compulsive; devoted; talented; magnetic. (Lusty; stressed love; sadomasochism; vulgarity; excessive desire.) Lover; pornographer; menstruating woman; artist.

VE/NO   Love union; adaptation; universal love; ties; obliging; artistic communities. (Isolation; separation; unhappy affair; flighty.) Lover; married couple; single; art groupie; gallery owner.

VE/AS   Harmonious love; beauty; attractive personality; adornment; art; taste; gentility. (Bad taste; desertion; unsociable; wasteful; indulgent.) Woman; mother; wife; lover; artist.

VE/MC   Objective love; affection; benevolence; artistic; attached; attractive individual. (Vanity; conceit; jealousy; dissipated.) Lover; artist; admirer.

♂ MARS ASPECTS

MA/MA   Energy; activity; work; aggression; impulse; resolve; will; decision; accomplishment.

MA/JU   Successful creativity; joy; activity; organization; prowess; rebellion; practicality. (Conflict; estrangement; precipitancy; haste; restlessness; dispute.) Manager; organizer; jurist; judge; official; athlete.

MA/SA   Inhibition; endurance; danger; fanaticism; spartan life; ascetic; tough. (Destruction; danger; death; impotence; obstinacy; separation; tests; dispute; illness.) Laborer; miner; fighter; killer.

MA/UR   Applied effort; intervention; courage; independence; operation; revolutionary; birth. (Argument; obstinacy; emotional tension; stress; nerves; operation; injury; accident.) Surgeon; violent person; revolutionary; reactionary; driver; fireman.

MA/NE   Inspiration; desire; sensitivity; escapism; romanticism; fantasy; denial. (Destruction; infection; misdirection; drugs; inferiority; smoking; paralysis; narrowness.) Sick person; addict; sailor; pathologist; dealer.

MA/PL   Superhuman force; violence; vigor; great ambition; success; obsession; research. (Cruelty; assault; aggression; injury; sadism;

homicide; ruthlessness.) Dictator; disabled; nuclear scientist; politician; general.

MA/NO   Physical collaboration; team spirit; union; shared success; progeny; betrothal. (Quarrels; lack of fellowship; disrupted meetings; asexual; dissolution; dissociation.) Collective; communist; socialist; eunuch.

MA/AS Fighting spirit; forced will; teamwork; attainment; resolution; creative work; surgery. (Caesarean; forceps birth; operation; fighting; aggression; conflict; dispute; quarrel.) Surgeon; soldier; colleague; boxer.

MA/MC   Ego-conscious action; order; decision; success; resolution; occupation change; prudence. (Excitable; stress; premature; purposeless; fever, fraud; agitation; murder.) Organizer; leader; politician; leading personality.

♃ JUPITER ASPECTS

JU/JU   Contentment; optimism; luck; financial gain; religion; philosophy; social life. (Unlucky; losses; pessimism; illegal; extravagant; materialistic; greedy; corpulence.) Lawyer; judge; banker; insurer; physician; uncle; grandparent; publisher.

JU/SA   Patience; perseverance; industry; diplomacy; seclusion; duty; philosophy; calm; real estate. (Vacillation; discontent; upset; failure; illness.) Professor; teacher; lawyer; official; politician; relatives; tenant.

JU/UR   Optimism; fortunate ideas; perception; sudden recognition; bliss; invention; change. (Independence; opposition; magnifying matters; arguments; tension; stress.) Organizer; inventor; adventurer; optimist; religious zealot.

JU/NE   Speculation; imagination; metaphysics; idealism; luck; ethics; generosity; profit. (Susceptible; dreaming; unreality; enmity; insult; losses; swindlers.) Speculator; dreamer; mystic; visionary.

JU/PL   Plutocracy; spiritual-mental power; leadership; regeneration; organization; transfusion. (Fanaticism; losses; guilt; failure; legal liability; bankruptcy; exploitation.) Organizer; professor; teacher; speculator; dictator; propagandist.

JU/NO   Good contact; adaptability; tact; common interest; fortunate union; life force. (Lack fellowship; anti-social; selfish; conflict; lifeless.) Philosophical community; fellow; partner; associate.

JU/AS   Agreeable; favorable influence; generosity; wealth; cure; success; easy birth; teamwork. (Waste; friction; rebellion; hypocrisy; conceit; bragging.) Generous person; wealthy person; uncle; grandparent; aunt.

JU/MC   Philosophical objectives; conscious aims; contentment; bliss; success; purpose. (Risks; unclear aims; changes in lifestyle; desire for importance.) Successes; philosopher; psychologist; priest.

 SATURN ASPECTS

SA/SA   Restriction; patience; concentration; industry; crystallization; earnestness. (Hindrance; illness; developmental crisis; depression; inefficiency; sorrow; paralysis.) Inhibited person; scientist; father; elderly; farmer; miner; businessperson; doctor.

SA/UR   Tension; determination; collected thinking; calmness; technical affairs; travel; endure. (Emotional tension; provocation; force; backlash from past; limitation of freedom.) Violent person; the dying; amputee; chronically ill person.

SA/NE   Renunciation; suffering; sacrifice; caution; method; duality; asceticism; patience. (Insecurity; illness; pestilence; habit; neuroses; emotional inhibitions; insecure.) Ascetic; chronically ill person; elderly person; druggist.

SA/PL   Cruelty; hard labor; tenacity; self-discipline; adepts; martyrdom; struggling; silence. (Egotism; violence; divorce; slow separation; murder; self-destruction; loss of money.) Scientist; murderer; reactionary; martyr.

SA/NO   Isolation; inhibited union; maturity; sponsorship; mystery. (Difficulty adapting; difficulty cooperating; death of relatives; depression; inhibition.) Elderly person; mourner.

SA/AS Inhibited personality; difficult birth; early maturity; lonely; isolated; inmates. (Depression; wrong outlook; poor family; disadvantages through others; segregation.) Inmate; patient; lonely person; doctor; hospital staff; grandparent.

SA/MC Serious objectives; slow development; separation; self-preoccupation; experience. (Emotional inhibition; dejection; illness; insanity; loss of consciousness; despondent.) Inhibited person; patient; burden.

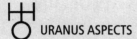

URANUS ASPECTS

UR/UR Suddenness; ambitions; enterprise; creativity; crisis change; reform; many plans. (Hard conditions; change; catastrophe; nervous crises; suicidal thoughts; danger.) Reformer; inventor; technician; revolutionary; astrologer; healer; physicist.

UR/NE Unconsciousness; inner vision; inspiration; mysticism; art; research; journeys; spirit. (Instability; confusion; death; revolution; crisis; incapacity; confusion psychically.) Mystic; medium; psychic; revolutionary.

UR/PL Transformation; revolution; innovation; mobility; reform; mutation; explosion; changes. (Impatience; mania; destruction; upsets; subversive activities; enforcement; explosion.) Pioneer; reformer; genius; explorer; gunman.

UR/NO Shared experience; sudden attraction; unstable relations; variety; innovation; activity. (Disturbance; quarrels; separation; restlessness; flighty; irritable; incidents; dreamy.) Politician; labor union; excited family; nervous person.

UR/AS Environmental response; invention; new contacts; original; nervousness; rearrangement. (Excitable; inconstancy; disquiet; accidents; quick changes; compulsion; rudeness.) Excitable person; original; eccentric; technician; neurotic.

UR/MC Original objectives; assertion; fortunate changes; organizing; successful; stress. (Tension; prematurely; unreliability; temper; upsets; sudden turns of destiny.) Yogi; guru; inventor; physicist; musician.

♆ NEPTUNE ASPECTS

NE/NE   Spiritual development; intellectual perception; travel; empathy; mysticism; drugs. (Hypersensitivity; nervousness; confusion; health crisis; deception; addiction; deceit.) Medium; fraud; sensitive; perceptive person; spiritual person; addict; dreamer.

NE/PL   Supernatural; intensification; active imagination; psychics; parapsychology; evolution. (Confusion; torment; obsession; craving drugs or alcohol; loss; possession; falsehood.) Mystic; astrologer; psychic; occultist; medium; addict; gambler.

NE/NO   Idealistic associations; sensitive groups; mysticism; utopian associations; spiritual. (Antisocial; deceptive; cheating others; deception; sleeplessness; disturbed dreams.) Groupie; psychic group; mystical organization; magic circle; coven.

NE/AS   Impressionability; sensitivity; sympathy; strangeness; refinement; idealism; water birth. (Betrayal; weakness; confusion; disappointment; escapism; fraud; illusion; drugs.) Anesthetist; sensitive; medium; addict; psychic; mystic; weak person.

NE/MC   Uncertain objectives; vagueness; peculiar ideas; utopian; supernatural; artistic. (Feigning; falsehood; acting; numbness; strange ideas; depression; deception.) Utopian; parapsychologist; weakling; actor; the mentally disturbed; psychotic.

♇ PLUTO ASPECTS

PL/PL   Inner change; metamorphosis; transformation; propaganda; mass influence; power lust. (Ruthlessness; fanaticism; agitating efforts; weakness; coercion; indoctrination.) Dictator; hypnotist; politician; magician; public speaker; actor.

PL/NO   Collective destiny; public figures; influencing others; group associations; movements. (Tragic destiny; karma; being cramped by others; antisocial; suffering; suffocation.) Crowd; mass meeting; army; political party; union; multinational.

PL/AS   Fascinating personality; ambition; magic; unusual influence; control; transformation. (Changing environment; dictatorship; ruling others; repulsion; readjustment; injury.) Great specialist; fascinating personality; star; politician; public figure.

PL/MC   Transformed objectives; individuality; strength; growth; authority; expert knowledge. (Misused power; resistance; vindictiveness; anti-social conduct; recuperation; destiny.) Transformer; authority; specialist; magician; surgeon.

☊ NODE ASPECTS

NO/NO   Unions; connections; junctures; communication; approach; groups; clubs; fellowship. (Limitations; antisocial; incompatibility; unsocial; not adaptable.) Contact; mediator; relative; family; association; colleague.

NO/AS   Fellowship; personal relationships; family contacts; social conscience; charm; love. (Short relations; estrangements; disturbed domestic relations; antisocial; difficult.) Family; associate; workmate; fellow; friend.

NO/MC   Group objectives; individual relationships; astral relationships; mutual understanding. (Inconstancy; differing; individual over collective; difficult collectives; Marxists.) Association; political party; union; friend.

AS ASCENDANT (AS) ASPECTS

AS/AS   Acquaintance; location; surroundings; the place; body; social relations; personal relations. (Maladjustment; feeling lost; misplaced; difficult birth.) People in the environment; doctor; midwife.

AS/MC   Individual synthesis; higher self and lower self; personality and ego; integration. (Impossible synthesis; irreconcilable goals; lack of direction.) Synthesizer; strong personality with direction.

MC MIDHEAVEN (MC) ASPECTS

MC/MC   The ego; spiritual, intellectual and social impressions; goals; objectives. (Egoless; materialistic; goalless; insane.) Egotist; person who lives in the moment; goal-oriented person.

NINE

CONCEPTION AND GESTATION: MOTHER'S REALM

Once we begin to understand how to apply the signs and their personifications, the octaves of the life process around the houses, and the aspects and aspect patterns that connect planets, houses, and octaves to each other, we can start to look at the horoscope in more detail. We start before conception and go around the wheel, house by house.

Each octave qualifies the planetary meanings in its own way. Although the underlying dynamic action of the planets remains, the type of presenting form changes from octave to octave. This is because the people we know change as we age, and their impact upon us changes. It is as though we need to find or attract for ourselves new characters to play the inherent parts of us. For example, Venus or Mars during gestation are older siblings or friends who affect our mother. During childhood they are more likely to be siblings, cousins, or neighbors, but now they are transferring their energies to us. In maturity they can be almost anyone we meet in life who we consider a friend or intimate, but they primarily show processes we are developing ourselves. Later in maturity they can be our own children, as we transmit qualities to others around us. The archetype changes form as our needs and realities change.

When we look at a particular house in our horoscope we must take the following information into consideration.

1. Determine the date when the house begins and when it ends (you can read this directly from the list of life dates you have downloaded). Think about what happened during that time.

2. See which zodiac sign occupies the beginning of the house (its cusp), and the date when it changes to the next sign. For example, you might change from the expansive and outgoing sign of Leo on the cusp to the more critical, perfectionist, and detailed sign Virgo, which would lead to a more inward-looking stage of your life. When you pass from the passive Pisces to the outgoing and self-assertive Aries, you would feel reborn, etc.

3. Identify and date the planet or planets that occupy the house. Interpret this from the interpretation tables (chapter 8) by combining text paragraphs. You might see that you have Jupiter in Capricorn in the Sixth House at eighteen years old. Read and combine the paragraphs for Jupiter in Capricorn, and Jupiter in the Sixth House.

4. Note whether the planet rules the sign or house it is in, in which case its influence is stronger than usual, or if it is in detriment, opposite to this sign, in which case it is weaker than usual. This tells us about its strength. For example, Jupiter rules Sagittarius, where its expansive influence affects our larger view of life, and is in detriment in Gemini, where we expect to see a limited view of the world.

5. Identify which planets are in aspect to each planet in the house. Notice the houses and the octaves in which they

fall. This will tell us about earlier (and later) influences that are a part of the constellation, when they originate, who they connect with, and the nature of their influence. Find the Aspect Interpretation Tables (chapter 8) and the description of each aspect combination (chapter 7). For example, Jupiter might have a trine to Mars in the Second House in childhood, registering at two years old. The Mars/Jupiter aspect therefore links with the childhood octave, where it carries a primarily emotional influence, and in the Second House, where it affects our early attitude to physical things, our own body, and, by extension, our attitudes to property and possessions. Mars/Jupiter is a creative aspect, so this represents a creative opportunity that calls on skills you developed very early in life.

6. If there are no planets in the house, take the zodiac sign on the beginning cusp of the house and determine its ruling planet. Locate the ruling planet by octave and house. Following our example, if the sign Capricorn is on the cusp of the Sixth House and there are no planets there, we would look at its ruler Saturn, which is in the Tenth House during gestation. This implies that your work choices in life would be conceptual (from gestation) and also pragmatic (from the sign quality of Capricorn). The houses are interlocked with each other through their sign rulerships.

Each level of being has its own identity, needs, and relative force in the whole of us, as shown by which planets occupy that level. Some bodies are stronger than others, indicating phases of life that are more important in our overall development. More planets in childhood show a dominance of emotions, while more in gestation show a dominance of the physical body, and more in maturity make the mental body predominant. The location of the Sun and the Moon indicate the parts of us that our parents particularly determine. Either luminary in gestation tends to show that our parental legacy is genetic and physical—we may look like our father (the Sun in gestation) but think like our mother (the Moon in the maturity octave). Our bodies vary in their density and importance as they come into being in sequence as we age. Understanding this primary model informs us about our fundamental needs. The four bodies are the elements of astrology—earth, water, air, and fire—and are also the four octaves of development.

Contradiction is an essential element in the process of interpreting the horoscope. It would be nice to think that we do not have contradictions within us, but the reality is that we do. The contradictions are often the most interesting and challenging parts of us, and they are also potentially the most creative mechanisms in us. I have always been surprised throughout my astrological career as a counselor to discover again and again that those individuals who have apparently the most difficult horoscopes are also the most creative. They are forced to grow, to develop, and to work with what seem at first to be their most problematic issues. Creativity springs from such rich and perplexing soil.

Do not be afraid to see contradictory qualities. *The sequence is most important.* It is a problem when any one factor or part of us is isolated. This is the inverse of science, where a quality must be isolated in order to be studied. We must bear in mind that we move on to the next stage of our process. We want to see and understand not only what happened at a certain point, but also where the energy went next, as well as where it came from in the first place. The phasing, the sequential nature of reality, and the sense that, whatever happens there will be a resolution shortly afterward, is a saving grace. I hope you will sense this in the examples to follow.

For the purpose of this process it is a good idea to suspend judgment. Instead of trying to justify our own beliefs about what happened at various stages of your life process, it is a good idea to remain open-minded about everyone involved. I find this particularly true when we look at our parents in the horoscope. We tend to box them into viewpoints and categories that are not necessarily correct. This is especially true in the early stages of our life, before conception and during gestation. Give them a break; be open to what they were really like then, when their formative influence on us was paramount.

Life begins at conception, when our father and mother make love to create us. The event that starts our life is a metaphor for our sexuality and its higher octaves, our creativity and potential for integration. Since conception and gestation happen in our mother, we must try to understand what happened from her viewpoint. We don't have a choice about this.

We first explore which parent was responsible for the initiation of our conception by moving clockwise from the conception point to either the Sun or the Moon, whichever happens first. This shows the principle of our creation: who acted first and who was acted upon. Understanding gestation from our mother's viewpoint allows us to identify with the deepest levels of our being and also clarifies the role of our mother and father in life. This relationship is very important because it reflects the nature of the female-male integration that brought us into being and is therefore central to the relationships we make. When we can accept our parents without judging them or being prejudiced against them, we can begin to see them as they really are, and then see ourselves clearly in the present.

During gestation, we pass through the collective history of all humanity, as modern genetics shows. We must confront our mother, work with her, and learn to value her, if we don't already. Our personal integration requires that we learn to accept and understand exactly those people in our lives who are most difficult because they reflect what is most difficult in us. The events of gestation are indicated by the planets present there, are seen from our mother's viewpoint, and are embedded in the structure of our body. The planets in gestation are biological imperatives we carry, which are reflected in relationships of our mother and which we understand as our instincts. The four houses of gestation represent the process by which we continually come into being through our deepest creativity. Gestation is a symbol of our creativity.

Our parents conceive us in a sexual act, and then our mother carries us for about ten lunar months. We incorporate our mother's influences into our physical body. Everything she thinks (air signs in gestation, plus Mercury and Uranus), feels (water signs in gestation, plus the Moon and Neptune), intuits (fire signs in gestation, plus the Sun, Mars, and Pluto), and senses (earth signs in gestation, plus Venus and Saturn) is transmitted directly to us within her and is then stored within our body as instincts and deep primary urges.

The function of the process of life is to describe our life in time,

As an exercise, before interpreting your own horoscope, shut your eyes, go inside, and breathe deeply. Try to visualize your mother and father as they were around the time that you were conceived. Think of how old they were. Think about what they looked like, how they dressed. What was their relationship like? How does this make you feel?

but very few of us contemplate our lives this way. The only time we are likely to do so is when we are in psychological crisis, or just before we die.

The dates of the duration of the houses in the following descriptions are averages and are determined by twelve equal houses. You have your own unique house lengths and times of entrance and exit depending on the time and place of your birth.

BEFORE CONCEPTION

We first look before conception to see which parent had the impulse to conceive us.

When I first began doing astrological readings using my technique thirty years ago, I always started at the conception point. I discovered that when there were planets in the Eighth House just before conception, they often signified important events that happened just before conception. One case in particular concerned a woman who had a conjunction of Saturn (fate, depression, and sadness) and Pluto (dramatic changes, transformation, death, and rebirth). As this is a very powerful and yet hidden influence because of the Eighth House position, which is intense but has hidden qualities, I assumed it was something of which she was not aware, but I mentioned it to her anyway. She confirmed my instinct and told me that just before her conception her mother miscarried. Her parents were extremely upset because the previous child had almost gone full term and they had even thought of names for her. When her mother immediately became pregnant with her, they even gave her the name they had planned for her predecessor. For her entire life she had felt fated, without knowing why, and this was an astrological confirmation of that fact.

In the pre-conception time the Moon is our mother and the

Sun is our father. Any aspects that connect Moon and Sun show us their relationship at this time. What we do is start with the Ninth Cusp and move in a clockwise direction. If we come to the Sun first, our father was responsible for the impulse to conceive us. If we come to the Moon first, it was our mother.

> The first horoscope in your package is the Pre-Conception Horoscope, which shows only the Sun and the Moon in their signs relative to the Ascendant and the Midheaven. Use this diagram with the following paragraphs.

The location of the initiating parent will first tell us if he or she was conscious or unconscious of the impulse to conceive us. If the planet is below the horizon, in the First through the Sixth Houses, that parent acted instinctively or unconsciously. If the planet is above the horizon, in the Seventh through the Twelfth Houses, that parent acted consciously. For example, if the Moon is the first planet before the conception point and lies below the horizon, your mother acted unconsciously in initiating our conception. This implies that your sexuality is often initiated unconsciously, as is your creativity.

The process for determining conscious or unconscious motives is applied to the second luminary as the parent who is secondary to the process. The parent who has the impulse to conceive us may act unconsciously while the parent acted upon is conscious of the process. This is paradoxical but could be an accurate picture of how we conceive actions, creativity, and sexuality in our lives. We will unconsciously initiate relationships and then wonder why we didn't understand what we were doing.

The sign and house of the initiating planet tells us the state of the parent during the time before our conception. When the Sun or the Moon are in a fire or air sign, they tend to be energetic and outgoing, while in an earth or water sign they tend to be reactive and inward-looking. This quality is either supported or contradicted by the house position of the planet. If the Sun is below the horizon in the active sign Aries but is in the inward-looking Cancerian Fourth house, the father's incentive is paradoxical. He acts assertively but in an unconscious and inward-looking way. The Sun's house location and the fact that it is below the horizon "masks" the Aries Sun qualities. This might be the case if our father wanted us but felt that he could not show this desire. The Fourth House is conservative and domestic, so there may be family reasons why he cannot express his desire to have a child more openly. This dynamic would be a part of our own sexuality and creativity, and a probably frustrating quality in our relationship with our father. He might find it difficult to express his love for us directly, in return.

If, in the same example, the Moon as our mother were in a passive and analytical sign like Virgo and in an active and outgoing house like the Sagittarian Ninth House, there would be a paradox in our mother's behavior. She would be critical of our father as a reaction, particularly when he acts first. She might think of herself as the active parent, but she finds herself in the situation where our

Find the parent who had the impulse to conceive you by looking in a clockwise direction back from the cusp of the Ninth House. Determine whether he or she is conscious or unconscious, and look in the interpretation tables that follow to match the sign and house position it occupies. Repeat the procedure for the second parent.

father acts first instead. This could be a source of resentment or indeed a central trait of our parental relationship. Given the dynamics of this family system before conception, it would not be a stretch to imagine that we would have incorrect or misleading ideas about our parents and their relationship. We would tend to see our mother as the active parent, thwarted in her actions by our inward-looking father, who sits on his emotions. This way of seeing our parents' relationship before conception can correct or modify our prevailing attitudes to our parents.

Both luminaries (the Sun and the Moon) above the horizon (as in Figure 9.1) shows that both father and mother were conscious of the conception process and possibly even planned it. But how can we know for sure? The answer is that we see whether there is an aspect between the Sun and the Moon (there isn't). The type of aspect will show us the nature of the couple's relationship at that time. If there is no aspect, they feel separate and may want a child to bridge the gap. If they are conjunct, it would mean that our parents not only concurred in having us but could have had the impulse at nearly the same time.

The location of the Sun and the Moon by sign and house constitutes a major determining influence upon your masculine and feminine natures, as of course we all have some proportion of both. The sign of each luminary describes the *quality* of its creative influence and the house describes the *developmental stage*. The sign elements of the Sun and the Moon are further definitions. In Earth signs parental reasons for conceiving a child are material; in Air signs the conception functions as a means of communication; in Fire signs it is an energy exchange or common creation; and in Water signs the parents conceive in order to have someone to feel for or about. Parental motives influence not only your parental state but reflect the motivating force behind your creative activity

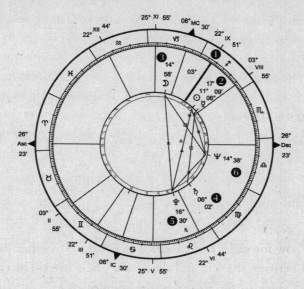

FIGURE 9.1: BEFORE CONCEPTION

We start by identifying the beginning cusp of the Ninth House, which is the conception point ❶. When we go back, we first come to the Sun/father in Sagittarius and the Eighth House ❷. The Sun and Moon/mother ❸ have no mutual aspect, showing that they feel separate. The father feels restricted and critical by the square to Saturn ❹. Both the Sun and the Moon aspect Neptune ❻ (uncertainty) and Pluto ❺ (dramatic changes in relationship).

throughout life. The elements correspond to those psychological types to which your parents respond.

In the example, the Sun is in the idealistic and optimistic fire sign Sagittarius, but in the closed Eighth House. He feels emotionally separate from the mother, as the Eighth House is the watery house of Scorpio and further inhibited and restricted by the square of the Sun to Saturn in the Sixth, the house of work. The father may feel financially inadequate but cannot talk about it. The Moon is in the stronger and more pragmatic sign Capricorn and in the Tenth House, which also corresponds to Capricorn qualities. The sequence of action is as follows:

1. The Sun/father in Sagittarius is responsible for the conception but feels separate. He is inhibited by the square from Saturn.

2. The Moon/mother is strong and independent yet does not know the father's wishes as there is no direct aspect between them, implying a lack of communication.

3. The mutual aspects from Neptune (uncertainty and insecurity) and Pluto (dramatic changes) imply that the child is not planned, that both parents are uncertain about their feelings about one another, and that the conception is a drama. I would assume they either were not married or that they were unsure about whether or not to have a child. (They were unmarried.)

4. When the mother discovers she is pregnant (at the Tenth House cusp), she will be required to take on the responsibility for the child within her.

In the example, I correctly saw that the parents were both unsure but neither communicated their fears or questions. When the mother realized she was pregnant at the Capricorn Midheaven and then the Moon registered shortly afterward, the implication is that she would have to assume responsibility. Indeed, the father was a foreign man with whom she had an affair, and he left shortly before she realized she was pregnant. This has the effect of inhibiting the creativity of the child as an adult and shows a tendency to not trust men. The implications of such early dynamics stay with us throughout our lives.

The following key words demonstrate the meanings of the signs and houses:

PRE-CONCEPTION PARENTS
Negative indications are in brackets.

House	Sign	Octave and Interpretation
		Gestation = Physical Body through Body
Ninth	Sagittarius	An aspiration to greater freedom, success in the future, a broader and richer life, and the need for children as a further exploration in life. Realized, free, exploratory, mobile, sporty, religious. (Material, split, careless, extremist, hedonist.)
Tenth	Capricorn	Pragmatic, rational, and austere in keeping feelings within the self, giving the impression of egotism and selfishness. Serious in the commitment to future material situations. Pragmatic, rational, logical, selfish, disciplined, tough. (Serious, inflexible, reserved, cautious, inhibited.)
Eleventh	Aquarius	Friendly to others; parental idealism is both a structure and barrier in relationships with others. Opinions and plans determine life structure but can leave the appearance of being quite detached or cold. Idealistic, humanitarian, sociable, civilized, intuitive. (Detached, cranky, frigid, rebellious, unreliable, insane.)
Twelfth	Pisces	Moody because of insularity and isolation but can be induced to be sympathetic to others. Feels overwhelmed by circumstances beyond control and accepts fate. Our own sense of "fate" is derived from this yielding nature. Solitary, reserved, absorptive, patient, secretive, open. (Druggy, inhibited, negligent, doubting, sacrificial.)
		Childhood = Emotional Body through Personality
First	Aries	Easily impressed and influenced; a self-aware, strong personality that extends power to others. Our spontaneous and emotionally powerful persona is inherited. Self-expressive, impulsive, self-centered, spontaneous. (Selfish, demanding, restless, tempered, tactless.)

House	Sign	Octave and Interpretation
Second	Taurus	Wants a stable home and an emotional relationship, with the focus on the physical. Beauty is enhanced by growth and depth of feelings. A strong physicality. Possessive, productive, physical, sensual, secure. (Indulgent, stubborn, jealous, grasping, withholding.)
Third	Gemini	Many aspects to the emotional expression, mobile and changeable, and vacillates in the commitment to parenthood. Fond of children, treating them almost as equals. Expressive, communicative, mobile, adaptable, active. (Superficial, nervous, dualistic, moody.)
Fourth	Cancer	Affectionate and impressionable, with deep feelings as the dark core to domestic attachments. Can be sensitive or smothering, always in an unconscious way. Determines our emotional security and depth. Familial, protective, sensitive, devoted, receptive. (Touchy, greedy, timid, overemotional, inferior.)

Maturity = Mental Body through Mind

House	Sign	Octave and Interpretation
Fifth	Leo	Plays with feelings, extends intuitions to evoke more confidence, and applies imagination and passion to relationships. Wishes for further means of self-expression, and is an expansive influence. Playful, impressive, self-conscious, leading, controlled. (Egocentric, fixed, conceited, dramatic.)
Sixth	Virgo	Head rules heart; practical considerations typically reign; pedantry and cold criticism to those close by. Demeanor is restrained and undemonstrative, and a critical emotional nature is derived from the influence. Orderly, diligent, discriminative, practical, perfected. (Critical, pedantic, suppressed, naive, hypochondriac.)

House	Sign	Octave and Interpretation
Seventh	Libra	Emotionally dependent and vividly expressive, but allows feelings to be largely determined by others. Life direction seems fated and in delicate balance. A balanced but dependent mentality is inherited. Harmonious, balanced, consistent, related, just, united. (Indecisive, vain, unreliable, shallow, lazy.)
Eighth	Scorpio	Feels separate from others, is intense and reserved, yet has a deep sensitivity that attracts power. Often resentful of the power and possessions of others. Penetrating, willful, separate, passionate, intense. (Fanatical, repressive, jealous, destructive.)

At this stage, our parents are described before either of them is aware that a conception is about to take place. The Sun or the Moon, or both, when situated exactly on the conception point, indicate a more spontaneous conception. The Sun or the Moon in either opposition or square aspects to the conception point shows their resistance to conception, and a constructive sextile or trine aspect shows their active support for the conception.

The aspect between the Sun and the Moon shows the relationship between our parents before conception, just as no aspect shows vagueness or separation. If the Sun and the Moon are conjunct, they have similar views and motives; in trine or sextile apart, they show a stable relationship and good communication. If they are in opposition, they may disagree profoundly about having a child; in square, they disagree but have the capacity to resolve their tension.

It is important to realize that we describe our parents' relationship at a time before either of them knows we are coming. Our being reflects the state of our parents' relationship throughout this time.

CONCEPTION POINT

The sign on the conception point describes our
mother's attitude at the time of conception. As it is the
event that begins our life, it has great importance as an
initiating influence in our life. The metaphor of our parents' coming together at conception affects, if not defines, our sexuality, our
creativity, and our drive for higher awareness through initiation.

If it is Aries, she initiates it and is self-assertive toward the father. If it is Cancer, she is reacting to the father and expects him to
act first, and so on. This dynamic reflects our own creativity, how
it it is initiated, and which parts of us function in which ways.

Planets that are conjunct the conception point affect us deeply.
If it is Venus, the conception is motivated by love and a sense of
merging, while if it is Saturn, the mother might accept it as a duty
and responsibility. I had a client who had the communicative
planet Mercury right on the Ninth House cusp, and when I mentioned that her mother was probably talking while she made love
to conceive her, she turned beet red and admitted that she could
not have an orgasm unless she or her partner were talking during
sex. Neptune conjunct brings a fantasy to conception and our sexuality, and can also imply that one or both parents were inebriated
at conception.

Planets are either square or in opposition to the conception
point show resistance to the conception itself, or to the sexual act
involved, depending on which planet makes the aspect. "Hard" aspects from Mars, Uranus, or Pluto can even show forced sex or
rape. The Sun is in either aspect to the conception point shows the
father resisting the conception, and when it is the Moon, it is our
mother herself who resists the conception. This shows a deep resistance to creativity.

CONCEPTION POINT SIGNS

In the following paragraphs we can see what the twelve signs on the conception point Ninth House cusp indicate for our mother and also for us. Planets near or in aspect to the Ninth House cusp are also covered under the sign they rule. See the appropriate paragraphs and blend them.

Aries or Mars Conception. Conception is an impulsive, spontaneous, and assertive act in which your mother expends much energy to express herself without much concern for your father. She is sexually demanding, restless, and selfish with her own pleasures. Your creativity is impulsive and sudden in its onset, and is primarily a response to the spontaneous need to express yourself without thought of its implications.

Taurus or Venus Conception. Conception is physical, possessive, and indulgent as your mother seeks sensual pleasure from sexuality. She finds her productivity and security through basic means. Your creativity is the result of a drive to secure a basic physical sense of security, and to produce some real material evidence of your success in life. (See also the house where Venus resides.)

Gemini or Mercury Conception. Conception is an active communication initiated by your mother as a sisterly gesture to your father. They are mobile, adaptable, and extremely facile about the sexual experience. You seek versatile and changeable means to express your creativity, but do not linger too long as you get bored very easily. (See also the house where Mercury resides.)

Cancer or Moon Conception. Conception is initiated by your mother to create a family she can nurture, protect, and possess. The conception is a means for her to express often contradictory feelings to your father in a safe space. Your creativity must be nurtured carefully and your innate conservatism overcome in order to express yourself fully outside your home. (See also the house where the Moon resides.)

Leo or Sun Conception. Conception is a playful, expressive, and extrovert act initiated and led by your mother and engaging your father. She exteriorizes herself in sexuality and revels in the energies liberated. Creativity and sexuality are very important to you as a primary means to express yourself and to overcome your natural self-consciousness. (See also the house where the Sun resides.)

Virgo or Mercury Conception. Conception is approached in an orderly, practical, and detailed way by your mother, who is, however, very critical of your father. She is a perfectionist about creative and sexual matters because she retains an essential naivete about such affairs. Creativity is achieved by attention to detail and perfectionist planning, with the valuable addition of self-analysis. (See also the house where Mercury resides.)

Libra or Venus Conception. Conception is an attempt by your mother to achieve balance between your parents, with her making the first move. She is willing to sacrifice her position to make sexuality harmonious, consistently pleasurable, and a true unity. Creativity is an intuitive search for harmony against which the rational part of you is resistant. (See also the house where Venus resides.)

Scorpio or Mars or Pluto Conception. Conception is a passionate and willful act, initiated by your mother to overcome her feeling of separateness from your father. Their tense and magnetic relationship brings strong feelings to the surface, and it can be a forced or violent act. Your creativity is impulsive and intense, and can be fanatical in trying to attract the attention and love of others. (See also the houses where Mars and Pluto reside.)

Sagittarius or Jupiter Conception. Conception is an exploratory, active, and open-minded communication initiated by your mother, intended to integrate her life with her ideals. She is pleasure-loving, natural, and sexual in her self-expression as a way of being in the world. Your creativity is the physical expression of your philosophy of life. (See also the house where Jupiter resides.)

Capricorn or Saturn Conception. Conception is a rational, logical, and pragmatic way for your mother to achieve a stronger position with your father. She overcomes her natural reserve and conservatism to achieve a physical expression of her desires. Your creativity comes from a material need for expression demanded by necessity. (See also the house where Saturn resides.)

Aquarius or Saturn or Uranus Conception. Conception is an idealistic, humanitarian, sociable, and intuitive way for your mother to express her link with your father, although she detaches from him and the sexual relationship is quite abstract. Your creativity is a process of transforming the ideal into reality but carries an inherent detachment with it. (See also the houses where Saturn and Uranus reside.)

Pisces or Jupiter or Neptune Conception. Conception is a solitary, secret, and sacrificial act as a response to situations beyond your mother's control. Sexuality is an area of fantasy and unreality because of the necessary lack of volition. Your creativity depends on agencies apparently outside of you and is a way for you to overcome isolation. (See also the houses where Jupiter and Neptune reside.)

PLANETS IN GESTATION

Gestation is the period from conception until birth, when we develop within our mother's womb from a fertilized ovum to the complex being we are. We receive influences from the outside world exclusively through our mother, yet it is a two-way process— she filters everything we experience and we receive everything she experiences. During these nine months we repeat the entire evolutionary process, from being a one-celled ovum to birth as a modern human. Each evolutionary stage leaves traces in our body and psyche, especially in our convoluted brain structure. We are a walking biological record, as modern genetic research can verify. In its psychological implications, gestation is what Jung called the *collective unconscious*—the primal inheritance common to all humanity from which derive the materials of our individual psyche. The collective traits of all humanity flow through us as our instinctive and autonomic reality.

Throughout the entire gestation process our mother receives influences from us as well as from people and situations she experiences. Our deepest reality is a blend of these influences.

Working with gestation influences teaches us much about our psyche and our memories. I always believed that astrology described objective reality in the scientific sense, until I realized, as modern scientists have confirmed, that there is no objective reality: All is subjective, relative to an observer. We perceive and feel whatever happens to our mother during gestation from her viewpoint. What actually happens is less important. This principle is also very true for us in our lives. It is what we remember and how we perceive our reality that matters more than what objectively happened. What others imagine we should feel may not correspond to what actually happened.

We can benefit from identifying the origin of the influences that affected our mother during gestation, as strange a concept as this is.

> *My father was a bomber pilot based in England during World War II and left five weeks after my mother became pregnant, but before she or he knew. As he was posted on sensitive duty running raids over U-boat command in northern Germany, my mother didn't know where he was for weeks at a time, during the most ferocious fighting of the war and a time when the Allies were losing many planes daily. I therefore carry the sense of separation from my father that my mother felt as*

one of the first and deepest influences in my life. This appears in my horoscope as the Sun in Leo (a leader) the Ninth House of foreign countries and influences, registering just after the conception point but before the Midheaven, when the mother realizes she is pregnant. The Sun is sextile Saturn, interpreted as "separation; the missing father," and square Mars in the Sixth House, as it was his job and duty to be there separated from her; the aspect means "the fighter; violence." The interpretation of a missing father in a foreign country during the critical early stages of realizing the pregnancy creates a deep craving for acknowledgment of creativity in me and probably was instrumental in leading me to create this "new vision of astrology."

Planets in the gestation houses and those that aspect them show influences that affect your mother. They describe both the nature of the influences and the people around your mother who carried them. Whether they are internal or external depends on the signs they are in (fire and air tend to be external, and water and earth are internal) and also, if they are aspecting planets, whether they are above the horizon (conscious and external) or below the horizon (unconscious and internal). This in turn indicates whether they affect you in inner or outer ways.

The Sun during gestation is your father and his relatives; your mother's consciousness; her vitality; and your father's (and father's family's) support for mother. The Sun can be your mother's father or her father-in-law, or both if it is in a double sign, particularly since grandparents are often possessive of their grandchildren. When Saturn or Jupiter are also present the influence is exaggerated. The Sun can also be a doctor; the inclusion of Mars often implies he is a surgeon rather than a general practitioner, which can produce fear in our mother. The Sun in the double signs shows a split masculine side. While practicing astrology in England in the

1970s, I discovered that many born there during World War II, when conscription was common and American allies were present, have paternity issues. Positive positions and aspects to the Sun show that your father supported the pregnancy, while tension aspects indicate paternal disagreement or resistance. He is your masculine essence within.

The Moon during gestation is your mother and her relatives; it describes her feelings and emotions and also her relationships and instincts. The Moon also shows genetic influences received from your mother's family. The Moon is other women: midwives, nurses, woman doctors, friends, and any maternal or nurturing figures, those who teach birth exercises, counselors, or other women who are mothers themselves. She symbolizes your deepest feelings.

Mercury during gestation is your mother's ability to express herself, which has a profound impact on your own creative process. Mercury is friends, siblings, and others that bring insight to your mother. It is the mental environment in which your mother finds herself. Her reading, talking, and access to cultural values stimulate intellectual roots in us. Mercury is those who encourage her to express herself and by extension those who enable your deepest ideas to surface.

Venus during gestation is beauty, harmony, love, adaptation, relationship, and sociability. She is often a woman friend, associate, or sister of your mother who acts as a prototype for taste and cultural sense. She is passive sexuality that accepts what exists, and also your mother's reaction to her own changing appearance.

Mars during gestation indicates a desire to change, activity, conflict, and will as personified by doctors and midwives. If squared by Mercury, your mother is nervous, and if opposed by Saturn, she resists the restrictions. Mars is an intervention in the process.

Jupiter during gestation is your mother's ability to accept gestation philosophically, through her own religious beliefs, her particular psychology, or those who protect her during this time. Jupiter is carried by those who are generous, supportive, optimistic, and expansive—typically aunts, uncles, grandparents, counselors, or the religious. Expansion in your mother's viewpoint and her physical size are indicated when Jupiter registers. Its influence is noble and good-humored, and broadens her horizons.

Saturn during gestation is worrying, pessimism, restriction, and seriousness, which are often imposed upon your mother by doctors, her parents, financial restrictions, and your father. Saturn is personifications who are older, sicker, negative, depressive, or limited in perspective, and who obviously or inadvertently transmit these qualities. Your mother may have to continue working or be isolated, in the care of her parents, depressed, or forced to economize, so the impact of Saturn is to narrow her perspective and make her aware of her limitations, though not necessarily in a detrimental way. Constraint upon relations with others may derive from forced tightness or social limitation, or from within your mother herself. Saturn has its strongest effect when it is near the Midheaven or the Ascendant, reflecting an actual or expected limitation of mobility and life as a result of the creative act of gestation.

Uranus during gestation institutes reform ranging from expressive creativity to disruption transmitted by revolutionaries; reformers; creative people who do things their own way; and friends who are independent or inspired and encourage your mother to be so herself. As Uranus is the first of the generational planets, its influence is often carried by more than one person. The sexual and creative appetite shown by Uranus becomes very active during gestation and unless sated manifests as rebelliousness or secretive behavior. A change in rhythm is Uranus's most frequent indication, and eccentricities in thought, action, and diet result, if not accidents that threaten our mother's well-being. As a generational influence Uranus also governs prevailing birth and gestation attitudes of the public, birth technology, and those who support new techniques or modern scientific attitudes.

Neptune during gestation increases your mother's sensitivity on the physical and psychic levels. It is her fantasies, dreams, and psychic life. She is sensitive to the effects of diet, drugs, tobacco, and the psychic influence of others, particularly in the early stages of pregnancy. Intangibility characterizes Neptune influences, which are transmitted by those around your mother who dispense food or drugs, are sensitive, and have similar ideals.

Pluto during gestation is dramatic changes and transformations of mood that lead your mother to question her motives and her life direction, and to make drastic alterations to accommodate them. A craving for a better understanding of the world leads her to attain higher knowledge. Inner regeneration and pioneering spirit allow religious or philosophical beliefs to be attained, social habits to change, and superior power to become possible.

The Node during gestation is utopian ideas, plans for communal or idealistic groups, and a focus on family responsibility. Educational interests interface with dreams, fantasies, and expectations of deep revelations.

The Ninth House (Sagittarius and Its Natural Ruler, Jupiter)

From conception until seven weeks after conception

After conception, the entire energetic and karmic pattern of our lifetime registers as a pattern in time. The ovum forms three spiral germ layers that are patterns for our skeletal, organ, and nervous systems. The short lifetime of the ovum is a microcosm of our lifetime, compressed one thousand times, reflecting the nature of a logarithmic scale that begins with 1 rather than 0. The fertilized ovum travels out of the fallopian tube into the mother's uterus and attaches itself to primed uterine wall. By the end of the Ninth House our major body systems are fully operative, our liver can process waste, and the embryo technically becomes a fetus.

Women discover they are pregnant within days or weeks after conception. The more sensitive our mother is to the subtle energies of her psyche and body, the greater the likelihood that she discovers our existence early in the Ninth House, and the more sensitive we are to these influences. It also implies that our own self-realization tends to happen relatively early in life. Biologically, during the first seven weeks, after the journey of the sperm to the ovum and then the journey of the fertilized ovum to the uterus, we are primarily a brain with a vestigial body attached, as we metamorphose through fishlike and reptilian stages of evolution. We develop the earliest brain components—the R-complex, the limbic system, and the neocortex—recapitulating their evolutionary sequence. Because of the molecular rate at which the embryo develops, perceptually we experience a greatly accelerated early evolution of our species within the womb.

This confirms the meaning of the centaur symbol of Sagittarius, which is half human and half horse. Indeed, we emerge from our primal animal roots and become fully human during this first house of gestation. The Ninth is the traditional house of long journeys, and both sperm cells and the fertilized ovum embark on long journeys that determine our very existence. Our propensity for developing higher mind, philosophy, and religion is stored in our brain structure.

Our mother's hormones transform her body and her life. Her attitudes register upon us deeply during this time: The way in which she realizes that something is happening, the symbolism that comes to her, who she turns to for verification and support, and the overall quality of these circumstances provide keys to our own

FIGURE 9.2: SAGITTARIUS CENTAUR

Sagittarius and the Ninth House symbolize our emergence from the earliest stage of evolution, as we transform into human form with a higher purpose. The symbol shows both our biological reality and our potential transcendent and healing function. Centaurs were Greek mythological healing gods.

philosophy of life. Her attitudes toward religion, parental wisdom, and individual philosophy during this first phase of gestation are very intense and important.

The horoscope of the ethno-anthropologist Terence McKenna (Figure 9.3) shows the powerful planets Saturn and Pluto in Leo just after his Leo conception point, which shows adepts and magicians, and also the deep study of science. Both planets are in aspect to Neptune, showing his great interest in psychotropic plants from the Amazon. The following Virgo Moon is his mother realizing her pregnancy very early in the process. McKenna was an extremely entertaining and deep thinker, and he had profound ideas about the spirits of the psyche and our inner connection with the world of nature. As Saturn/Pluto is also considered a highly "fated" aspect, it is ironic that he died of a brain tumor that also falls under the governance of Saturn and Pluto in the house when the early or "primitive" brain evolves.

The Ninth House is our ability to orient within the world as a reflection of our mother's realization of her pregnancy and her acceptance of our existence. It is our tendency to be able to transcend by linking our primitive and higher brain functions.

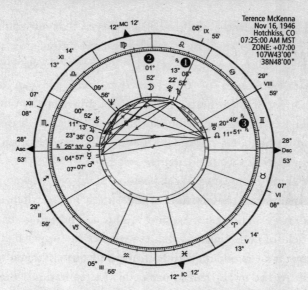

FIGURE 9.3: HOROSCOPE OF TERENCE MCKENNA

Terence McKenna had Saturn and Pluto register just after his conception, showing a deep and powerful experience within his mother at that time. His mother is the Virgo Moon registering immediately afterward, showing that she realized she was pregnant and was quite critical. The aspect of Saturn and Pluto to Uranus registering in his thirties shows the eccentric and profound impact of his books and lectures.

THE MIDHEAVEN

Seven weeks after conception or thirty-three weeks before birth

The Midheaven (in Latin, *Medium Coeli*) registers about forty-nine days or seven weeks after conception. We look and are recognizably human for the first time; our gender is differentiated (we are all genetically female until males diverge). Around this time our first true bone cells start replacing the cartilage skeleton that we initially create. Our mother often already knows she is pregnant; this is when she confirms it and expresses it to the outside world.

In Hinduism and Buddhism it is believed that our soul enters the physical body forty-nine days after conception after passing through the *Bardo state* between lives.[20] We accept the *karmic* traces (Sanskrit: *samskaras*) of our past lives, which is an ancient metaphor for the synthesis of our genetic inheritance, our soul's unfulfilled urges from previous incarnations, and the astrological pattern in time that describes our lifetime. In my estimation we are an integration of these informative systems.

The Tenth House cusp is the position of the Midheaven. As our ego, it symbolizes the position of the Sun at noon, when it is directly above us, and is hottest and brightest. The ego is the center of the field of consciousness that constitutes the upper half of the horoscope, and is our objectives in life and our ability to exercise our will. As the upper half is our collective aspirations, the ego is the center of such needs to manifest in the outer world.

The sign of the Midheaven and the planets in aspect to the Midheaven determine the quality, strength, and complexity of our ego. Planets conjunct the Midheaven show what directly influences our ego, symbolized by people around our mother and later we ourselves, while aspects of other planets to the Midheaven show more indirect but still important influences on our ego.

The element of the Midheaven shows us the psychological function motivating our ego awareness. When it is airy we define ourselves by our thoughts and ideas, when earthy by our material wealth or possessions; when it is fiery we create energetic patterns of creativity, and when watery we feel, therefore we are. When the Midheaven is in the double sign Pisces, for example, our emotional objectives might bifurcate or split due to our need to be all things to others; when it is in Virgo, our goals are based upon our perfectionist criticism.

Planets near or in aspect to the Midheaven show objectives we manifest. The more planets around and aspecting the Midheaven, the more complex are our objectives and the parts of ourselves we bring into the equation. This almost always involves contradiction because there are inevitably various types of aspects and planets refining the Midheaven qualities. When planets aspect the Midheaven from below the horizon it indicates unconscious or introvert responses to our being that feed our objectives in life, while planets aspecting the Midheaven from above the horizon show conscious and extrovert attitudes and are more aware. Planets in aspect to the Midheaven from the left half of the horoscope are selfish motives, and those on the right half are more motivated by others' expectations. These qualities show influences that affect our mother during gestation and also us in our outer self-expression in life.

Our mother becomes conscious of us in a way similar to that by which we become conscious of ourselves. Making this discovery because of her own realization, requiring outside opinions, and not trusting herself are all metaphors for our own route to self-discovery.

The Tenth House Cusp and the Midheaven in the Signs

The Midheaven through the twelve signs shows our mother's reaction to her pregnancy, and planets in aspect to the Midheaven are the reactions of others around her. Combine the paragraphs for the sign on the Midheaven and the planets either conjunct or in aspect to it.

Midheaven in Aries or in Aspect to Mars. Your mother intuits that she is pregnant with you, and it constitutes proof of her ability to successfully establish her individuality in the world. She is ambitious and projects her ambitions onto you within her. To successfully establish your individuality is your main objective in life, and your ambitious and actively assertive aims bring you recognition and a strong sense of purpose. (See also the house where Mars resides.)

Midheaven in Taurus or in Aspect to Venus. Your sensitive and productive mother senses that she is pregnant and sees it as a stabilizing and secure manifestation of her creativity. Tangible and practical objects attract her love, and she treats her process in basic physical ways. In order to feel recognized in the outside world, you present a productive and stable attitude toward your career, and love clothes and objects, which represent stability, and use your strong willpower artistically. (See also the house where Venus resides.)

Midheaven in Gemini or in Aspect to Mercury. Your mother thinks she is pregnant and, once she accepts the reality, is ambivalent about what she has helped create. Her changing goals and indecisive nature make for confused and chaotic communications in all relationships, and you do not clarify things to her. Multiple professional interests, focused on the media and the sphere of communication, convey your multifaceted intellect, and you need to keep your finger on the pulse and stay well informed. (See also the house where Mercury resides.)

Midheaven in Cancer or in Aspect to the Moon. Your mother feels deeply that she is pregnant and is overwhelmed with motherly, nurturing, and protective emotions. She becomes devoted to what is inside, is simple and caring in her expression of love, and becomes conservative to support her safety. Caring and protective energies create your position in the world, and you make devoted and nurturing efforts in your career to be receptive to others, and are recognized for doing so. (See also the house where the Moon resides.)

Midheaven in Leo or in Aspect to the Sun. Your mother intuits that she is pregnant and exteriorizes herself in the world. Often your father is significant in the discovery and can even see it before your mother. As a result she worships you within as an expression of her own creativity and sovereignty. She has high aspirations and immediately organizes her environment to support her goals. The showing of your extrovert intuitive qualities marks your appearance in the world at large as a leader. High aspirations lead to a desire for creative self-expression and a leadership role in any organization. (See also the house where the Sun resides.)

Midheaven in Virgo or in Aspect to Mercury. Your mother senses that she is pregnant, and her first impulse is to expect perfection of her own creative expression. She may have morning sickness, and she immediately places great importance on her sensitivity to diet, health, and other physical aspects of her environment. Sensitivity and a careful approach to health, as well as desiring order and perfection in the outside world, contribute to your critical and overly fussy nature. Few can live by your perfectionist high standards. (See also the house where Mercury resides.)

Midheaven in Libra or in Aspect to Venus. Someone around your mother thinks that she is pregnant before she herself realizes the fact. She is balanced and relaxed, but requires others to see her clearly, and she finds reflection difficult. She craves recognition in her relationship, yet also wishes to be a true, reliant partner. Reflection induces harmony in design ideas or artifacts, presents your influence on others, and satisfies your need for recognition. (See also the house where Venus resides.)

Midheaven in Scorpio or in Aspect to Mars or Pluto. Your mother feels separate from the creativity within her at the recognition of conception. She is willful and passionate about her emotions and will not allow herself to be possessed, fights the very thought, and as a result might even consider abortion. There is suspicion surrounding the conception, and she hides information about herself. Powerful desires are serious, and a transformative influence leads you to create several beginnings and endings in your professional life as you change and grow in your effort to maximize your considerable energy in the outside world. (See also the houses where Mars and Pluto reside.)

Midheaven in Sagittarius or in Aspect to Jupiter. Your mother intuits that she is pregnant and sees you as a savior and manifestation of her philosophy of life. Her attention is split between the physical and the religious, and she is always trying to realize herself and expand her mind. The world is your oyster, as expansive enthusiasm and optimism are used to good advantage in your working life to create popularity while you strive for security, always aware of the moral stance you are taking. (See also the house where Jupiter resides.)

Midheaven in Capricorn or in Aspect to Saturn. Your mother senses she is pregnant and treats her pregnancy as a purely physical process. Her pragmatic worldview centers around her own ego, discipline, and toughness in dealing with others. You are an opportunity for her to bring her own views into reality. You present yourself as a veritable rock of society to the world at large, as you have a healthy respect for the establishment in whose ranks you belong. Discipline, pragmatism, and cautious reserve get you where you want to be. (See also the house where Saturn resides.)

Midheaven in Aquarius or in Aspect to Saturn or Uranus. Your mother thinks that she is pregnant but is so abstract and detached from her own feelings that she is not initially sure. She concentrates her energies upon being a social animal and loves being the center of attention. She immediately plans your position in life far into the future, and leaves it to you to live up to her ideals. Humanitarian goals and the need to reach many people rather than the few spurs you on in your quest for recognition in the world and your career. Idealism and sociability enable you to mix business with pleasure and to meet groups who invest in your futuristic ideas. (See also the houses where Saturn and Uranus reside.)

Midheaven in Pisces or in Aspect to Jupiter or Neptune. Your mother, upon feeling that she is pregnant, attributes it to the influence of your father and the pressure put upon her by others. She reacts sensitively to the expectations of others and is devoted to doing what is intended for her. Her inner peace and fantasy life often betray her isolation from the real world. Always being sensitive to others leaves you feeling isolated and lonely, a dilemma with which you have to grapple in your career. Consciousness of your goals and throwing out muddled thinking may lead to a clarity that others will recognize. (See also the houses where Jupiter and Neptune reside.)

For example, the Sun as the father opposite the Midheaven at the bottom of the horoscope would imply that he was opposed to the conception itself, which could indicate a resistance to masculine acceptance in later life. If the Sun is near the Midheaven, the father would identify with the child the mother carries and might even believe it was his impetus that brought you into being.

THE TENTH HOUSE (CAPRICORN AND ITS NATURAL RULER, SATURN)

Thirty-three weeks to twenty-eight weeks before birth

The Tenth House (and the opposite Fourth House) is traditionally our parents and often begins with our mother telling our father of our existence, which transforms our existence from an interior and unknown reality to complete acknowledgment. Although archetypally the father, it is often the parent of the opposite gender, just as the Fourth House is the parent of the same gender. We see our home life in the Fourth House as we relate to the same-sex parent, and the outside world in the Tenth House as the opposite-sex parent. Our mother announces the change in her life as she adopts a new set of physical conditions and prepares for our arrival. Our parents must handle practical matters, including the choice of doctor or midwife, dietary and physical regimes (the

Moon, Virgo, or Taurus), and whether to deliver in hospital or at home and mechanically or naturally. There are many decisions to make, and adjustments in lifestyle and practical issues to confront. Indeed, our inner security is defined by the planets and signs here.

As the Ninth House is the creation of our brain and our transformation through the various early evolutionary stages, the Tenth House is when we achieve structural stability through our teeth and skeletal system, when our sexual glands form and our pancreas begins to function. These biological mechanisms are very appropriate to the Saturnine structural quality of the house.

Our parents' concerns foreshadow our ability to achieve success in the world (Jupiter) and to receive recognition (the Sun) for our skills and goals. When our mother is reluctant about telling our father about her pregnancy, due to either a sign uncongenial to the Moon, like Scorpio, or difficult aspects from the Moon to a planet in the Tenth House, it follows that we (particularly the feminine in us) resist making our creative objectives known to others. When our parents broadcast the fact, shown by Mercury or the Sun connections, we expect great publicity to attend our life objectives and often manifest this. A neutral response, shown by few aspects to the Midheaven or no planets in the Tenth House, implies little impact upon the outer world and not much support from others. If our parents did not want us at all, when there are oppositions or squares to the Sun or the Moon or both, we will feel threatened by the world. The realizations and actions that follow can range from open to totally suppressed, and from natural to superficial. An instrumentally determined pregnancy, shown by Uranus or Pluto or Aquarius contacts, would predispose us to a life influenced by machines. The way our mother deals with our existence determines our attitude toward our life objectives.

In the horoscope shown in Figure 9.4, Neptune is in Libra and the Tenth House, opposite the Aries Moon in the Fourth. In this case the father is missing, creating insecurity in the natural place of the father, and the mother is forced to compensate for his absence. This creates idealism about career and outer-world expectations, and a tendency to associate with spiritual matters. The trine to Pluto in the Eighth House, registering just before conception at the Ninth House cusp, is the knowledge of the father's leaving before the fact as a "fated" and powerful event. The Moon and Neptune in opposition also indicates psychic powers and great sensitivity to emotional relationships. This constellation of planets is simultaneously sensitive and also powerful. Since Neptune and Pluto were in such a sextile aspect for everyone born during the '40s, '50s, '60s, and '70s, it has affected entire generations of people. Where such

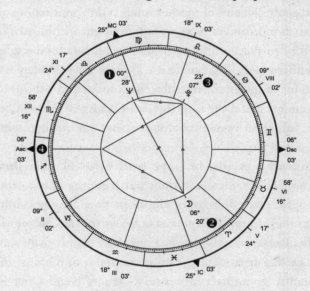

FIGURE 9.4: TENTH HOUSE PLANETS

Neptune in the Tenth House ❶ shows a missing father (the mother knows he is leaving before conception, shown by the sextile to Pluto in the Eighth House ❸). The mother compensates and must take control, shown by opposition Neptune ❷ in the Moon's natural house. The loss is acutely felt around the Ascendant ❹ birth time and therefore affects the personality deeply.

combinations occur in our horoscope and how this connects to the other planets shows to what extent we partake of such generational qualities.

The Tenth House is our ambitions and achievements, as determined by our parents' reactions to the discovery of our existence and their subsequent actions.

THE ELEVENTH HOUSE (AQUARIUS AND ITS NATURAL RULERS, SATURN AND URANUS)

Twenty-eight weeks to seventeen weeks before birth

The beginning of the Eleventh House is the "quickening," when our mother recognizes movement within her. The placenta is of primary importance now as an intermediary between our mother's body and our fetus. The placenta exchanges carbon dioxide for oxygen and waste for nutriments, and provides minerals, vitamins, and hormones for fetus and mother. We begin to respire, and our involuntary movement system becomes functional.

Our mother projects her expectations onto us during this time, concerning our gender, appearance, character, and life. She thinks about our future while beginning to prepare for our coming into the world. Our mother experiences the initial limitations of movement (Saturn), although she does not show her pregnancy until the end of the Eleventh House. This corresponds to the dual rulership of Aquarius by Saturn's conservative structure and Uranus's individualistic desire to go beyond existing structures. Our mother is increasingly freed from her usual responsibilities, her relationship is less sexual (Saturn), and the focus is upon friends (Mercury, Venus, or Mars). She may join a support group (the Node or Jupiter) or learn to understand (Jupiter, Mercury, or the Sun) the demands of the birth process. Her responses to the possibilities of this time can range from ignorance of any relationship at all (negative aspects to Mercury, Moon, or the Sun) to a profound recognition of the interconnections permeating every step in the gestation process. She can focus upon herself (Saturn) or upon the universal state of childbearing and birthing (Uranus).

Toward the end of this house, she not only feels different from others but also is physically, emotionally, and mentally separate from her former self. This can lead to a unique understanding of others, compassion and sympathy for people in general, and progressive thinking, all transmitted to us.

The Eleventh House is our ability to abstract and detach ourselves from the physical world and to ascend into the realm of ideas and plans.

The Eleventh House Cusp

The Eleventh House cusp is when we quicken within our mother; she acknowledges our being and makes projections and plans for our life in the world. It is idealism, planning, expectations, groups, and our ability to imagine our being in the world.

Eleventh House Cusp in Aries or in Aspect to Mars. Your mother's ideals are affected by her drive for you to succeed, supported by her assertive manner. She feels alone and must depend upon her own energies and skills to survive. (See also the house where Mars resides.)

Eleventh House Cusp in Taurus or in Aspect to Venus. Your mother feels secure and has stable surroundings as well as much love to sustain her, and she projects positively upon your life in the world. She is optimistic and solid in her love of you within and radiates an inner beauty. (See also the house where Venus resides.)

Eleventh House Cusp in Gemini or in Aspect to Mercury. Your mother is ambivalent about her pregnancy and procrastinates continually about what she wants and who you will be. She has many odd and talkative friends and communicates constantly, not bothering about whether she is consistent or not. She somehow sees you as a potential sister or brother and may spend time with either your siblings or hers. (See also the house where Mercury resides.)

Eleventh House Cusp in Cancer or in Aspect to the Moon. Your mother is nurturing, takes very good care of herself, and has conservative and domestic plans for you. She loves motherhood although it is still very idealistic to her, but her warmth is reflected in her loving others. (See also the house where the Moon resides.)

Eleventh House Cusp in Leo or in Aspect to the Sun. Your mother is extrovert and acts as though she can deliver you herself, and she acts experienced, whether or not she actually is. She is a consummate actress and carries you with aplomb and great gravity. She is proud and almost refuses attention from others. (See also the house where the Sun resides.)

Eleventh House Cusp in Virgo or in Aspect to Mercury. Your mother is critical and perfectionist about others but also herself. She is reliant upon others and feels that her work is carrying the burdens of those around her. She is naive about the process and yet understands what is demanded of her. (See also the house where Mercury resides.)

Eleventh House Cusp in Libra or in Aspect to Venus. Your mother sublimates herself in favor of friends, family, and husband, balancing herself with them. She feels a kinship with her child within and often cannot separate herself from what is within herself. (See also the house where Venus resides.)

Eleventh House Cusp in Scorpio or in Aspect to Mars or Pluto. Your mother feels emotionally and possibly physically separate from those around her and also distant from you within her. She is secretive, perpetuates the feminine mystery, and has deep feelings that are rarely expressed to others. Her intensity is transformed within. (See also the houses where Mars and Pluto reside.)

Eleven House Cusp in Sagittarius or in Aspect to Jupiter. Your mother sees gestation as a rebirth of herself into a new life, and she is optimistic, expansive, and outgoing about her beliefs, aims, and attitudes. She plans you as an extension of her worldview, and you are a natural advocate for her. (See also the house where Jupiter resides.)

Eleventh House Cusp in Capricorn or in Aspect to Saturn. Your mother is firmly in control of her world, her friends, and her ideals, which are becoming more practical and pragmatic in their focus. She almost takes on the fatherly role in the family system and does not express her needs adequately. (See also the house where Saturn resides.)

Eleventh House Cusp in Aquarius or in Aspect to Saturn or Uranus. Your mother is idealistic and spends more time looking into the future than attending to the present and its realistic demands. She creates structures and then feels trapped by them, so she tries to be unconstrained. (See also the houses where Saturn and Uranus reside.)

Eleventh House Cusp in Pisces or in Aspect to Jupiter or Neptune. Your mother is affected deeply by external influences, over which she feels little control. Her pregnancy is a time of fantasy, with an active dream life, spiritual energies swirling around, and profound effects caused by diet and environmental influences. She is very sensitive and open to everyone around her. (See the houses where Jupiter and Neptune reside.)

THE TWELFTH HOUSE (PISCES AND ITS NATURAL RULERS, JUPITER AND NEPTUNE)

Seventeen weeks before birth until birth

Our mother gains water weight (the Moon, Jupiter, and Neptune) during this water sign time, which restricts her mobility (Saturn). The amniotic fluid in which we swim supports us in many ways. We live within this watery capsule totally protected from the outside world. Our mother becomes more and more dependent upon others (the Moon, the Sun, and Neptune) and as her water weight increases, so her sensitivity to external influences increases, as does psychic contact (Neptune) with us. The symbolism of the two fishes tied together by their tails reflects in an uncanny way our attachment to our mother via the umbilical cord.

As birth approaches, the self-sacrificial qualities (Neptune and the Moon) of the Twelfth House become more pronounced. Examinations by the doctor or midwife (Mars, Uranus, or Pluto) become more regular, as does the realization that birth itself is approaching. As our mother's psychic faculties (the Moon and Neptune) and fantasies and dreams (Neptune) are all in full operation, her absorption in the birth is complete. While her husband (the Sun), friends (Mercury, Venus, or Mars), midwife (the Moon or Mercury), doctor (Mars, Saturn, or Uranus), and other children (Mercury, Venus, or Mars) support her, she realizes that she will give birth alone (Neptune). The acceptance and release (Jupiter and the Moon) of her deepest instincts coincides with our final development. The inability of the uterus to expand any further heralds the pre-delivery time. She is ultimately alone, yet she carries us in her. Her choice of delivery method (the Ascendant) and environment (the Moon and Saturn) reflect our later reliance upon or independence from the inner life. The more she bypasses her own instincts (the Moon or Venus) and relies upon mechanical direction (Uranus and Mercury), the weaker will be our instinctual contact.

Neil Armstrong (Figure 9.5) was the first astronaut to set foot on the Moon in 1969. He has the Moon in Sagittarius, the sign of long journeys, registering at the exact age he went to the Moon. This would show that it was a highly emotional moment for him and in many ways defined him for the rest of his life. What is fascinating is that he was psychologically prepared, as shown by the Moon trine his Node in Aries in the Twelfth House when he swam in the amniotic fluid within his mother. The Moon in the sign Aries shows that he is self-assured and spontaneous in his actions, especially when subject to forces beyond his control. Also of interest is the trine to Mercury and Neptune in the Fourth House, indicating both the standard communication and the psychic experiments that were conducted on the Moon journey. This shows his need to link back to home and family while being distant from them. It also demonstrates how outer events can interface with the inner qualities we carry that date back to our gestation period.

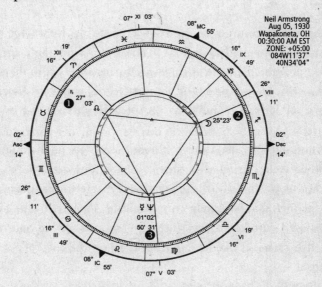

FIGURE 9.5: HOROSCOPE OF NEIL ARMSTRONG

Neil Armstrong was the first astronaut to set foot on the Moon in 1969. He has the Moon in Sagittarius, the sign of long journeys, registering at the exact age he went to the Moon. He was psychologically prepared, as shown by the Moon trine his Node in Aries in the Twelfth House, when he swam in the amniotic fluid within his mother.

The ten degrees immediately above the Ascendant correspond to the final six weeks of gestation, and show hidden aspects of our personality: dreams, fantasies, illusions, and idealistic expectations that lie near the surface of consciousness, as represented by the Ascendant/Descendant axis, across the horizon. Our mother's instinctive physical responses are the best outlet for these influences, and natural birth tends to allow these instincts their proper role so that we also can call on our inner physical guidance in tense life situations.

The Twelfth House is relationships between forces acting upon us that affect and guide our inner psychic attitudes.

Signs on the Twelfth House Cusp

The Twelfth House cusp is an inward-looking, final stage of gestation when our mother feels us inside and is vulnerable and subject to outer influences as our inner life forms and is completed. It is a self-sacrificial, mystical, and fantastic time, with her dreams coming true. It is our ability to accept and nurture our own inner world.

The signs on the Twelfth House cusp show us the qualities our mother feels during this time and also our attitude to what is within us psychically, those secret and mysterious urges and deepest feelings that we rarely communicate. Planets in this house are associated with their sign rulerships, so that having Saturn in the Twelfth House is like having Capricorn on the cusp of the Twelfth House.

Twelfth House Cusp in Aries or in Aspect to Mars. As your mother withdraws from the world, she asserts herself and becomes stronger and more vital. She revels in her isolation and finds it a time to contact her true inner nature. She may be alone at this time and find she likes it. (See also the house of Mars.)

Twelfth House Cusp in Taurus or in Aspect to Venus. Your mother feels secure and stable as she withdraws from the world, often implying that her material needs are met and she lacks for nothing. Pregnancy is a tangible and sensual experience for her, and she is likely to stress the practical considerations of the process. (See also the house of Venus.)

Twelfth House Cusp in Gemini or in Aspect to Mercury. Your mother communicates with friends, immediate family, and others to express herself, and she tends to see her relationship as brotherly-sisterly at this time. She may even anticipate you as a sibling for her on mental levels. (See also the house of Mercury.)

Twelfth House Cusp in Cancer or in Aspect to the Moon. Your mother is emotionally changeable and tends to emphasize issues that trigger her feelings. She may exaggerate and blow out of proportion any maternal issues, and she controls her family in deep and conservative ways. (See also the house of the Moon.)

Twelfth House Cusp in Leo or in Aspect to the Sun. Your mother plays with her role and acts the part of being in control and knowing what to do, whether or not she does. Her extrovert and powerful sense of seeming to be totally aware might be misleading, yet her poise is undeniable even in isolation. (See also the house of the Sun.)

Twelfth House Cusp in Virgo or in Aspect to Mercury. Your mother is very critical and perfectionist about her choice of influences, friends, and ideals at this time, as she goes within herself. She protects herself by her criticism of others, although much of it turns back onto her, and the criticism often originates in her own naivete. (See also the house of Mercury.)

Twelfth House Cusp in Libra or in Aspect to Venus. Your mother is very much reliant upon her partner and lessens her own needs in favor of what is inside. She might experience frustration at not getting enough attention, although she is very social and open to the influences of others. (See also the house of Venus.)

Twelfth House Cusp in Scorpio or in Aspect to Mars or Pluto. Your mother feels separate as she goes into seclusion, although she revels in her aloneness. She goes inside and in the process forms deep and strong bonds with you. (See also the houses of Mars and Pluto.)

Twelfth House Cusp in Sagittarius or in Aspect to Jupiter. Your mother is very philosophical and optimistic about her isolation and accepts her fate. She fluctuates between concern for the physical reality within and her higher, more spiritual aspirations. She feels foreign and strange, and is active even in her acceptance of the isolation. (See also the house of Jupiter.)

Twelfth House Cusp in Capricorn or in Aspect to Saturn. Your mother feels trapped and controlled by the gestation process, and perhaps oppressed by the prospect of doctors being in control of the birth. She may even experience depression or exaggerated isolation in this last stage. (See also the house of Saturn.)

Twelfth House Cusp in Aquarius or in Aspect to Saturn or Uranus. Your mother is reserved and lonely during the seclusion of the last stage. She might be nervous and more timid than usual, fearing failure and tending to retire rather than accept the sacrifice she is to make for you. (See also the houses of Saturn and Uranus.)

Twelfth House Cusp in Pisces or in Aspect to Jupiter or Neptune. Your mother is deeply emotional and revels in her hidden life, caused by modest circumstances. She may be around unreliable people and can indulge herself, but her vision of the future remains intact. (See also the houses of Jupiter and Neptune.)

BIRTHING INTO CHILDHOOD

*Who shows a child as he is? Who places him in a
constellation and hands him the measure of distance
and interval?*

RAINER MARIA RILKE, *DUINO ELEGIES*

The birth process corresponds to our Ascendant, or Rising
Sign. We express this transition in our personality, modified
by the Ascendant and the planets near it. Think of the meaning of
the Sun signs and apply it to a birth situation. A long labor and a
mother's resistance, characterized by Saturn or a Saturn-ruled sign
such as Capricorn or Aquarius on the Ascendant, brings a careful
and retrained persona, while an easy, natural delivery, typical of
Jupiter or a Jupiter-ruled sign like Sagittarius or Pisces, creates an
open and expansive nature. When the mechanical and technological Uranus is involved, the birth happens quickly, is an intervention, and applies these qualities to the personality as eccentricity
and individuality, as well as an attraction to technology. Neptune
and the Moon both lend watery and feminine qualities to the
birth, which often occurs with anesthetics or their natural equivalent of water birth, and increase the sensitivity and psychic abilities. Each of the planets near or in aspect to the Ascendant are
components of our birth and exist as subpersonalities.

It is of interest that our personality comes into being at birth itself. If we think about it, in the time leading up to birth we don't
have a personality at all, and at birth and afterward we distinctly

do have one that continues to develop. Influences in the preceding gestation octave are stored in our physical body as somatic or instinctive traits, while those in the childhood octave that starts with birth are stored in the personality.

Other contemporary astrological systems, even those that grade the horoscope circle, do not even mention conception and gestation, much less recognize their importance in interpretation and in life.[21] Most current psychological theories also ignore development prior to birth, with the notable exception of Dr. Stanislav Grof's work. It involves perinatal matrixes, which are "nearly universally accepted among perinatal psychologists as unconscious forces, factors, matrices that exist in us all as a result of a human birth that is unique, by comparison to *all* other species, in its degree of trauma and hence of its impact or imprint on what we might call—dare I say the word—our 'human nature.' "[22] Even though Grof applies his ideas to phases of the birth process, he is clearly including influences back into gestation. The qualities of our gestation and birth process affect us profoundly—not only our personalities but also our ability to experience our life in time.

Those who participate in our birth and who affect it at a distance show up as distinct subpersonalities, parts of us that have quite specific roles in our self-image. While usually one or two dominate, all want and need their say. The blend of personality traits we carry is complex, and yet we can live each part of us out. Psychosynthesis, where subpersonality is central, has distinct phases for integrating the subpersonalities. They are:

1. Thorough knowledge of one's personality and subpersonalities.

2. Control of the various elements of the personality.

3. Realization of one's true self by the discovery or creation of a unifying center.

4. Formation or reconstruction of the personality around a new, higher center.[23]

THE ASCENDANT—BIRTH AS

Our astrological birth is the germ of our personality, and whereas gestation was of necessity seen from our mother's viewpoint, we come into our own existence in the world here. Our parents are still extremely important because we are largely governed by them throughout childhood, but we are also simultaneously freeing ourselves from their influence. For example, John Lennon has his Libra Sun opposite his Aries Ascendant, showing that his father was at sea in the merchant navy at his birth: His mother did not want to be pregnant in the first place, and he never really connected with his father. The lack of recognition by his father meant that all the recognition he received from the world made little impact on his life and was ultimately unsatisfying. It is often the case that planets show us individuals who affect us profoundly by not being present, which is seen in oppositions and squares to planets in the four houses of childhood.

The complexity or simplicity of our Ascendant and its planets is a guide to how our personality operates and expresses itself. The planets are really subpersonalities, as we have seen before, with the additional impact that they are directly integrated (or not) with our personality as a whole.

Birth occurs when we draw our first breath, although the Ascendant governs the entire time before and after the process. The manner of birth and its implications determine the way in which our personality functions. The body that formed during gestation is tangible and physical and continues to develop, change, and mature. The process by which the essence of our personality begins forming at birth develops throughout childhood. Our personality is a mask that contains instincts, habits, mannerisms, expressions, and fantasies, and is our way of adapting to our world.

Our personality is related to the environment into which we are born, the nature of our birth, physical appearance, and gender, and the actions and projections of those present or affecting the birth from a distance. The zodiac sign on our Ascendant shows the atmosphere and attitude existing in the birth environment. Cancer shows warmth, maternal influences, and emotional reactions as environmental and then personal qualities. Scorpio shows separations in birth and subsequent medical treatments. Taurus determines a physical view of birth and of the personality. We continue to act as we came into the world.

As personality is a process, the process of birth itself is a key to understanding the Ascendant. When birth is rapid and easy, the resultant personality manifests itself fluidly in both short-term and long-term situations in life. Whether in the local pub or in lifelong working associations, personality flows easily. A difficult labor that requires great effort by the mother produces a hardworking personality. The longer and harder the labor, the more stressed our personality. When a doctor or midwife must help delivery, our personality requires assistance from others to assert it. When forceps or caesarean section is part of the birth process, we require the physical intervention of others to allow our personality to function. When an entire team of doctors and hospital staff is necessary, the resultant personality needs collective situations for awakening personality, such as mass movements, gurus, or religious revivals. The more people present at a birth, the greater the collective influences upon the personality.

In addition to the physical conditions of delivery, the reactions to our birth and to us of those present determine our reflection in the world around us. Modern birth movements stress the importance of who is present at birth and the general atmosphere of all births. Anesthetics, local or general, produce numbness, vagueness, or great sensitivity to certain influences. Induction exposes our personality to an overstimulation by external forces and generates a compulsive attitude. We would feel that others were compelling us through external circumstances to emerge from within, before our time. These birth "complications" are interventions in what should be, but rarely is, a natural process. The medical profession has accepted and encouraged such intervention as routine, and as a result implicates itself in the problematic and violent personalities exhibited by many people today. The degree and manner of involvement of those present at our birth determines the closeness or detachment of our personality to others. If the doctor hurries things along so that he can play golf, our personality reflects this by continually rushing into self-expression.

The Ascendant also governs the personality aspects of physical appearance, gender, and initial health. When her family and friends surround our mother, sympathetic supporters respond to us after birth. Reactions to our gender and appearance should be various and full, although in institutional births these responses are lacking. The closer we are to others at birth, the more related we feel to our gender and body.

The implications of birth and subsequent treatment have such a profound influence upon one's whole view of life that attitudes toward childbirth affect entire generations of children. Natural methods and the increasing awareness of women and men create natural awareness in children. Rigid, suppressive, assembly-line birth techniques produce zombies.

The Ascendant is our personality, which derives from the manner of our birth and the influences of those participating in and surrounding it.

The range of interpretations describes personalities as derived from the nature of the birth environment. The choices as to which words are most apt are made in relation to the planets around the Ascendant, the circumstances described in gestation as leading up to the birth, and the planets that are in aspect to the Ascendant.

Planets conjunct your Ascendant show people and influences affecting your birth and personality. Conjunctions, when a planet is right on the Ascendant, show the most immediate and direct influences, which are often indistinguishable from the personality as a whole. Close conjunctions indicate a lack of boundary between the qualities involved. When a conjunction is before (above) the Ascendant, external influences affect the triggering of your birth or personality; when after your Ascendant, the influence is strongest after birth and is an aftereffect of your personality. The closeness to the Ascendant shows the strength and bonding of the qualities.

Planets near the Ascendant show people apart from the mother who are present and become direct components of one's personality. Often subpersonalities reflect the delivering doctor, an anesthetist, worried grandfather, or pushy grandmother. Planets in aspect to our Ascendant show people who have an indirect influence upon our birth. If the aspecting planet is below the horizon, the influence upon our personality is unconscious; if it is above the horizon, it is conscious. These influences might emanate from a nervous father at home or younger children wondering what was

In rebirthing or primal scream therapies the individual attempts to recreate the birth circumstances and its feelings and associations. Shut your eyes, go inside, and try to feel your birth based on what you know of your own circumstances. Include the people who were there at the scene and see what imagery or feelings emerge. It is very useful to process and work with such imagery.

happening. All the influences coming directly from those present and those making distant projections determine the subpersonalities we exhibit. Once we identify these influences, we can discover exactly who these individuals were and how we carry them within our own being.

The table of Ascendant birth interpretations given later in the chapter shows the influences of each sign on the Ascendant as modalities of the birth process and also their traditional "ruling planets," which dispose Ascendant influences. Planets that either aspect the Ascendant or are rulers of the Ascendant sign also signify individuals who are present at the birth or who affect it by their absence. Thus with an Aries birth we can expect a doctor or surgeon to be present, while a Taurus Ascendant is more likely a feminine, Venusian influence like a midwife, nurse, or nurturing mother of the mother. After seeing the sign of our Ascendant, we also look to see where the planet ruling that sign is located in the horoscope. This shows an area and time of our life when our personality manifests itself particularly significantly. If we have a sign with double rulers like Scorpio (Mars and Pluto), Aquarius (Saturn and Uranus), and Pisces (Jupiter and Neptune), we must see the houses and signs and aspects of both rulers. Naturally this brings a duality to the personality that is so marked also in the double signs (see chapter 1).

THE ASCENDANT (FIRST HOUSE CUSP) THROUGH THE SIGNS

The Ascendant is our birth and begins the First House, which is our bonding process with our mother. Our personality is affected by our birth circumstances and environment, our physical appearance, and the reaction of those around us to our coming into the world.

Ascendant Birth in Aries

The environment into which you are born has qualities of restlessness, energy, impatience, and self-assertion, all qualities that are a part of your personality. Your mother concentrates upon her own needs, finds it difficult to adapt to the requirements of others, and wants the birth to happen on her own terms. There is a dramatic and exuberant quality to the delivery, and a sense of "I can do it on my own" pervades the event. Yet there is a great likelihood that an aggressive person is present who attempts to dictate the pace and rhythm of the birth process itself, and hurries it along as much as possible. (See also the house where Mars resides.)

Your Arian personality is decisive, active, and very direct about expressing your own needs—you do not like others telling you what to do and see yourself as the be-all and end-all of existence; your needs come first. Physically you are lean and spare, strong in an unobtrusive way, and fiery in all ways. Any activities that allow your self-assertion are accepted.

After birth you are very self-assertive in making your mother aware that you have needs that must be met immediately. The bonding process is very strong, but your mother is highly independent and has her own concerns, which sometimes compete with yours. You are the center of the universe and glow with the attention you get.

Ascendant Birth in Taurus

The environment into which you are born is stable, controlled, secure, and quiet, and the focus is on the physical, practical aspects of the birth process. Your mother is surrounded by women friends, relatives, midwives or nurses, and wants the birth to happen slowly and without pressure. There is a sense of her wanting the birth to happen to her rather than initiating the activity herself.

Our Taurean personality is secure, fixed, earthy, and sensual, supported by a need for financial and physical well-being and material support. Life is tangible and very real, and the possessiveness your mother felt for you after birth can bring possessive qualities to you. You create habitual patterns that bind you to set routines that change only under great duress. Artistic qualities are dominant, and you spend time and effort on appearances. Physically you are robust and broad, physical, sound of body and attractive in an earthy way.

After birth you are treated like an object, fondled, and held, and your bonding is very secure and tangible. The physicality of the world is immediate, and breast-feeding is a reinforcement of the stability you receive after making your needs known to your mother. (See also the house where Venus resides.)

Ascendant Birth in Gemini

The environment into which you are born is unstable, mobile, adaptable, and versatile in coping with a basic ambiguity that your mother feels about the birth. The process is talked through, which gives a nervous and superficial slant to the proceedings. There are a variety of people present who have constant, light conversation with your mother, some who hurry through and many who just want to gossip with her.

Your Gemini personality is full of diverse interests stemming from the need to express yourself and make contact with virtually everyone around you. Content is less important than the act of communication, and you transmit information from place to place and person to person. Physically you tend to be lithe and agile, with a tendency to change your appearance regularly. Writing, musical, linguistic, and artistic abilities are available if your application is sufficient.

After birth you are one among many who need attention, and often surrogate mothers, maybe older sisters or friends of your mother, substitute for her. You become accustomed to being talked to as well as held, and you begin trying to communicate very early as a way of asserting your needs. (See also the house where Mercury resides.)

Ascendant Birth in Cancer

The environment into which you are born is simple, homely, conservative, and warm in response to your mother's classically maternal attitude to childbirth. She relies heavily upon others, especially women, around her to aid and nurture her during the process, and is particularly sensitive to what others feel about her. Your mother may feel vulnerable or insecure and compensate by adopting a rigid attitude and withdrawing back into herself.

Your Cancer personality is two-sided, often changing feelings rapidly and extremely, sensitive to the opinions of others and receiving psychic contact constantly. Feelings are more important than ideas or material goods, although a natural possessiveness is part of your personality. Physically you are receptive, round, and absorptive, and can become corpulent with age. Artistic and musical talents vie with a natural feeling for psychology and counseling skills.

After birth you are nurtured, held, cuddled, and warmly loved in every way by your mother, who becomes enamored of you. Your sense of belonging is heightened by her tendency to treat you as a possession or extension of herself. Your needs are supported by instinctive responses, and security is there for you. (See also the house where the Moon resides.)

Ascendant Birth in Leo

The environment into which you are born is open, active, and has within it an air of authority. Your mother is self-confident, joyous, and proud, sensing that she will have the child herself. She is not prepared to rely upon others and is the absolute center of attention to the point of being bold and domineering with others. Even if she is not as confident as she might be, she appears and acts totally in control of herself and others. She is special, unique, and extravagant and dramatic as an individual. A flood of energy is directed to you upon birth, and you are treated by her as royalty.

Your Leo personality reflects the phenomenal attention and love lavished upon you early in life, a dominant but warm nature prone to making yourself the center of all affairs, allowing others into your own great light if they warrant or deserve it. Physically you are robust, fiery, open-faced, strong, and vital to the point of exaggeration. Any activities that allow you to express yourself and to be central in a group of people is attractive and indeed necessary to you.

After birth your mother acts as though you are the center of the universe, and you bask in the love and attention. Your bright and sunny disposition is extrovert and positive, and brings joy that you reflect back onto others. (See also the house where the Sun resides.)

Ascendant Birth in Virgo

The environment into which you are born is nervous, unstable, and cautious. The focus is upon the physical aspect of birth, including a pedantic attention to hygiene. Your mother is naive and tends to see the birth process as an idea rather than a physical action, and yet is intensely critical of others around her. She is surrounded primarily by staff or nurses whose function is to analyze and define the birth conditions and to practically manage them rather than be concerned with the feelings of your mother. The focus is upon reacting to what "is" rather than making situations manifest in a certain way. An almost obsessive attention to correct and exact details leads to overlooking the more important human issues.

Your Virgo personality is critical, discriminative, and introspective about the parts of your whole rather than able to understand the larger picture. You are a natural observer, critic, and team worker. Physically your attention is upon diet and digestion, bringing an attractive appearance under the microscope and yielding a delicate and distilled physique with pronounced mental and intellectual abilities. The rigidity and need for formal structures will attract interests that require grading, criticizing, categorizing, or ordering.

After birth your mother is highly critical of you in many ways and chooses to concentrate upon the practical details of your early being. The natural responses to your demands for attention and loving touch are hygienic and antiseptic in quality, which leaves you dissatisfied with what you get. (See also the house where Mercury resides.)

Ascendant Birth in Libra

The environment into which you are born is balanced, harmonious, homely, obliging, and deliberate. Your mother is highly influenced by what others tell her about what she is supposed to do, and most likely a doctor or authority figure takes control of the birth process for her. She wants attention and to be noticed, but ultimately she bows to the need to work with others, to be part of a team, to have others direct her during birth. In turn, she is obliging and chatty about how she feels. Her thoughts are determined by prevailing patterns and her own social habits. Her system of values is strong, she follows the norm, and she makes a very strong bond with you and assumes you will accept her value system as well.

Your Libran personality is similarly obliging and social, and you accept and work within existing normal patterns of interaction at all costs. The set of values you accept determine your life and behavior to a large extent, and idealism pervades all aspects of your being, as you can understand many contradictory viewpoints and can vacillate from one to the other regularly. Relationships are essential, and your life will revolve around them. Physically you are tall, elegantly formed, quite beautiful or handsome in appearance, and generally clear and fine of line. Any activities that involve relationships and social skills will suit you.

After birth you and your mother have a strongly synergistic relationship in which balance and mutual support are dominant in every way. Asserting yourself brings an immediate, if sometimes detached and idealistic response, and your instinctive needs are met easily and lovingly by your mother and her surrogates. (See also the house where Venus resides.)

Ascendant Birth in Scorpio

The environment into which you are born is aggressive, disharmonious, hostile, separate, and potentially dangerous. Your mother is quite separate from you and scared of the birth process, a fact that is heightened by those present at your birth, particularly a doctor or assertive midwife. The birth is an emergence from darkness that is a struggle and requires great effort and energy, and brings passion from others. There is distinct danger from a hospital delivery and a great potential for forceful birth techniques, such as forceps or surgical delivery. As a process of life and death, your birth is highly stressful to your mother and threatening to you.

Your Scorpio personality is intense, hotheaded, and passionate beneath a cautious and conservative exterior. The outer and inner parts of you create tension, and often inner feelings force themselves into the light of day and create explosions of feelings. Physically you are strong, compact, and intense, and have an inner darkness that attracts, yet evokes caution in others in its penetrating and forceful glance. You like depth and passion in all affairs and matters of the world.

After birth you are separate from your mother, and may be given into the care of others who are not as passionate in responding to your needs. Often breast-feeding ceases very early on, and your powerful expressions of need are ignored. (See also the house where Mars and Pluto reside.)

Ascendant Birth in Sagittarius

The environment into which you are born is enthusiastic, expansive, naturally social, lively, and adventurous. No standing on formality or ceremony here—your mother sees the birth as an athletic contest in which a positive outcome is assumed and assured. She has great energy and receives strong support from relatives, friends, and all others around her. She feels foreign but pushes through the differences with good humor, joy, and pride of achievement. Her worldview encompasses all accidents and unusual occurrences, and the birth is exciting and lively, if a little messy.

Your Sagittarian personality is tolerant, optimistic to a fault, open-minded and liberal about foreign influences, and accepting of different attitudes and beliefs. Physically you are strong, active, well-formed, athletic, and handsome. Although lengthy, your posture is stooped and less forceful than your size implies. You like expansion and flexibility in viewpoint, and you work in conformance with your philosophy of life.

After birth you and your mother move around and are very active and open with many other people. Physically secure, you are mobile and flexible, and the generally expansive atmosphere around you is invigorating and enervating. (See also the house where Jupiter resides.)

Ascendant Birth in Capricorn

The environment into which you are born is serious, practical, pragmatic, and anxious. Your mother is concentrated on the task at hand, which is expected to be difficult, and her inhibition and strain encourage a long labor. The circumstances of your birth are methodical, attended by older, unemotional, and cold assistants, and the absence of warm women is noticeable. Your mother is reserved, conservative, and restrained, and she bows to the experience of men and allows them to take responsibility for the delivery itself. The birth is perceived as a physical process devoid of emotion.

Your Capricornian personality is unemotional, highly defined and rigid in value, habitual in the extreme, and often stern in manner, all of which conspire to give an impression of discipline and control. The rules of the society and the laws of the authorities are respected and worked within, bringing a high estimation of self-worth as a result of abiding by existing structures. Physically you are muscular, boney, dark, narrow, and sturdy in a slanted way. Particularly, facial angles are prominent. You accept the seriousness and need for structure in life, and you like professions that require feelings to be repressed and reality to be kept constantly in mind.

After birth you are dealt with pragmatically, as a business proposition, and the tangible aspects of your needs are met at the expense of a lack of adequate emotion. The coldness is evident, and your craving for love goes beyond these outer and unsatisfactory gestures. (See also the house where Saturn resides.)

Ascendant Birth in Aquarius

The environment into which you are born is communal, convivial, sociable, and sympathetic, which supports your mother's need for friends with whom she can talk, parents to oversee matters, and an idealistic context in which to express herself. The paradox of the situation requires that within the rigid structure and need for technological and mechanical support, which is carefully planned, there is a need to be eccentric, independent, and detached from it all. The birth is assisted, and a wide range of people participate in bringing you into the world.

Your Aquarian personality is unique, original, unusual, and prone to individual statements, in contrast to habits and manners that are dependent upon the acceptance and support of others. You continually create social structures that you immediately wish to dissolve and free yourself from. Physically you are well put together, rather tall, delicate, and clear, but without distinct features. You like any activities that involve you in determining the structure or freedom of your and others' lives.

After birth you become part of a family and social life that bring you into contact with many different people and surrogates of your mother, so that the bond is multiple from the beginning. The rigid structures of your mother's habits are restricting but secure. (See also the house where Saturn and Uranus reside.)

Ascendant Birth in Pisces

The environment into which you are born is obscure, uncertain, subject to myriad outer circumstances beyond anyone's control, and yet progressive, uninhibited, and gentle. Your mother relinquishes any semblance of control and allows situations to emerge from the unconscious. There is a possibility of drug inducement or anesthetic, which heightens the sensitivity, vulnerability, and extreme openness that allows the birth to happen. The context is institutional in that it is isolating and dreamy, and satisfies your mother's need for reserve, vagueness, and an absence of expressed emotion. There is a contrast between your mother's fantasies about you regarding your entrance into the world and the reality evident at this time. She is merely the medium or channel by which you become.

Your Piscean personality is self-sacrificial, easily seduced and influenced by forms and feelings, religious and devoted in an uncertain way, and utopian in all matters. Physically you are delicate and sensitive, and you tend to absorb all in a sleepy and indistinct way. As an eternal victim of the ways of the world, you adopt lifestyles that suit whatever conditions prevail.

After birth you are insular and isolated, often left on your own except when your mother feeds and nurtures you. You are dreamy and sleepy, and often accept prevailing conditions without negative response. The sensitivity you have to milk is related to your emotionally receptive nature. (See also the house where Jupiter and Neptune reside.)

INTERPRETATION OF ASCENDANT PLANET AND RULER

Aspect	Personifications	Influences
Sun/Ascendant	Father, men, doctors, grandfathers.	Relationships to men, recognition, popularity, personal attitudes to others, self-confidence, physical relations, the public, masculinity. (Defective or dysfunctional sense organs, paralysis, weakness of cells.)

Aspect	Personifications	Influences
Moon/Ascendant	Mothers, grand-mothers, midwives, nurses, women.	Personal feelings about others, feminine influence, maternity, protection, breast-feeding, sensitivity, receptivity, adaptability. (Alkaloids, induction, anesthetics, drugs, watery birth.)
Mercury/Ascendant	Friends, talkers, nurses, young children, gossips.	Thoughts at birth, definition, talking, changing views, ideas, criticism. (Sense stimuli, nerves.)
Venus/Ascendant	Women, sisters, nurses, girls, attractive people, lovers, midwives.	Harmonious personality, loving atmosphere, art, adornment, beautiful surroundings, easy birth, pleasure, even-tempered. (Good complexion, general appearance, proportions.)
Mars/Ascendant	Surgeons, doctor, midwife, men, fighters, aggressors, male children.	Fighting, teamwork, forceful success, physical strength, restlessness, decision. (Surgery, force, circumcision, violence, episiotomy, forceps, facial scar, accidents, cesareans, birth apparatus.)
Jupiter/Ascendant	Doctors, midwives, uncles, aunts, grandparents, team, positivists, priests.	Easy birth, pleasant experiences, agreeable manner, compromise, generosity, correct acts, successful operations. (Large baby, jaundice, difficult breast-feeding.)

Aspect	Personifications	Influences
Saturn/Ascendant	Doctors, hospital staff, grandparents, serious people, inhibitors, lonely people.	Isolation, restriction, inhibition, seriousness, experience, hindrance, depression, seclusion. (Separation, isolation, long labor, birth apparatus, skin trouble, blockages, tension, amputation, sensory dysfunction, facial mark, premature birth, stillbirth, lack of attention.)
Uranus/Ascendant	Excitable people, innovators, originals, technicians, orderlies.	Excitement, originality, scientific birth, movement, rhythmic, incidents, disquiet, sudden events, unexpected circumstances. (Quick birth, short labor induction, machines, monitors, headaches, forceps, accidents, sensitive skin, responsive nervous system, circumcision.)
Neptune/ Ascendant	Anesthetists, nurses, psychics, sensitives, druggists, mediums.	Impressionable, sensitive, insecure, peculiar contacts, disillusionment, sympathetic, exploitation. (Inducement, anesthetics, alcohol, drugs, peculiar birth, dreaming, water birth, sensory deception, malformations, incubators.)

Aspect	Personifications	Influences
Pluto/Ascendant	Doctors, staff, powerful people, authorities, fascinating people, those in control.	Fascinating personality, ambition, psychic forces, unusual influences, readjustment, dramatic changes, radical alterations. (Force, cesarean, forceps, brutal birth, forced birth, physical transformation, surgery, accidents, circumcision.)
Node/Ascendant	Family, friends, nurses, colleagues, fellows, social workers.	Collective contacts, personal relations, family influences, social contact, teamwork, relating. (Respiration, metabolism, hospital birth, antisocial behavior.)

As an example, see the horoscope (Figure 10.1) of a woman given up for adoption at birth. Neptune before conception ❹ shows a seduction, and in Scorpio, so possibly forced. Her adoption was negotiated at birth, as shown by the presence of Saturn ❸ just before the Ascendant/birth moment ❶, which shows restriction and inhibition and also authority figures. Mercury on the Ascendant shows an act or a negotiation. Mars just after birth is the care of a doctor and Jupiter a journey to a foreign country. She was flown to another continent and taken in by a grand family in the new country. The genesis of her birth shows clearly. Her new parents are shown by the Moon and the Sun conjunct in the First House ❷. We could expect psychological issues to arise when the aspects to three early planets register with the Node, Uranus, and Pluto in the Seventh House ❺ from twenty-three to thirty-eight years old. All three of these are in retrograde movement, which means they are moving backward at the time of birth. Retrograde planets show

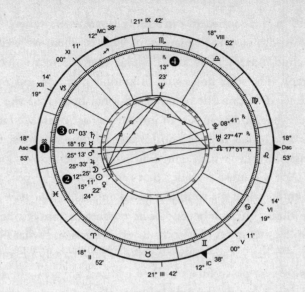

FIGURE 10.1: ADOPTION AT BIRTH

Neptune before conception ❹ shows a seduction, and in Scorpio possibly a rape. The presence of Saturn ❸ just before the Ascendant/birth moment ❶ shows restriction and inhibition, and also authority figures. Mercury on the Ascendant shows an act or a negotiation. Mars just after is the care of a doctor, and Jupiter a journey to a foreign country. The new parents are shown by the Moon and the Sun conjunct in the First House ❷. We could expect psychological issues to arise when the aspects to these early planets register in the Seventh House ❺ from twenty-three to thirty-eight years old.

looking back into the past of an issue, in this case probably a therapeutic look at the circumstances of her birth and early adoption, and maybe even a search for her actual parents.

CHILDHOOD

During the first seven or so years of life (the duration depends upon the size of our first four houses), our personal way of being and seeing ourselves gradually unfolds within the context of our family system—its values, beliefs, conditions, dramas, and separations. This is where we create our "inner child," a resonant and popular concept in modern psychotherapy. The four houses of childhood monitor and measure the gradual development of our emotional body and the family characters that either support or impede us (or both). We rarely remember much that happens in this critical time; we must rely on our parents' stories, which dangerously favor their choices and attitudes. And we must consider that our parents were probably in their twenties when we were conceived and born, but now we see them in their fifties or beyond. The reconstruction of our childhood evokes memories of who really affected us and what part our family really has in our emotional life. These largely unconscious patterns are very powerful and, when realized, are great allies to our whole being, whether they are traditionally positive or damaging. Either way, we learn a way of being just as we start to leave the family and go off to school. Childhood determines our emotional "set."

Planets in childhood and their aspects from the other two octaves represent people around you and those upon whom you base your personality. They are models of behavior that we accept, reject, exclude, or integrate, and probably some combination of all these. Most childhood influences originate with those in our family circle; our family conditions our attitudes. We may not be free to adopt our own ways of being, as our family's values often qualify this, as well as determining what we push off against. An important issue here is to understand what our family is and which of its attitudes affect us. We believe ourselves to be separate from the family, but its coherence is usually larger than us. Therapist Salvadore Minuchin, in Philadelphia, created his family systems therapy and believes that our early psychological issues are inseparable from the dynamics of our family system as a whole.

Freud postulated that in childhood we recapitulate the development of all humanity. Early developments of humanity are mythological, and childhood events carry a mythological and fantastic atmosphere.

The Sun during childhood is the vital relationship to your father. His influence during gestation is indirect until you gradually realize his role in the family. Often fathers have little direct contact with us until we begin to speak or even later. Your father exerts a strong influence upon your personality when the Sun occurs in childhood. Naturally your grandfathers and uncles also take on solar qualities. Aspects from the Sun to planets in childhood show indirect paternal qualities.

The Moon during childhood is early feelings about your mother during this bonding and nurturing stage. In childhood your mother nurtures your personality development with her care and love, and yet you begin to detach from her early in the process. At birth and shortly after you do not differentiate yourself from your mother because the natural instincts are to bond with her. Theoretically there are no boundaries and it is an unconditional relationship, while in reality your personality is determined by exactly those issues. When you begin to separate from her and her influence you evolve and develop, but her attention is your emotional foundation. By the end of childhood you are able to distinguish yourself from her and from other women, but early on she can be interchangeable with nannies, grandmothers (Saturn or Jupiter), aunts, surrogate mothers (the Moon or Neptune), and even older sisters (Venus or Mercury).

Mercury during childhood is your ability and desire to communicate, primarily with other children, and the effect information has on you. When Mercury aspects the Sun or the Moon, your primary communication is with a parent. Mercury is other children at home, while aspects from Mercury to planets in childhood are children outside your immediate family. Planets aspecting Mercury qualify its personifications, so when Mercury and Saturn are in aspect to a planet in childhood, the communication may come from a talkative grandparent.

Venus during childhood is your ability to relate with young women or children who affect your love, aesthetic sense, and creativity. In aspect to the Moon these qualities come from your mother. Venus is people and objects you wish to merge with and become. You want to accommodate yourself to them if possible. Your early drawing, painting, and musical skills are determined; your taste in clothes and the look of your family's world affects these profoundly.

Mars during childhood is the desire to change what you experience, to push away from the family and its values. Mars is active and willful, and can be destructive; however, when its considerable energies are harnessed through discipline (Saturn), we can create more stable situations and order. It governs accidents and childhood illnesses that define us.[24]

Jupiter during childhood is expansion or support from family friends or those outside the family, particularly grandparents, aunts, and uncles. It is primarily your religious attitudes as you begin to understand belief.

Saturn during childhood is restrictions that limit and then define you. You are shy or isolated, withdrawn and concentrated on your own way. Its influences are serious, concentrated, pessimistic, or negative, and may derive from family finances, status in the community, and your locale. Saturn may be the family doctor.

Uranus during childhood is fierce independence, eccentricity, and disruptive tendencies that break or redefine your family's rules or perspectives. You are likely to be restless, highly strung, and erratic, and enjoy rhythmic influences in your pattern-breaking. You accept and work easily with technology and computers at this time.

Neptune during childhood is your sensitivity, receptivity, and psychic links within your family. As a young child you are apt to have powerful and informative fantasies, imaginary friends, toys, or animals that have their own identities. In some ways you dream your world. Neptune may not be real, but it accumulates an inner world. Freud observed that when family situations are difficult, we create a parallel fantasy world that we inhabit as a release. Occasionally this mirror life remains until adulthood. Your fancies are exaggerated during illness or times of weakness.

Pluto during childhood is your relationship to the public outside your family, often through television and other media, which expose you to the rules of the world at large. Pluto also carries prevailing attitudes toward child-raising, and may indicate violence or abuse.

The Node during childhood is your ability to adapt to your family, relatives, neighbors, and friends. Its quality tells us the kind of groups you are drawn to.

THE FIRST HOUSE (ARIES AND ITS NATURAL RULER, MARS)

Birth until seven months old

While we immediately form a bond with our mother at birth and after, our primary needs are nourishment, warmth, and attention. The Ascendant shows the nature of the bond and ultimately our ability for intimacy. We need to learn to express our needs (Mars and Jupiter), and our treatment at the hospital (Saturn and Uranus) and then at home (the Moon) determines our ability to assert ourselves and have our needs met during life. If we are coddled, watched, and surrounded by a supporting family and parents (Sun or Moon) we expect such support throughout life. If our mother rejects us (Pluto or Uranus), cannot or will not breast-feed (negative aspects of the Moon or Venus), or leaves us in the back room, we feel isolated (Neptune) whenever we try to assert our personality.

We are not free to move our own body and must have others satisfy our basic needs. We typically don't focus light until we are about three months old, so we identify others on an energetic [SOUND] level, then visually, accepting those who satisfy our needs. Our ability to get security and satisfaction through our instinctive interactions with our mother, then our father and others, relates directly to our personality. Our instincts determined at this time affect our ability to be intimate, to trust others, and to have the security to know our needs will be met.

Our self-image is often intimately tied up with First House matters. In the example horoscope of a notable artist (Figure 10.2), he was largely ignored after his birth by his mother and immediate family, as shown by Neptune. His mother withdrew her attention and affection from him, which would make him question his very existence. The root of this problem is seen in the aspects of Neptune, most of which have already happened during gestation. The planets Uranus, Saturn, and Pluto all register in gestation, indicating that not only did his mother reject him after birth, but she was already irritated and wanting him not to exist throughout the entire gestation process. Uranus near the conception point shows that his conception was almost certainly accidental. Saturn just after the Midheaven is depression and inhibition after discovery of the pregnancy, and Pluto is even consideration of an abortion later in the process. It is truly a difficult gestation, loaded with three traditionally difficult planets. What is fascinating is the final inconjunct aspect from Neptune ahead to the Moon in Taurus in the Eighth House that registers at fifty-one years old, which indicates emotional seclusion and which led him to become estranged from his aging mother and family and a virtual hermit.

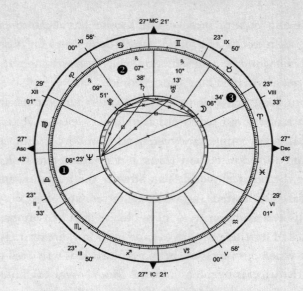

FIGURE 10.2: NEPTUNE IN THE FIRST HOUSE

Neptune ❶ registers just after birth during the bonding time of the First House. The bond was tenuous and insecure, primarily in its aspects to three difficult outer planets in gestation ❷. The mother did not want the child and ignored his early needs. The later aspect to the Moon in the Eighth House ❸ saw a reclusive and solitary emotional set emerge, and estrangement from the aging mother completes the loop.

The First House is our ability to assert our needs within the family.

The Second House (Taurus and Its Natural Ruler, Venus)

Seven months old until one year eight months old

As Piaget describes it, we gradually realize that we are objects in a world of other physical objects. Our body is the primary object, and we investigate everything with our developing senses as we taste, touch, observe, and put down everything we can get our hands on. Our mother has already weaned us and we begin taking solid food, which determines our taste later. We live in a world of pure sensation, where everything is an extension of ourselves, including other people.

We gradually gain control over our body and extend and amplify the range of our sensations as much as we can. We try everything but reject unpleasant tastes, odors, and textures, and we appreciate and attract good tastes and pleasant sensations as we navigate the physical world. The broader the range of sensations that we access, the freer and wider is our sense of physical security. Our senses remain open to new objects and sensations; being touched and touching in turn (Venus and Mars) are primary transactions. When our access to the physical world is restricted (Saturn or negative aspects to the Sun or the Moon)—for example, when we are put in a crib or harness to play, our connection with the physical world is similarly restrained. These sensory mechanisms determine our later attitude to property, possessions, finances, and the physical world. If we cannot gain access to the physical world around us, we abstract it (Neptune), reject it (Pluto), or become inhibited (Saturn). Generous family and relatives (Jupiter and Venus) facilitate our access to the world and show us feelings associated with matter. If we grow up in a large family we might have to learn to share early in life (the Node and the Moon), or communicate through our senses (Mercury and Uranus).

The Second House is the ability to apply our energy to the physical world and learn the use of our senses.

Signs in the Second House

The Second House is the discovery of the physical world through our senses. We begin taking solid food, focusing early, crawling, and identifying objects by applying our energy to them. This time determines our attitude to our body, to possessions and steward-ship.

Second House Cusp in Aries. Forthrightness in discovering objects in your environment and using a great deal of mobile energy leads to fits of temper with your mother if you cannot get the object or physical contact you desire. You are self-assertive about the physical world and possessions. (See also the house where Mars resides.)

Second House Cusp in Taurus. A love of the feel, smell, and texture of objects and a possessiveness toward them gives you much contact and many warm relationships. You have a natural affinity with the physical world and create material wealth later on in life as you naturally acquire things. (See also the house where Venus resides.)

Second House Cusp in Gemini. You flit from object to object, from sensation to sensation, and it is difficult for you to settle on any one thing. Your restless appreciation becomes easily stifled by boredom and requires constant stimulation and variation. You may make money from several different endeavors running concurrently. (See also the house where Mercury resides.)

Second House Cusp in Cancer. You develop emotional attachments to the objects around you and sympathetic receptivity to the people in your family. You have an instinctive sensitivity to caring for others through which you can gain stability in life. (See also the house where the Moon resides.)

Second House Cusp in Leo. All the objects around seem to belong to you, are there for your creativity and amusement, and make you feel powerful when you master their shapes and names. Your natural authority and the ability to earn money mirrors the same easy action in the physical world. (See also the house where the Sun resides.)

Second House Cusp in Virgo. You love separating objects, putting each in its own place, and feel safe within that organization. You need to classify, and prefer detailed work and creating order within larger structures in a disorganized world. (See also the house where Mercury resides.)

Second House Cusp in Libra. Color and form, beauty and attractiveness draw you toward certain objects and to sharing these. You feel needed being in a team in business ventures and balancing personalities or books most of the time. (See also the house where Venus resides.)

Second House Cusp in Scorpio. You develop deep feelings of love or hatred toward objects you cannot have, and destructive tendencies can be taken out on pets or toys. Things that are lying around and ignored by the rest of the family are singled out for your attention, and you can see a value in them that others miss. You are frustrated by the elusiveness of what you want and desire in the physical world. (See also the houses where Mars and Pluto reside.)

Second House Cusp in Sagittarius. You expend an abundance of energy on the objects around you, many of them involving diverse images and interests. Your values develop along philosophical lines, and you support religious and educational institutions with effort and money. (See also the house where Jupiter resides.)

Second House Cusp in Capricorn. Your slow recognition and serious appraisal of objects around you, and a need for the sense of order and structure they provide is central. You are realistic and pragmatic, and have a careful approach toward material things. (See also the house where Saturn resides.)

Second House Cusp in Aquarius. Your approach to objects is original as you want others to appreciate them; at the same time, idealizing them creates values that are very difficult to satisfy. You very much need to be appreciated by the group or family with which you are involved. (See also the houses where Saturn and Uranus reside.)

Second House Cusp in Pisces. Objects are given away, imbued with mystical feelings, and fantasized about because of their distance from you. Your attitude to releasing money and nourishment comes back to you from other sources and directions. (See also the houses where Jupiter and Neptune reside.)

The Third House (Gemini and Its Natural Ruler, Mercury)

One year and eight months until three years and six months old

By two years old our focus is on communication. Our relations, particularly with brothers and sisters, begin to matter more. We vacillate between seeing objects and people as extensions of our reality and allowing them to have their own independence. This very Geminian subject-object duality is the most prominent characteristic of this time, in which we learn by mirroring, mimicry, and copying the behavior and language of others.

Names are the people and things themselves; a name becomes our access to the person or object it describes. These associations lead to our first abstractions of the world. We learn to walk (Jupiter or Mercury), and our range of impressions increases dramatically. We learn our first ideas and abstractions through language (Mercury or Uranus) and learn to apply actions to objects (Mars and Pluto). We are less dependent on the structure (Saturn) of our parents, although they provide standards of literacy and creativity. At this age, because of the logarithmic scale of our perceptions, our parents' time sense is so much faster than ours that our primary models are other children. A child at this age experiences the passage of time ten times more slowly than a thirty-five-year-old adult. When we watch our parents read a newspaper, it seems to take them hours.

Having a good balance between child (Mercury, Venus, and Mars) and adult models (the Sun, the Moon, Jupiter, or Saturn) achieves the widest range of experience in communication. When our parents talk baby talk we learn an irrelevant vocabulary, for whatever means of communication we observe, we mimic and integrate. The more content and the higher the quality, the better it is for us. Many planets here bring a profession of writing or professional communication, and media begins to affect us profoundly.

Whenever the outer world becomes too difficult to understand, we enter a parallel, magical inner world (Neptune or the Moon) where images are consistent with our feelings of them. Our verbal faculty relies upon transferring rhythmic movements (Mercury and Uranus) into language.

A young man who was an unwanted child (Figure 10.3) became a disciplinary problem starting at the age of nine. What was the cause? His problems started when he was at the exact opposite point to Neptune ❻, which would lead us to assume it was involved in some way. We notice that Neptune is part of a constellation including a T-square involving the Moon square the Ascendant ❹ square Saturn ❷ right on the conception point, and also the Sun. To discover the origin of the problem we would go back to the earliest influence, Saturn on the conception point in Scorpio. His mother is the parent responsible for the impulse to conceive him (she is the first luminary counterclockwise back from the cusp of the Ninth House), but at the actual conception she felt inhibited and depressed, confirmed by Saturn. The conception point is quincunx the Sun, showing the father's frustration with their contact and maybe even their sex life, while his mother as the Moon is opposed to the contact. I wouldn't think either parent enjoyed the conception and may even have resented each other at that time. She felt emotionally separate from the father, and there-

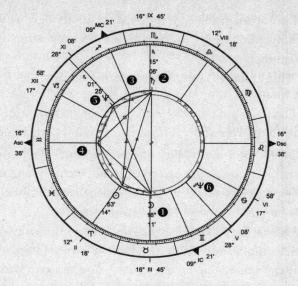

FIGURE 10.3: UNWANTED CHILD

This child became a disciplinary problem throughout school age, starting at about nine, when the opposite point to Neptune ❺ registered ❻. What brought him to do this? The parents could not figure it out, blaming his school environment. Yet the cause is in the parents' relationship. The Moon opposed to Saturn ❷ at conception is the mother giving a mixed message: She initiates the conception but does not want the child (trine Neptune).

fore their son partakes in this separateness of not being wanted and carries it deeply within his body, because it occurred at gestation.

As a young child the boy's parents became more and more distant from each other, although he had much attention from them, shown by the Sun and the Moon in the early houses of childhood. When the Moon registers, the parents talked of divorce, just as he was learning to speak. He started to talk quite late, as we can see because the first two houses are quite large. What brought this about? The parents could not figure it out, blaming his school environment. Yet the cause is in the parent's relationship. The Moon opposed to Saturn at the conception is the mother giving a mixed message: She initiates the conception but does not want the child (trine Neptune).

The Third House is our ability to communicate.

Signs in the Third House

The Third House is our ability to communicate. We begin walking and talking, objects are perceived simultaneously, and the relativity of people makes sense. We model behavior on our family members and develop ways of expressing ourselves.

Third House Cusp in Aries. Strong and outgoing energy shows in your first communications in the form of quarrels with siblings and insistence that your ideas are right. You disagree with established ways of thinking, which can make you a creative ideas person. (See also the house where Mars resides.)

Third House Cusp in Taurus. You are slow and deliberate in communicating, expressing yourself more easily through pictures and objects, which you love. Your thinking is directed in a material way toward moneymaking or artistic endeavors. (See also the house where Venus resides.)

Third House Cusp in Gemini. A true chatterbox, loving to communicate with everyone, especially brothers and sisters, about everything, you are versatile in expressing ideas, although there are so many of them that they need to be focused to take shape. You are a natural communicator and revel in expressing the multiple sides of yourself. (See also the house where Mercury resides.)

Third House Cusp in Cancer. You communicate with your siblings and family by expressing how much you care for them. Taking care of dolls or animals is the first sign of your nurturing nature. You change from reaching out with words to withdrawing from all emotive contact. (See also the house where the Moon resides.)

Third House Cusp in Leo. You express great energy communicating in a positive and gregarious manner, displaying a dramatic sense and experiencing a wide range of mentally ingenious activities. You are able to transfer multiple interests into artistic expression connected with pleasure and love. (See also the house where the Sun resides.)

Third House Cusp in Virgo. Precision in speech, order with words, and a practical manifestation to your ideas makes you seem intelligent for your age. A love of learning stays with you always. Your criticism is directed toward siblings and others as a way of defining yourself. (See also the house where Mercury resides.)

Third House Cusp in Libra. The graceful and diplomatic expression of your ideas and the way they are communicated produces harmony between others and makes you popular at home. You enjoy travel and literary friends who express themselves gracefully. (See also the house where Venus resides.)

Third House Cusp in Scorpio. You have a snakelike tongue that can spit venom or soothe troubled ears, as you are either intensely sweet as a child or destructively angry in communication, but always with frankness. You express yourself only in intense and controversial ways to others. (See also the houses where Mars and Pluto reside.)

Third House Cusp in Sagittarius. Happy-go-lucky, chatty, and outgoing initially, you are stimulated by changes of location and new faces. You learn to transfer your ideas into philosophical avenues, and your love of travel and seeking new destinations satisfies your need to diversify. (See also the house where Jupiter resides.)

Third House Cusp in Capricorn. Rather quiet and reserved in expressing yourself as a child, you lack spontaneity, and choose your words very carefully and deliver them with precision and structure. Your self-expression is very practical and honest, and excessive discipline inhibits your freedom. (See also the house where Saturn resides.)

Third House Cusp in Aquarius. You reach out to people in your family and want to communicate in original ways, which makes you seem amusing and original. You have odd relationships with siblings, who come and go. Flashes of intuition and progressive thinking are put to practical use. (See also the houses where Saturn and Uranus reside.)

Third House Cusp in Pisces. Sensitive and gentle communication as a child makes you shy and not easily heard or noticed. Highly emotional inner thoughts make you seem magical and mysterious, and your ideas are based on intuitive insights. You enjoy having time alone for thinking about and planning your idealistic directions in life. (See also the houses where Jupiter and Neptune reside.)

THE FOURTH HOUSE (CANCER AND ITS NATURAL RULER, THE MOON)

Three years and six months old until seven years old

In the Fourth House we start to have emotional responses to our communication. We begin to see that words produce reactions from our parents and siblings: Some provoke laughter, others anger, and still others a reprimand. We play with this, circling around the feelings we evoke, and learn to elicit those feelings that work for us—that is, unless our family system is too restricted (Saturn) or has too little structure (Uranus, Mercury, or Neptune). Home should be a place where our full range of communication can be expressed, but the contrast between what we want to say and what we are allowed to say determines our emotional "set" for life. The issue at stake is emotion. We learn how we feel (the Moon or Neptune) about home (the Moon), parents (the Sun or the Moon), family (the Moon and the Node), church (Jupiter), country (Pluto), or nature (Venus or the Moon)—those attitudes, emotional patterns, and profound triggers that prevail within our family and originate with our parents, who have such a profound effect on how we feel.

We begin to experience that our family system is a self-contained world (Saturn) without being able to take that in, or that our family's views bear little resemblance to those of the world outside (Uranus or Pluto). When our family does not permit us to question its attitudes, we reserve our feelings (Saturn and the Moon) and do not express them easily (difficult Mercury), or we rebel against them (Uranus or Pluto). We also experience emotional changes; the crab symbolism shows the whirling and changing polar emotions, spinning around us. I always recognize that the Cancer way of being is such that whatever feelings are expressed, they are breeding the opposite and contradictory feelings in the unconscious. The wheel turns and the Moon goes through its stages. The tarot card of the High Priestess shows the Moon phases arcing through the sky (Figure 10.4).

Our parents influence our feelings, as their attitudes are guidelines, whether we accept or reject them. Our emotional patterns are a blend of and compensation for our parents', and we realize

FIGURE 10.4: THE HIGH PRIESTESS TAROT CARD

The arc of Moon phases shows the Cancerian qualities of emotional change that create richness and variety and that force us to understand the entire cycle of this natural emotion. *From* The Mandala Astrological Tarot, *by A. T. Mann, 1987.*

that the family system holds together by feelings that are not necessarily consistent or just. We may relate more easily or strongly to one parent or the other, but we must gradually take our relationship with both parents into consideration. Our ability to comprehend these complex relationships determines the kind of home and family system we seek or avoid in later life. The parent with whom we create the strongest bond is often the carrier for our eventual marital role. In single-parent families, one parent must portray either both roles or neither role.

Among astrologers there are many opinions about the association of the Tenth and opposite Fourth Houses with father and mother. The oldest view is that the Tenth House is the father and the Fourth is the mother, primarily because the Tenth House is associated with Capricorn and its ruler Saturn, who is considered masculine and controlling, while the Fourth is associated with the sign Cancer and its feminine ruler, the Moon. But there are differences of opinion, and astrologers such as Liz Greene believe the opposite.[25] I have found that the most satisfying solution is that the Fourth House is the parent of the same sex, after whom we pattern our attitude to home and family, while the Tenth House is the parent of the opposite sex, after whom we pattern our attitude to the outside world. This means that in a woman's horoscope the Fourth House is the mother and the Tenth is the father; for a man it is reversed. When the Sun or the Moon is in either house a parent may be reinforcing the role or substituting for the other. For example, if the Sun is in the Fourth House of a woman's horoscope the father provides the nurturing and love rather than the mother, and there is a likelihood that the woman would seek either a man with a highly developed feminine side or a lesbian relationship.

The Sun and the Moon are the influences of our father and mother in the horoscope, and their placement conditions these parental-emotional valuations. The position of these luminaries can exaggerate, parallel, negate, or have no effect upon this house, according to their positions.

Emotions are the glue of family relationships, and our feelings are important for our family as well as for us. When our feelings are blocked or unexpressed, we revert to the Third House of instinctive thinking—we just do not feel at home.

The horoscope in Figure 10.5 is that of a woman who suffered an abusive relationship in childhood. It is shown by the Moon in the Fourth House, conjunct Saturn, and in opposition to Pluto on the Midheaven. This implies that the abusive context probably originated in gestation, as that is when it initially registered and when we see the Midheaven from the mother's viewpoint, with the Moon opposite the Midheaven and Mars in square to it. The sig-

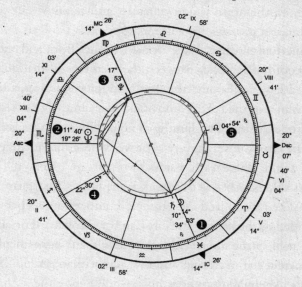

FIGURE 10.5: CHILDHOOD ABUSE

An abusive relationship at six years old is shown by the Moon in the Fourth House conjunct Saturn. The telltale signals are the opposition to Pluto on the Midheaven and the trine to the Sun in the secretive Twelfth House. Very probably abuse was characteristic of this woman's gestation, as this is when the constellation has its origin.

nal of abuse is that the Moon/Saturn conjunction is in trine to the Sun/father in the hidden and secretive Twelfth House. The fact that Neptune is also there further supports the idea. The abuse was unknown until it emerged in group therapy when the woman was thirty-two-years-old, at the age point of the Node in Gemini pointing back to the Moon.

The Fourth House concerns feelings about our ability to communicate within our home and family.

Signs in the Fourth House

In the Fourth House we become aware of our parents, and our family system and the complex relationships within it, and begin to recognize the importance, structure, and status of our parents, home, objects, possessions, and money.

Fourth House Cusp in Aries. Home is a battlefield, and strong expressions of individuality between the members of the family can cause sparks to fly. Family members fend for themselves, and independence is expected. Your unconscious feelings are self-assertive, aggressive, and fiery, manifesting as a need to be emotionally free. You are a family rebel or very creative, with effusive energy. (See also the house where Mars resides.)

Fourth House Cusp in Taurus. Your family is well provided for and lives in a warm and comfortable home with a feel of luxury, surrounded by music and art. The family is a solid, secure, and materially stable structure, and Mother dominant. Your unconscious feelings are sensitive, secure, and practically impregnable. (See also the house where Venus resides.)

Fourth House Cusp in Gemini. Your family has multiple faces and places, reflecting the duality of the home environment and your ambivalent attitude to your parents. Your love of literature in the home and concern for domestic affairs is emphasized. Your unconscious feelings are dualistic, as you want to identify your family but also be free of it. (See also the house where Mercury resides.)

Fourth House Cusp in Cancer. A nurturing home environment, dedication to the family, and a strong mental influence creates powerful instincts. You consider your home your base of operations, in which your mother is dominant and feelings are strong glue holding things together. Your unconscious is grasping, possessive, and reliant upon the nurturing support and love of others. (See also the house where the Moon resides.)

Fourth House Cusp in Leo. Your sense of power stems from home and family, and elaborate acts, habits, and decoration express the creativity and status of your parents. They entertain lavishly and treat visitors with warmth. Your unconscious is highly expressive and self-aware, and easily puts an act on to show your apparent confidence. (See also the house where the Sun resides.)

Fourth House Cusp in Virgo. Work, health, and hygiene are priorities for your family, as well as a love of critical discussions that create an atmosphere of perfection. Details are valued over the larger picture, and your values are often passed by. Your unconscious is naive and perfectionist in wanting ideal siblings and parents, but getting neither. (See also the house where Mercury resides.)

Fourth House Cusp in Libra. Art, beauty, and refinement, as well as harmonious conditions, surround your home life. The family is considered a partnership, and there is strict justice for all members. Your unconscious is balanced and mentally identified with ideal relations. You attempt to recreate this same harmony for yourself. (See also the house where Venus resides.)

Fourth House Cusp in Scorpio. You take out the cares of the day at home as an expression of your father's influence in the family system. Your parents are very possessive and protective of the family but are really separate from you. Your unconscious requires distance from the passion of family life as a result of early difficulties at home. (See also the houses where Mars and Pluto reside.)

Fourth House Cusp in Sagittarius. Your spacious and comfortable home environment, which allows freedom of thought, allows expansive and foreign ideas to become natural. Any visitors are treated generously and with hospitality. Your unconscious vacillates between the achievement of an individual philosophy of life and material security. (See also the house where Jupiter resides.)

Fourth House Cusp in Capricorn. Your authoritarian father and emotionless family makes you difficult to please and distant from desired warmth. The home is practical and pragmatic as a secure material structure that is paternal and disciplined. Your unconscious wishes your emotional life to be seen as a sacrifice to material security and stability. (See also the house where Saturn resides.)

Fourth House Cusp in Aquarius. You come from an unusual and distinctive home environment that includes people from all walks of life. Idealistic attitudes and far-reaching plans produce independence but abstraction in relationships. Your unconscious inspires you to create a home for yourself that becomes a meeting place for groups of people with similar ideas. (See also the houses where Saturn and Uranus reside.)

Fourth House Cusp in Pisces. Home is a special, meditative place where you escape from the mundane realities to a more soothing realm. You are emotionally subject to feelings imposed upon you by others, and you retreat inside to escape. Your unconscious inspires artistic or healing qualities and interests. (See also the houses where Jupiter and Neptune reside.)

ELEVEN

MATURITY IN THE WORLD

Our school years are a transition from our parents' domain to the broader values of the outside world, and they may be either a smooth or tragic transition. The mental body is our ideas and our ability to express them, our worldview and mutual relationships with others. This is in keeping with the Eastern concept of "mind" as more than just thinking: it is our conception of the world. Our games become occupations, and our competitors and teammates become relationships; we create a way of being and seek our careers, partners, and also our reflections in others. Our powers peak in life, and our upward cycle morphs into a giving back of all we have taken on, beginning with children, health, and senses in our midlife crisis. We then either resist or gracefully accept our progressive distancing from reality and then life as we approach old age and death.

The planets in maturity are, of course, aspects of us, signposts in our process through life, but initially we may identify them with our parents, then teachers, coaches, mentors, partners, therapists, religious guides, or initiators who induct us into life. We learn by our relationships with others, at first tentatively and abstractly, and then more intimately, until we make commitments for life. That is the ideal, but our reality is highly conditioned by the process we have taken to get there. The nature of our earliest relationships beyond the family often condition later ones, and it is these seminal people whom we see identified in our horoscopes in these years. The nature of our ways of playing and the values we bring to simple pleasures often determine the qualities that are evoked in our relationship to our body, to working relationships and our life partners.

We move through the initiatory stages of the life journey by working, living with mates, and creating children and creative paths that express and reflect our inner needs or compromise those needs. The equilibration of inner and outer is critical, as it often shows us whether we are satisfied with our life journey or not, and if not, what to do to correct the perspective. Readers can begin to conceptualize their own relationships as part of a sequential flow of events through time, leading to higher and freer modes of being. Instead of remembering dates, we are sequencing our development in life, maybe seeing the whole for the first time.

This ascending process takes us through our entire life and ends only in death. Maturity is relationship.

PLANETS IN MATURITY

The planes registering in maturity are particularly important because they describe higher manifestations of each planetary quality. Your entire previous life is the background for this third stage of development, and planets have a particularly potent effect. Whereas in the earlier stages the planets are primarily other people in your life, in maturity the planets are distinctly you, and events are determined and acted out by you, starting with the child leaving the family to go into the world of education in adolescence. One object of maturity is to manifest ourselves as completely as we can, to experience as much of the world as we dare, and to grow as much as our being allows. We take initially personal models, integrate them into our whole, and find our center. We go into the heart of our environment, heredity, parents, and friends, and into the sacred and timeless realm of the realized self. It might even be said that we have the potential to create our mythic realities here; the highest aspirations come into being through our soul path.

The Sun during maturity is the conscious, masculine focus of your life and vitality. The influence of your father declines as you take back and then integrate fatherly reality into your own creativity. The gradients of this transition may be from the protective father at the end of childhood, to the teacher in the Fifth and Sixth Houses, to the father in you in the Seventh and Eighth Houses. The Sun is your drive for maximum consciousness, for creativity and self-expression, recognition, acknowledgment, personal focus, and strength. Your goals are manifestations of your individuality and sense of self-esteem as well as your ability to meet the practical goals in life of success, health, and the creation of a family life. The Sun's most natural place in maturity is the Fifth House, associated with Leo.

The Moon during maturity is transferring your maternal self-image from your mother to others with whom you make the deepest connections. Your mother's influence is strongest and deepest in gestation, and protective during childhood at home; during maturity it is reconstructed in your choice of partner and your desire for intimacy in relationship. You gradually leave the influence of your mother, but you strive to find your soul in the process. Your mother outside becomes a mother within as you express your feelings in the context of your working and social life in the world. The Moon is your feelings and protective instinct, your ability to nourish yourself and others and to mother your children; on the higher level, it is your higher emotional reality as a summation of your hereditary disposition.

Mercury during maturity is your ability to communicate with friends, students, workers, associates, salesmen, agents, mediators, intellectual leaders, organizers, partners, and friends, and their effect upon your mind. How you communicate who you are is reflected in the people with whom you base your expression, and with whom you express your thoughts. You need to learn and assimilate the ideas you are exposed to in school and then to formulate your own mental landscape. Hopefully you carry your ideas forward through reading, writing, or other creative acts. Mercury's most natural place in maturity is the Sixth House of the magnetic Virgo.

Venus during maturity is your relationships, those you find attractive and who find you attractive—initially school friends, but later artists, musicians, lovers, and sexual partners. It is your ability to merge with others, to integrate with them in intimacy. In some ways you might want to become your lovers. Venus is the environment you create around yourself, exploring your taste and touch with the physical world in your social life, entertainment, cultural venue, and friendly relationships. It is associated with your values, and therefore relates to children, financial security, and your appearance in the world.

Mars during maturity is the desire to change your world with athletic, sexual, mechanical, skillful, and aggressive activities. Mars is an expression of your physical fitness, athletic competitiveness, and sexuality, which later transforms into your desire for energetic business, marriage, and associations. Doctors, surgeons, craftsmen, and soldiers fall under the influence of Mars. If your energy or relationships are blocked, you may channel it into workout routines, diets, physical therapies, or sexual relations outside marriage. If you cannot redirect your vital energies, they are drawn inward and may create physical afflictions. Mars is your mobility, and its most natural house in maturity is the Eighth House of the magnetic Scorpio.

Jupiter during maturity is the development and growth of your worldview and those others who influence it. Its influence can be religious, psychological, philosophical, or financial, and promotes expansion and optimism. You open yourself up and try to connect with a profession or career, at first in school and later out in the world. Jupiter is religious guides, gurus, psychologists, psychiatrists, those of high character, wealth and esteem, speculators, healers, and all people who make fortunate connections.

Saturn during maturity is your responsibilities made manifest through your sense of security and community. You come into contact with cultural values in school and then create your own structure of life in your home and society. Saturn is those who maintain these organizational systems, like doctors, bank managers, employers, partners, and associates, as well as those who are serious, older, strict, conservative, hardworking, and mature. You first become a parent, and then toward the Eighth House, you may become a grandparent, representing an existing or declining order.

Uranus during maturity is the force of emerging individuality that leads to sudden changes, inventions, independence, erratic drives, and all influences that serve to break up rigidity and patterns in your life. These influences are carried by reformers, eccentrics, inventors, unusual teachers, therapists, and unusual associations or partners. Uranus ranges from submission to teachers or gurus to exerting a transformative influence upon your own life and that of those around you.

Neptune during maturity is the gradual transformation of youthful fantasies and ideals into increased sensitivity that may ascend to spirituality. You might value your meditations and dreams, and envision higher values in your life. Your concern for society and its highest values is characterized by idealists, romantics, sensitives, mediums, and spiritual people, and is rejected by alcoholics, mediators, hypochondriacs, and seducers. Neptune's

influence extends to negative drug experiences and mystical rever-
ies, as well as confusion and wondering that result from misdi-
rected higher energies.

Pluto during maturity is your relationship to the collective values and changes in your society. Pluto is carried by personal and
public people who understand or engage in collective values. You
might change dramatically, move to a foreign country, make profound choices, or transform yourself. Pluto symbolizes revolutionaries, transformers, reactionaries, fundamentalists, and terrorists, as
well as those who exert psychic or magical influence over the
masses, the media, politicians, gurus, domineering partners or employers, and those who promote or force change. Pluto generates
changes in job, residence, partnership, and your overall view of life.

The Node during maturity indicates the groups toward which
you are drawn, and it influences teamwork, your family and alliances, collaborations, marriages, and the partnerships you form.
Professional associations, political parties, labor unions, and groups
all show the influences of the Node.

THE FIFTH HOUSE (LEO AND THE NATURAL HOUSE OF THE SUN)

Seven years old until thirteen years old

In the first fire house, just after birth, we assert our energies in the world, and here in the Fifth we exteriorize
the personality we created in childhood into the outside
world and become self-conscious. This coincides with our primary
education. Throughout this time we transform from child to ado-
lescent as puberty approaches. This house is therefore associated
with the emergence of our inner child into adulthood.

The most important and often first way to interact with others outside our family is playing games. We choose certain games because they provide us with a way of expressing our needs and having those needs met. We gravitate toward games that reflect the sign or signs in the Fifth House. If it is Aries, we tend to prefer individual competitive sports, while Capricorn probably shows that we own the ball. Virgo is a natural referee or judge, critical of the proceedings, while Aquarians are team organizers. The types of games we attract reflect our need to define our relationships. I might be attracted to you because we like the same games, and this gradually metamorphoses into a relationship.

Some of us prefer to make up our own rules (Leo, Aries, Scorpio, or Sagittarius), some of us only play by commonly accepted rules (Virgo, Libra, Capricorn, or Aquarius), some want to be told the rules by others (Pisces or Capricorn), and some refuse to play at all (Scorpio or Pisces). The kinds of games we play and our attitude toward making rules determine our personal relationships (the Moon and the Sun), our boundaries (Saturn), and our ability to make our individuality known (the Sun). Those friends with whom we play and establish rules are those with whom we form affectionate contact. Personal relationship is the acceptance of game-playing.

The games we play may exchange energy (the Sun or Mars), demonstrate physical proficiency (Mercury or Jupiter) or intellectual superiority and invention (Mercury or Uranus), provide an outlet for emotions (the Moon or Venus), or any of these in combination. The best games contain all of these. The framework within which relationships develop is school (Mercury, the Sun, and Saturn), where we learn the rules that our social class, religion, geographical area, or country holds to be important. We choose to abide by certain conventions, while we ignore or resist others. For example, with Libra in this place we tend to associate being liked with playing strictly by the rules. The open-mindedness of games contrasts with the rigidity of school discipline (Saturn). A well-adjusted child (Venus or Jupiter) balances the two.

Once out of our parents' domain, teachers (Mercury or Saturn) and those who play games for a living (Jupiter or Pluto) become primary role models for action and thought. This tends to hero worship (the Sun or Pluto) of ideal individuals. Our preoccupation with school or games sets a pattern that we follow in later life, in relationships and, especially, sexual relationships (Venus or Mars). When game-playing and school are difficult (Saturn or Neptune), we regress to the security of home and mother in the Fourth House.

Figure 11.1 is the horoscope of a young woman who discovered at age nine that she had digestive problems that progressed to Crohn's disease in her teens. As the cause of digestive or colon illness is often traced to emotional issues, it is easy to see here why she felt unloved and not supported by her family. First, she has a very complex horoscope, with every planet a part of one constellation, which promises complexity but with the potential for resolution. The earliest indication we can see is that Neptune ❶ is square the conception point ❷, showing that her father is the parent who wanted her and her mother was uncertain and insecure. When the mother realized she was pregnant at the Midheaven in the fated and resigned Pisces ❸, her reaction was disappointment and anger at the apparently forced child, shown by the opposition to Uranus and Pluto ❹ in the critical sign Virgo. All this becomes interiorized and inherent in the physical body of the young woman, waiting to be triggered. The mother may have even considered an abortion, but she certainly wished what was within her belly would go away. This thought form was probably responsible for the pain and rejection this young woman experienced. A further factor is that the Fifth and Sixth Houses are very large, indicating that she is expected to "grow up" earlier than usual. For example, her Fifth

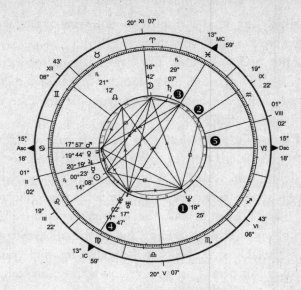

FIGURE 11.1: CROHN'S DISEASE

This young woman has a very complex horoscope, where every planet is connected in one constellation. It is complex, but the potential for integration is there. She was found to have Crohn's disease and had part of her colon removed at seven years old when Neptune registered.

House cusp registers at four years old rather than the archetypal seven. However, at the opposite point of Mars ❺, around the age of twenty-three, she discovered a clinic that was able to treat her with colonic irrigation, diet, and supplements to control her disease. She later had children and achieved a full, rich, and normal life.

Signs in the Fifth House

In the Fifth House we learn to learn, accept, play, and master games as a way of expressing ourselves and forming relationships with others outside our family. Primary schooling is a framework within which our mind and spirit develop ways to contact others and begin creative work on ourselves.

Fifth House Cusp in Aries. You form relationships with others with passion and dynamic force, and show leadership qualities in the first exchanges of energy outside your family. (See also the house where Mars resides.)

Fifth House Cusp in Taurus. You are warm and affectionate as you form associations with attractive friends and begin to feel possessive about them. You value stability and loyalty beyond all qualities except appearances. (See also the house where Venus resides.)

Fifth House Cusp in Gemini. Your expression is self-conscious in your use of words, sharing of ideas, and participation with as many people as possible at school. You love learning, and your quick mind makes this period progressive and active. You learn games quickly but get bored easily. (See also the house where Mercury resides.)

Fifth House Cusp in Cancer. You are shy and sensitive in the playground as you prefer to be approached rather than take the initiative yourself. A love for female teachers may supplement your mother while you are not at home. You prefer just being to winning in games. (See also the house where the Moon resides.)

Fifth House Cusp in Leo. You wish to be king of the castle, warm and gregarious in relating to others in your first friendships, which leads to creative self-expression and multiple contacts in the outside world. You develop an "act" of confidence that everyone except you accepts readily, and only winning reinforces it. (See also the house where the Sun resides.)

Fifth House Cusp in Virgo. A logical approach to creative expression leads to an orderly academic approach at school and a need to choose friends who are articulate and intelligent. You grade others, have perfectionist criteria, and are basically naive, which combines to distance you from the norm. (See also the house where Mercury resides.)

Fifth House Cusp in Libra. Seeking grace and balance at school, and wanting to create harmony with your friends makes you popular. You are very sensitive to what others want you to be and are willing to make the diplomatic compromise. You enjoy music and dancing and have a creative approach to self-expression. (See also the house where Venus resides.)

Fifth House Cusp in Scorpio. You are intensely emotional about games and relationships, and feel the need to dominate others. You become a loner in the playground, or choose only a few friends, to whom you are extremely loyal but with whom you also feel competitive. Secrecy accompanies your movements. (See also the houses where Mars and Pluto reside.)

Fifth House Cusp in Sagittarius. Gregarious behavior with others, sports, and generosity allow your entry into the world of primary school to be met with enthusiasm and largesse. You spoil your friends and expand through anyone who comes your way. (See also the house where Jupiter resides.)

Fifth Cusp in Capricorn. Serious attitudes to expressing yourself at school make your disciplined and concentrated. It is hard work and probably is most difficult to reach out to other children to make friends, as you appear cold. (See also the house where Saturn resides.)

Fifth House Cusp in Aquarius. Unusual friends and an interest in the group aspect of the classroom is appealing. You are a joiner but always ultimately detached from the groups you create. Mental discipline makes learning easy, but restlessness and boredom counteracts this. (See also the houses where Saturn and Uranus reside.)

Fifth House Cusp in Pisces. You are sensitive and sacrificial in making friendships outside home and family, which can lead to hurt or disillusionment. Dancing or artistic endeavors are important attempts at self-expression, and you are highly subject to the attitudes and patterns of others. (See also the houses where Jupiter and Neptune reside.)

The Fifth House is to accept and play games as a way of expressing ourselves and forming relationships with others.

THE SIXTH HOUSE (VIRGO AND THE NATURAL HOUSE OF MERCURY)

Thirteen years old until twenty-three years and five months old

As adolescence approaches, our bodies undergo a profound change as our sexuality blossoms. The sign Virgo is appropriate symbolism, as we are literally virgins as the house begins. During this time we begin to make the choices that will determine our subsequent life and affect our career, work, and health.

We begin to break away from our parents' domination (the Sun, the Moon, or Saturn) in our early life, and we tend to transfer the responsibility onto our teachers (Jupiter, the Sun, or Saturn) or heroes. As the Sixth is an earth sign house, our body is the focus, and the way that we relate to our body determines the nature of our work relationships. If we feel that our body and its needs govern us, then we expect to work for or to serve others. If we feel that we control our body with our mind (Mercury and Saturn), we can expect to manage others and have them work for us. We have to make choices about what to eat (Jupiter is nutrition); what to wear (Venus and the Moon); how to clean, care for (Jupiter), and dress our body, or not; and we gradually accept responsibility (Saturn) for our own decisions—all of this becomes the foundation of our physical reality.

Our health and our attitude to it reflect the overall importance we give to the body. The games upon which we relied in the Fifth

House become more serious as we must find out what to do with our life.

It is not possible to separate our perfectionist ideals from reality, and they therefore collide during our late teens and early twenties. We come up against limits and boundaries (Saturn and Pluto) that we and others impose, until tangible impediments intervene, such as mental (Mercury or Uranus) or physical limitations (the Moon, Saturn, or Mercury), lack of financial mobility (Venus and Capricorn), or class barriers (the Moon and the Node). We rely more and more on the systems (Saturn) we learned to adapt to the reality of the world. We must begin to learn how to channel game-playing attitudes and techniques into working situations as we take our first jobs and learn to work for others. Whereas our world values specialization (Mercury), we must make choices that can be binding for the rest of our lives. In the Sixth House, we either accept or reject control over our own lives.

We experiment with relationships (Mercury or the Moon) within or beyond familial codes (Cancer) and social codes (Libra). Our sexuality (Mars, Venus, and Pluto) is mainly fantasy at the beginning of this time, and we gradually mature, whether we want to or not. Often our choices are binding—as, for instance, when we have children due to early sexual experiences. If we resist taking chances due to our naivete, we are seen as being backward, but unreasonable experimentation also produces premature commitments. It is a delicate balance (Libra and Venus). Our ability to synthesize the impressions of our early life, to organize ourselves into a consistent whole rather than a collection of parts, is the object of this time. We tend to be extremely critical of others, which masks our own self-criticism. We may be accurate and objective about others, but rarely about ourselves. If we cannot make choices or organize ourselves, we revert to the game-playing attitudes of the Fifth House.

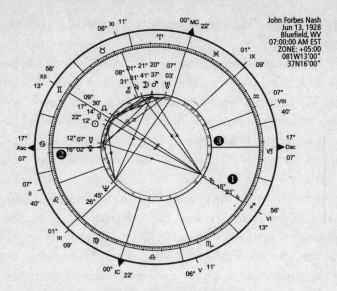

FIGURE 11.2: HOROSCOPE OF JOHN FORBES NASH

Nash discovered mathematics at the time Saturn registered in the Sixth House. It became his career and obsession. He first started experiencing nervous breakdowns at the opposite point to his traumatic Plutonic birth ❷, in the Seventh House, in his early twenties ❸.

The mathematician John Forbes Nash, the subject of the film *A Beautiful Mind,* is a perfect example, as he discovered mathematics at the age of about twelve, exactly when the inhibited and structured Saturn ❶ registered its age point in the expansive and profound sign Sagittarius. It is the only planet on the western, right half of the horoscope that shows our relationship to the outer world. Nash's mind and his math were his only channels to the world and might help explain his mental difficulties. Most of his planets are in gestation, which shows that his interior life was paramount and that he often acted on deep instincts. It is as though Saturn must compensate for the entire rest of the horoscope.

John Lennon is another good example, as his very long Sixth

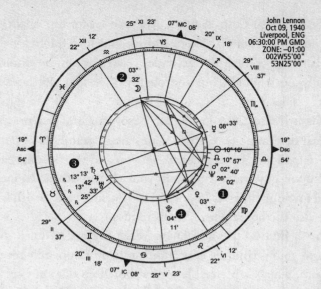

FIGURE 11.3: HOROSCOPE OF JOHN LENNON

John Lennon's horoscope shows his career Sixth House ❶ as central to his life. It was the time of his greatest creation and growth. His mother did not want him (Moon ❷ in gestation), shown by the opposition to Pluto ❹ in the family Fourth House. He was raised by his grandparents ❸ and then his mother's sister from immediately after birth.

House saw the creation of his own languages when Venus registered, meeting Paul McCartney when Mars registered, and forming the Beatles at the Node. By the time the Sun registered at the age of twenty-one, he had performed at the top of his profession.

Signs in the Sixth House

In the Sixth House we enter puberty, develop physically and mentally, and make the transition to adulthood. Our education reaches completion, and we begin making decisions that will affect our occupation, tastes, health, and emotional relationships.

Sixth House Cusp in Aries. Assertive leadership qualities force you to apply yourself. There is drive and forceful creative energy available for competitive activities. Your choices are intuitive and usually not thought out thoroughly. (See also the house where Mars resides.)

Sixth House Cusp in Taurus. Perseverance and a practical approach determine your attitude to school, exams, and your choice of occupation. Appearances attract you and you become easily fixated upon physical attributes in yourself and others. Monetary reward for your efforts is important to you, and your health is robust. (See also the house where Venus resides.)

Sixth House Cusp in Gemini. Versatility and a quick mind are keys to your secondary education, and you can handle several jobs at once, which is preferable so that boredom does not set in. Difficulties come with the necessity for decisions. The ability to communicate with co-workers makes for excellent management skills. (See also the house where Mercury resides.)

Sixth House Cusp in Cancer. You enjoy being surrounded by people, taking care of them, and treating them as family members during your school years, and your choice of occupation reflects this concern. Your emotional state is a strong contributory factor to your health, and you desire committed relationships at an early age. (See also the house where the Moon resides.)

Sixth House Cusp in Leo. You can prove to be domineering as you enjoy a feeling of authority. You apply tremendous creative energy to gaining attention and recognition, as virtually any area is ripe for your talents at self-expression. Relationships must revolve around you. (See also the house where the Sun resides.)

Sixth House Cusp in Virgo. Care and precision is taken in all your work, but a constant search for perfection can make you fail to complete tasks, as your standards are too high for you to match. You are interested in health and diet, as you feel that a healthy body makes a healthy mind. Naivete is interspersed with nit-picking to make you hard to please. (See also the house where Mercury resides.)

Sixth House Cusp in Libra. A well-balanced approach to work, including consideration for co-students and co-workers, aids success. A socially oriented work environment or one that is aesthetically pleasing either literally or emotionally suits your artistic receptivity. Your creativity functions best within structures created by others. (See also the house where Venus resides.)

Sixth House Cusp in Scorpio. Through application to study or work you regenerate yourself, and your intense will power makes you concentrate deeply on the task at hand. Your drives are directed to unachievable goals; if you do reach some goals, others immediately replace them. The expression or repression of your desires reflects on your health. (See also the houses where Mars and Pluto reside.)

Sixth House Cusp in Sagittarius. Your generosity in helping others expand will make you popular at school and afterward. You attract luck but must feel free to follow your inspiration. A positive outlook attracts you to faith-healing, and foreign experiences broaden your attitudes. (See also the house where Jupiter resides.)

Sixth House Cusp in Capricorn. Serious, practical, and hardworking attitudes in secondary school and after helps you up the ladder of success. You are highly disciplined and may be too rigid for any other than arranged relationships. A strict approach to health and diet, or giving in to Dionysian excesses are both possible. (See also the house where Saturn resides.)

Sixth House Cusp in Aquarius. Your original and creative approach to learning and your ability to treat co-workers as part of a group of friends ties in with community awareness. You thrive in large groups of people. You use unusual and progressive methods in your day-to-day functioning and health. (See also the houses where Saturn and Uranus reside.)

Sixth Cusp in Pisces. Unselfish devotion and giving yourself completely to causes marks your educational experiences and extends toward companions. You accept the conditions of others in all you do. In order to avoid an overload of work that was taken on thoughtlessly or to avoid confrontation, your health may suffer through nutrition or eating disorders. (See also the houses where Jupiter and Neptune reside.)

The Sixth House is our ability to adapt to the world in physique, health, work, and sexuality.

THE SEVENTH HOUSE (LIBRA AND THE NATURAL HOUSE OF VENUS)

Twenty-three years and five months old until forty-two years old

At the Descendant we are directly opposite the time when our personality registered at birth. The way we see ourselves is the opposite of the way we really are, and this polarity promotes objectivity. Our parents, brothers, and sisters condition our personality, and now we must reconcile ourselves with the outside world. The equilibrium we seek between inside and outside manifests in our choices of partnerships, both marital and professional. We leave the subjectivity and unconsciousness of the lower half of our horoscope and emerge into the upper, conscious, and objective hemisphere. Of course, we must blend and integrate them. The synthesis involves blending both positive and negative traits developed and enacted during our first twenty-three years and five months.

Partnerships are a summation of our appearance, parental relationships, education, ability to communicate, attraction, ambitions, and conflicts. Our partner is the balancing agent in this complicated equation as someone who seems to possess the characteristics we lack yet desire to possess. We project these characteristics onto our partner, whether or not he or she actually carries them. Often it is more important to discover what we think and feel about a partner than who he or she really is.

The houses around the life cycle are related intimately to their opposites. The Seventh House of partnership is opposite the First House, which governs self-assertion just after birth. The more attention and projections we receive in the First House, the more likely we are to seek a partnership that counterbalances these very qualities. Like everything else, it is critical to realize that it is the process of partnership that is important; the growth it allows and encourages is essential to our development. The Seventh House and its natural sign Libra are about sublimation, balance, and the integration of opposites, as well as justice. Excessive strength or weakness in ourselves or our partners reflects a similar imbalance within each of us.

The nature of relationship at this time is fascinating. Say we are twenty-four years old, working in a city and looking for a life relationship. We are overly self-critical and insecure after having completed our Virgo Sixth House time, and so we compensate by trying to appear in control of ourselves. We dress up as smartly as we can, act like we know what we are doing, and go out on the town. Across the room we see the someone we are attracted to, who appears to be in control of their world, dresses the right way, and is in the right place at the right time. We have selected someone who seems to manifest all the traits we ourselves feel deep down that we lack, and we think: She (or he) has all those qualities I need in a partner, with the confidence I lack, the savoir faire I want, etc. What is important is that we attract a partner who expresses what we project onto the world, and once we begin a relationship with them, they will discover that we express their projections. Both of us are compensating for our perceived weaknesses and looking for such support, yet we find the so-called "shadow" side of ourselves, carrying all the negative traits we ourselves have but cannot come into contact with. This is the true nature of relationship. We must not only embrace our shadow through our partners, but must learn to integrate them and make them a part of ourselves. The irony is that we can easily find we don't need the partner any longer once that process has happened throughout the Seventh House.

Marriage is a contract subject to moral and legal controls, and many marriages are transactions in which there is little interchange beyond an outer sharing of lodging or children; there is an agreement not to go within. Our relationships should allow both partners to grow, yet we must also bond in intimacy, whether our relationships are straight or gay. It is necessary to define our roles and then play them. The success of relationships hinges around our foresight in determining the interweaving demands of each individual as well as the whole marriage. The liberation of women and men from stereotyped family roles is important, but we must remember that we ourselves make or break these roles and rules.

When our personality is very complex, it becomes necessary to expand beyond a nuclear relationship. This may mean a succession of growth partnerships or a desire to form a relationship with the world itself. Public figures often sacrifice personal relationships in favor of career.

This house also governs our business relationships, which parallel our personal relationships; we must often sublimate our own individual drives for the good of the whole. Yet we all want to advance in the world and have our own influence. Our individuality therefore arises from our ability to withdraw our projections, to integrate them into a workable whole, and to make a relationship with the world.

An inability to relate to others forces a regression back into the unconscious lower half of the horoscope. We may then find that partnerships become work (Sixth House), game-playing (Fifth), protection (Fourth), childlike (Third), or purely physical (Second), or that we are alone in self-assertion (First). At best, all the elements described by the early houses are present in a blended form.

The horoscope in Figure 11.4 shows a man who, while in a happy marriage, began cross-dressing in his thirties at the age point of the Moon in Taurus ❶. The sequence of his conception bears on our evaluation of causes. First we see that the Moon is the first luminary back from the conception point and therefore initiated the conception, probably as part of the mother's marital responsibility. The Uranus ❺ registration just before conception in the Eighth

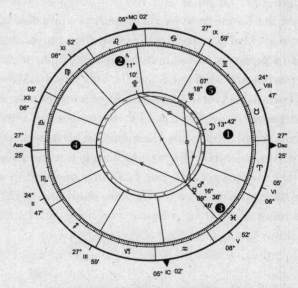

FIGURE 11.4: ORIGINS OF A CROSS-DRESSER

Despite a happy marriage, this man began cross-dressing in his thirties when the Moon in Taurus registered ❶. The Moon makes a square back to Pluto in Leo ❷ just after his mother realized she was pregnant and a sextile back to the hermaphroditic Mercury ❸ at the age of nine. His only access back to his Ascendant ❹ is via Mercury. At the Uranus ❺ age point he began recognizing the eccentricities of his ways.

House may indicate an accidental action, and since it is in Gemini there is a duality in her actions. Just after his mother realized she was pregnant, Pluto in Leo ❷ in the Tenth House squares the Moon, showing that the required transformation shown by Pluto is resisted (the square to the Moon). The mother may have wanted a female child like herself (the Moon aspects the Midheaven). When the hermaphroditic Mercury ❸ in the reflective and feminine water sign Pisces registers at the age of nine, it shows ambiguity, affecting this man's selfish relationships, his sense of self-love, and his acting skills and game-playing. Mercury is flexible, dualistic, and communicative, and also looks ahead to the Moon as a principle of emotions affecting mental choices (Mercury/Moon aspects).

When the Moon registers at thirty-three years old, this man's emotional life changes, reflecting his deep life patterns, and he discovers an alternative female persona that he begins expressing in special moments. Of interest is that the only way the Moon energy can get back to his Libran Ascendant ❹ personality is via Mercury. He incorporates, quite literally, all these components into his alter ego, whom he naturally calls Harmony, which is word equivalent to Libra. At the Uranus ❺ age point he began recognizing the eccentricities of his ways and gave Harmony more of his energies. Often what may seem to be bizarre paths in life are the natural and organic result of previous patterns combining and permuting to form who we are.

The Signs in the Seventh House

The Seventh House cusp is opposite our birth and is the time when we begin to develop a higher awareness of ourselves in the world as we move above the horizon in the horoscope. We detach from family influences and begin to express ourselves, making occupational commitments and permanent emotional relationships, and defining our position and attitude about the world. All such contacts are ways of understanding qualities we ourselves possess and yet project onto others.

Seventh House Cusp in Aries. The opposite, selfish side of your harmony-seeking nature comes out in an ability to motivate others and an aggressive urge to gain the attention and co-operation of partners. You have a great skill in compromising with others to increase your own position. You seek the hidden balance and consideration in yourself through a partner who displays these qualities. (See also the house where Mars resides.)

Seventh House Cusp in Taurus. Wealthy partners and co-operative ventures that promote gain make up for the difficult and changeable circumstances that you constantly attract. Your partner is a reflection of yourself, so possessiveness and a profound emphasis on stability can be met through others. (See also the house where Venus resides.)

Seventh House Cusp in Gemini. Multiple partnerships with people who are intelligent and versatile satisfy your own need not to be tied down, and lead to competitive relationships. In dealing with public relations you are astute and perceptive, but tend to find focus upon one direction that is difficult if not impossible. (See also the house where Mercury resides.)

Seventh House Cusp in Cancer. There is a strong emotional attachment to partners, friends, and the public, and when these people become emotionally dependent on you this can cause problems. There is a balance between being practical and not letting any feeling through, and allowing feelings and attachments to cling to everyone with whom you come into contact. (See also the house where the Moon resides.)

Seventh House Cusp in Leo. Powerful and well-established partnerships balance your own need for independence, as those you

choose are usually self-sufficient. You have to search within yourself for personal power and inspired creativity, which is the other
side of the coin from your objective evaluation of abstract and distant concepts. (See also the house where the Sun resides.)

Seventh House Cusp in Virgo. Your partners are efficient and discriminative and can keep you within a structure that you may have
found difficult during the early part of your life. You attract those
who must bring you messages and are affected by others' standards,
which manage our practical affairs. (See also the house where Mercury resides.)

Seventh House Cusp in Libra. In the natural zodiac this is your
choice of partner, whom you allow to determine your life direction. The partnership model is really within you, and by attracting
someone who has a more gentle and conciliatory spirit, you bring
it out in yourself. You await the answer from outside or above. (See
also the house where Venus resides.)

Seventh House Cusp in Scorpio. Power and status are qualities
sought after in a partner as these characteristics boost your very
practical and everyday approach to life. This may bring out possessiveness and competitiveness, and a need for spiritual detachment could well be developed. Social relationships become
accepted domination and financial holds are particularly attractive.
(See also the houses where Mars and Pluto reside.)

Seventh House Cusp in Sagittarius. Religious or ethical values
are important to you in partners and associates, and you will link
up with types who represent these qualities for you. Although apparently directed, you find it impossible to make firm commitments and often harbor unspoken misgivings about others. You
attract luck to yourself from the public in general. (See also the
house where Jupiter resides.)

Seventh House Cusp in Capricorn. Your cautious and reserved
approach to partnerships and relations with other people in the

world requires security as a pressing issue; a partner of status fulfills this requirement. Your decisions in emotional and practical areas are pragmatic and often leave us cold but secure. (See also the house where Saturn resides.)

Seventh House Cusp in Aquarius. A desire for freedom within a structured partnership and always wanting to know about members of the family are the two opposite poles of this particular way of relating. You are detached and idealistic about relationships that make for good form but lack adequate warmth. (See also the houses where Saturn and Uranus reside.)

Seventh House Cusp in Pisces. Through partners you expand into new fields, and also meet a more disorganized but perhaps creative individual who has your opposite qualities. As you enter relationships, merging and remaining separate are constant opposing conditions. You tend to want to settle for another's vision of life structures. (See also the houses where Jupiter and Neptune reside.)

The Seventh House is our ability to form permanent relationships.

THE EIGHTH HOUSE (SCORPIO AND THE NATURAL HOUSE OF MARS AND PLUTO)

Forty-two years old until death

The Eighth House is the last house and governs middle age, the gradual withdrawal from life, old age, and death. In the Second House our senses herald access to the physical world, while in the Eighth House we release our grasp upon the sensual world. Often we lose the senses that were most prominent as we developed our personality during childhood, as our hearing and sight diminish. We experience the results of our life's work here, and ideally settle all our outstanding karmic and financial debts. We devote time and energy to "making our peace" with the world.

In our old age we gradually relinquish or delegate control (Venus and Saturn) of our life. In the Seventh House we acquire job, family, possessions, and financial security, and as we progress through the Eighth House we transform our desire to accumulate into a willingness to let it all go, although this particular trait is rare in our society. In India, Brahman men as householders traditionally structure their finances and family so that as their children reach maturity and take control of family and business, they can become *saddhus*, traveling holy men. They often leave home (Jupiter, Uranus, or Pluto) and retreat to mountain fastnesses to meditate (Neptune) and be at peace. Detachment from the world accompanies aging, and in our modern society diseases such as Alzheimer's (Neptune or Uranus) and Parkinson's (Mercury and Uranus) enforce the required detachment. We find ourselves depending on others' feelings (the Moon), thoughts (Mercury), will (the Sun), and even physical support (Saturn or Jupiter). After a lifetime of being in control (Saturn), it is difficult to relinquish this control.

Our energies, vitality, and sexuality decline and our activities (Mars and the Sun) reflect this. Our increased interest in metaphysics, the opposite of the physical world of the Second House (Pluto, Neptune, or Jupiter), religion (Jupiter), and the intangible is a way of transferring the focus away from youthful gratification. (Mercury and Venus) toward the symbolic acts of old age (Saturn and Jupiter). Friends (Mercury, Venus, and Mars) pass away; old places do not seem the same; the activities of middle age are tiresome; the physical world dissolves into an internal, spiritual world (Neptune or Jupiter) that lies behind appearances; or we become enslaved by medicines (Neptune), doctors (Mars and Pluto), and constant ill health (Saturn). In senility (also Neptune), the inner world literally encroaches upon and dominates the outer world.

Our time senses becomes highly compacted as our metabolism slows down almost to a stopping point, and the world around us seems to fly by. Our mind often moves faster than our body can react, and we find ourselves living in past memories. The deterioration of our senses coincides with our perception slowing down— our understanding just cannot keep up with the speed of our perceptions.

The Eighth House is death, and as it approaches we reconsider and reflect on our life. The Eastern idea of karma resonates as we hold on to those values that determine our next incarnation. Our ability to release control and our property, finally including our body, generates conditions for a positive death.[26] When we leave matters undone and continue to grasp for the world, release and death are painful torment. Our primary objective should be to channel our diminishing energies into intangible places, to pass on our understanding of life and the world to those who are younger, and to maintain an interest in the last great transformation. We often see planets in the Eighth House as indicators of a synthesis of earlier qualities, of activities that represent either terminations or new activities in the twilight of life.

In the horoscope shown in Figure 11.5, a successful businesswoman reaching the age of forty-eight discovered through her therapy the desire to teach and spread her acquired wisdom. As we can see, this happens as the Node in Scorpio ❶ registered on the cusp of the Eighth House. The constellation of planets in aspect to the Node makes it clear that this time in her life is a culmination and integration of many disparate events and states of being, all coming together in midlife. The Node makes aspect to Jupiter in gestation, to Mercury, Mars, and Pluto in childhood, and the Moon earlier in adolescence.

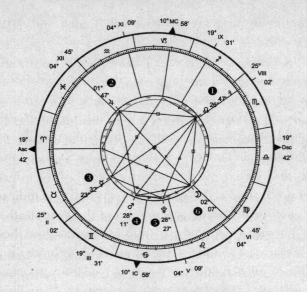

FIGURE 11.5: PSYCHOTHERAPIST

At the age of forty-eight, when the Node registered in Scorpio, the sign of deep emotions, this woman became a practicing psychotherapist. This late planet in the Eighth House shows the integration of a series of earlier events and experiences in her life. It is the culmination point of the constellation.

In order to understand the genesis of her choice, we would go back to the earliest planet in the constellation, which is Jupiter in Pisces ❷ in gestation. This is seen from her mother's viewpoint; from the opposition to the critical Virgo Moon ❻ (which could be her mother or mother-in-law), we can see that it was not an easy process, showing that the individual would not have been comfortable in her body due to deeply held stored pain and discomfort. In reality, her mother discovered that she was very ill, and she was obviously preoccupied and not able to give her child the proper attention. Her Aries Ascendant shows that from birth on, the little one was virtually on her own.

The trine from Jupiter ahead to Mars in the Third House ❹, when she learned to talk, shows that the childhood home was filled with anger and grief that was sublimated and rarely expressed. She discovered this anger during her gestalt sessions and training, when it emerged into the light of day. The Mercury opposition to the Node (the family) is a lack of communication and attention during the bonding stage, implying that her mother was not really interested in her and in some ways abandoned her, which is understandable but unfortunate. Pluto in Cancer signaled a critical time at the age of five years old, as it indicates the intense emotional turmoil accompanying the early death of her mother. The registration of the Virgo Moon therefore shows her father's remarriage and her stepmother, who was quite dismissive and uncaring of her. Indeed, it was her inability to experience and express love that led to her psychotherapeutic activities when the Node finally registered. Her therapeutic process uncovered many of these past threads of experience and allowed her to integrate them and pass on her experience and expertise to others. She ultimately led a very successful psychotherapeutic school in Scandinavia.

The release of a sequence of planets is very significant as it will guide our understanding of how we operate and also can guide a therapeutic process. We have already seen when in this woman's life their original registrations occurred. The list below shows the exact sequence in which they released. This process occupied eight years from Mercury to the Moon, and also a change of signs from Scorpio, which indicates darkness, emotional separation, and inner anger, to Sagittarius, which is higher mind, philosophical and psychological aspirations, and positive thinking. Using these dates makes the meaning of a constellation of planets very clear.

OPP	MERCURY	JAN	1984	23.31	SCO
***0	CUSP 8	JUN	1985	25.01	SCO
SSQ	MC	APR	1986	25.57	SCO
***0	N NODE	MAY	1986	26.02	SCO
SQQ	VENUS	JAN	1988	27.51	SCO
QNX	MARS	MAY	1988	28.10	SCO
TRI	PLUTO	AUG	1988	28.26	SCO
***0	O SAGITTA	MAR	1990	00.00	SAG
SQU	JUPITER	JAN	1992	01.46	SAG
SQU	MOON	MAY	1992	02.05	SAG

FIGURE 11.6: SEQUENCE OF RELEASE

The sequence of planets in the constellation release as shown by their dates in the printout. Note the change of house from the Seventh to the Eighth in June 1985, and the change of sign from Scorpio to Sagittarius in March 1990.

Signs in the Eighth House

The Eighth House cusp begins with the midlife crisis time and determines our metaphysical attitude to life. Our energy begins to decline, interests and priorities change, and the need to assert ourselves wanes in favor of higher and more personal values. We must learn to release control and accept a more sensitive stance. It is our acceptance of our separateness and unexpressed passion in life.

Eighth House Cusp in Aries. Regeneration is found through decisive action at the point in life when you are making reassessments and entering midlife. Joint finances or legacies can be the cause of this newly found assertiveness, and breaking free of prior commitments attracts you. (See also the house where Mars resides.)

Eighth House Cusp in Taurus. You adopt a peaceful attitude to the middle stage of your life, as you generate wealth from sources ignored by others. Tranquillity and an enjoyment of material comforts are a turning point away from the haste of acquisitive youth. (See also the house where Venus resides.)

Eighth House Cusp in Gemini. A youthful approach to middle age, many ideas regarding your resources, and an intellectual interest in death contribute to a varied and communicative later life. You create secondary occupations everywhere, and the alleviation of boredom is a primary concern. (See also the house where Mercury resides.)

Eighth House Cusp in Cancer. Your emotional approach to all aspects of your life and a wish to have secure circumstances colors your increasingly conservative attitude. Looking after people close to you becomes a priority, and nurturing younger associates is important. An interest in psychology and alternative therapies answer deep and unexpressed needs to express feelings more actively. (See also the house where the Moon resides.)

Eighth House Cusp in Leo. This period of life finds you at maximum effectiveness, as only now can you feel the confidence to really honor yourself. Generosity with resources but also a need to control dispensing them brings expansion and exteriorizing of your creativity. (See also the house where the Sun resides.)

Eighth House Cusp in Virgo. Your detailed concern over health makes you emotionally uneasy and intent on providing enough resources for the remainder of your life. Your perfectionist tendencies give way to pragmatic behavior and decisions. Alertness to dangerous situations where accidents may occur and practical help from partners are features now. (See also the house where Mercury resides.)

Eighth House Cusp in Libra. A renewed interest in art enriches the slower pace of your life, you have harmonious relationships with the people around you, and you enter joint endeavors, which can all create a sense of value for you. New and expansive partnerships accompany changes in position and attitude. (See also the house where Venus resides.)

Eighth House Cusp in Scorpio. An understanding of the deeper level of life comes to you through willingness to transform and change old habits. Your detachment becomes a final advantage as you accept what others cling to. The realization that you are part of an infinite cycle, passing through time and out again, becomes reality for you now. (See also the houses where Mars and Pluto reside.)

Eighth House Cusp in Sagittarius. Your concern with legal procedures, a philosophical approach to old age, and a return to religion is expressive of the next stage of maturity. You are intrigued by psychology and new ways of expanding your consciousness. Foreign travel and residence are attractive. (See also the house where Jupiter resides.)

Eighth House Cusp in Capricorn. A more serious image is one that fits you well; a prudent and security-minded approach to the later years and the desire to pass on the wisdom of our experience make this last part of your life journey an instructive time for yourself and others. (See also the house where Saturn resides.)

Eighth House Cusp in Aquarius. A strong spirituality, the development of mediumistic abilities, and being drawn toward groups supporting social betterment marks the most eccentric and individualistic phase of your life. (See also the house where Saturn and Uranus reside.)

Eighth House Cusp in Pisces. Merging back to the place of all beginnings may not be something you dwell on in the latter part of your life. Your interest in music and poetry increases at this stage, and you may also be inspired to help others, just as you want to withdraw from the world. (See also the houses where Jupiter and Neptune reside.)

The Eight House is the separation from life as we approach death.

This ends the octave of maturity and the qualities that we carry in our mental body.

TWELVE

STRIVING FOR TRANSCENDENCE

Spirit Song over the Waters
The soul of man
Resembleth water:
From heaven it cometh,
To heaven it soareth.
And then again,
To earth descendeth,
Changing ever.

JOHANN WOLFGANG VON GOETHE, 1789

Our materialist, mechanist culture encourages us to value money, property, and our ambitions and expectations in the world above all else, but more and more of us have a need to go beyond this. Material success just doesn't satisfy our deeper spiritual nature; we seek access to higher, freer states possibly the transcendence described by Eastern religions or the transpersonal realm of depth psychology. We do so through a return to our experiential roots, by rediscovering our suppressed feminine side or our inner child, or by finding meaning in our life.

In the 1980s and 1990s I became more and more interested in ecological and sustainable ideas in design and economics, and ran workshops in what I called "Designing Desires" for designers and architects. They examined, through personal values, guided imagery, studying symbolism, and meditation, whether we achieve satisfaction through the fruits of the material world, or rather seek the deeper values of intimacy, full communication in relationships, nurturing our children with our being and experience, and valuing our relationship rather than our work. The participants discovered that the sense of unreality they felt in this world could and should be transcended by going more deeply into themselves and understanding their true values. We all seek access to the transcendent domain, which is not above us in some inaccessible realm, but rather within.

When we begin to explore our earliest history and return to the realm of the mother we simultaneously recreate the dynamics of our conception. The fourth octave is the higher level of gestation. The pattern of female-male relationship established by our parents symbolizes the nature of our creativity, our striving for transcendence, and our mechanism of individuation. We hold within ourselves the keys to the path of our own initiation. We must go back to the beginning.

In our vision of our whole life, we come to realize that our greatest difficulties are often the keys to our deepest being. People we have rejected are parts of ourselves we have left behind. The anger and guilt we project onto parents or partners are aspects of ourselves we cannot integrate. The new vision of astrology guides us to find meaning in the darkness of our life and to find direction in the chaos we create. We come to value everyone who has interacted with us because they are vehicles of our own understanding. Astrology completes the loop of the healed life.

THE HIGHER OCTAVE

The process of life from the Ninth House cusp conception point until the end of the Eighth House of separation and death defines our mundane life. Life is a circle in time. In the East they symbolize it as the Wheel of Samsara, the round of illusion.

FIGURE 12.1: WHEEL OF SAMSARA

The Tibetan Buddhist Wheel of Samsara shows the stages of life as a circle that never ends as we reincarnate again and again, living through life without breaking through the cycles of ignorance, greed, and lust, symbolized by the animals entwined in the center.

In order to understand our life in full, we must see it in its entirety in time. We must unify all our joys, sorrows, meaningful moments, and trivial enjoyments, the complexity and simplicity, the loves and fears, protagonists and allies into a whole that we know works. The new vision we are describing is one way for beginning to be comfortable with the whole of life as a unity.

It is fascinating that many people want to be someone else. I believe that this is because they cannot really understand the depth and true significance of their own being. We feel stuck in a causal chain of events that we do not understand, yet those very influences, as random as they often seem, are the keys to our higher nature. Paradoxically, we must become ourselves fully in order to transcend ourselves. We must obey the laws of being, the dharma. I have found that thousands of my clients, simply by understanding the inner dynamics of their life, were able to forgive their parents, recognize the patterns of their life when they did not believe such a pattern existed, and recognize that they were not alone in the separation and the pain of life they experienced. We all carry such travails, and it is a relief to express them, even when we are learning astrology.

Most of us live mechanical lives: We are conceived, born, mature, and die. Although the circumstances of our lives change and are different from those around us, we all experience the same process. We feel alone, but we share this round of existence with all other humans.

Understanding our life as extended into a cylinder (see Figure 12.2) shows conception at the bottom and the transcendent octave at the top. As we live through our life the cylinder fills up with our memories. The deeper a memory is within us, the farther down in the cylinder toward conception it lies. Our present moment is the surface of the cylinder. The planets spiral along their inexorable paths within the cylinder, reflecting and synchronizing with our life pattern in time. The planets do not cause our life but are symbols that reflect it. If we are trapped by past patterns it is like being held underwater, unable to breathe and unable to swim. In this state of unknowingness, or sleep, as some consider it, we perceive our life as only the surface of the cylinder above a murky fluid. The "realized" person perceives a crystal-clear cylinder and can move backward to conception and even before that into previous lives, as well as forward into the future. We often hold ourselves in our lives, unable to escape.

When we see our life as a cylinder resonating with the spiraling solar system, we extend our perspective of the two-dimensional

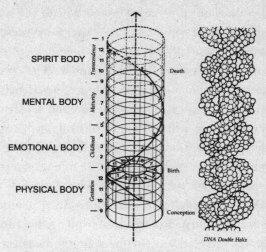

FIGURE 12.2: THE TRANSCENDENT OCTAVE

The transcendent octave is the fourth spirit body and is the higher octave of the events of gestation. We must go back to the very beginning of our life in order to break out of the causal confines of our existence and gain access to our higher nature. The spiral DNA molecule fits within the spiral of life just as the planets continue their transits up the cylinder.

horoscope into a higher dimension of reality: We understand relativity.

To gain access to the transcendent octave, we extend our reality beyond the confines of the three-dimensional world of our senses. Conception and gestation describe our coming-into-being, and this patterns our transcendent reality as well. The way our parents come together to create us is mirrored in our creativity and drive to transcendence. Of course, this means that our relationships are a key to our being. They are a spiritual domain in which life and spirit interpenetrate. The initiating action and relative dominance of our parents as they conceive us is a metaphor for the way in which our masculine and feminine sides blend creatively. The way our mother realizes our pregnancy resonates with the way that we discover our true nature; the process of pregnancy describes how creativity manifests itself.

The transcendent octave is the higher level of gestation, so when we reconstruct our gestation, we are experiencing a transcendent process. If our gestation was fluid and satisfying for our mother, then the same will be true of our transcendent reality. If she resisted the conception and was depressed during the pregnancy, we would expect such issues to arise in our own process. Indeed, the pathologies we carry are often triggers to higher awareness, if we can only learn to see them in that way and, further, utilize their inherent wisdom in our being. It is not accidental that sickness can be a potent metaphor for our transcendent octave. Sometimes we must near death in order to really begin to live. The events of gestation provide a pattern that we enact in living out our creative potential in life.

The gestation octave both begins and ends our life in time: It completes and encloses the circle, yet provides the possibility of being free of the circle. The point of access to the transcendent octave of the horoscope is the Ninth House conception point/death point. The gestation patterns that led our parents onward are often a crucial key to entering our own path. Simultaneously, we liberate ourselves from our parents' karmic influence by going more deeply into their being at that time. The irony is that we often flee the very influences that signal our freedom. The reliving of our conception and gestation is an initiation into a more holistic way of seeing.

The initiation process is available to us in ways we might not recognize. The most obvious initiation is a woman bearing and giving birth to her children. In ancient cultures the women's mysteries were a symbolic reenactment of the conception, gestation, and birth process. The series of initiations began with a young girl's first menstruation and culminated with the birth of her first child.

Menstruation is a biological signal that a girl can conceive. The first sign of creation within her led to a ritual separation—a symbolic "death" in relation to the tribe. She is never the same again. It evokes the Scorpio, Eighth House stage just before conception in a very appropriate way. Gestation is an initiation process to the mother.

A conception irrevocably changes the pattern and orientation of a woman's life, and in a way she dies to her former life. The risks of life and death affect both the mother and her child in the birth process. A woman relives her own gestation when she is pregnant.

The man's initiation has the same roots, but since men cannot bear children it is necessarily abstracted. Once again they are mysteries of creation that are idealized and made into a ritual. Parallel to the isolation of the female before conception, the male orgasm is a dying release. The test of strength in initiation evokes procreation and symbolizes our higher purpose in life.

There are many ways in which we can experience an initiation. A near-death experience that happens in the case of an accident, surgery, or critical illness can trigger such a process of death and rebirth. Psychedelic drugs and plants remove us from our mundane daily reality and allow us to experience a boundary-free reality for periods of time. Psychedelics have the primary effect of increasing our metabolism, and we therefore travel back through our life, encountering the planets in reverse order. Because our metabolism is faster in youth and decreases as we age, when our metabolism is artificially or organically accelerated, we begin to see the world as we did as a child. We travel clockwise back against the natural direction of the signs and houses in the horoscope, back to the Ascendant and our birth. In this sense it is like a therapeutic "rebirthing," in which the conditions of birth are duplicated and we experience our own birth process over again. Taking massive doses of such substances takes the individual back through birth itself, into gestation. Since our personality comes into being at birth, we therefore feel as though we are losing our personality. The early psychedelic prophets like Timothy Leary described it as ego loss, but it is more accurately personality loss. The proper understanding and administration of psychedelics provide an opportunity to relive life and experience existence without personality—a transcendence of ordinary life.

Sexuality also evokes conception and death. As we have mentioned, orgasm is often described as a little death and is certainly a symbolic death in which we give ourselves up; we relinquish our vital energy to our loved one. The nature of the sexual act between our parents symbolizes the connection between sexuality and creativity, evoked when we make love. Sexuality is a highly spiritual act and a profound initiation, as the practice of eastern Tantric yoga makes clear.[27] Reconstruction of the sexual act that conceives us is a key to our own creativity, sexuality, and entrance into the transcendent octave of reality.

Psychoanalysis, psychotherapy, and other analytical processes can also function as initiation. In these processes we go back into our life, sometimes in such a way that we step out of ourselves, with the therapist as a guide. We can see our entire being through processes of association, hypnosis, gestalt work, dream work, psychodrama, movement, words, or symbols, and it can happen in the presence of a sympathetic listener. Certain movements that occur in athletics, running, stretching, dance, golf, and sex can provide a breakthrough to transcendence. Yoga, martial arts, tai chi, meditation, and other techniques developed in the East are specifically oriented toward the identical aim of achieving unity.

Using *A New Vision of Astrology* can also provide a technique to guide the aforementioned techniques of experience and ecstasy. When we break through into the higher octave of transcendence, the four gestation houses take on a higher and more weighty meaning.

HIGHER OCTAVE CONCEPTION

Gestation begins with conception and ends with birth and is a pattern of our own creative processes, but it is also a pattern for our transcendent development. Conception, transcendence, creativity, and sexuality are all aspects of the higher life in the energies that drive these processes.

Our father and mother are the masculine/feminine, positive/negative poles in us. We can see by the signs and houses they occupy whether they are active or passive in nature, and also active or passive in their expression. A luminary (the Sun or the Moon) in an active sign (the fire and air signs) but a passive house (the even-numbered ones) can contradict the norm, and it is therefore possible that our father was active, passive, or a mixture, and the same for our mother. They can easily be contradictory. The significance is that our creative process echoes or mirrors this dynamic, whatever it was.

The parent responsible for conceiving us symbolizes our creative motivations, and the parent acted upon reflects our shadow side. Both are required for our wholeness. Our conception might have been accidental, planned, one-sided, equivalent, boring, highly sexual, asexual, purely physical, extremely emotional, detached and cold, intellectual, violent, attached, athletic, or lazy. Our higher nature and the process we take to get there reflect the nature of conception as a relationship between our parents.

The evolutionary process we experience in the womb corresponds to Jung's *collective unconscious,* the universal evolutionary consciousness we all carry, embedded in our genetic code and in our souls.[28] Genetic research bears this out: Every cell contains a genetic register of our collective heritage in our mitochondrial DNA, which passes down the female line directly to us. It is not accidental that our new vision amplifies the importance and relevance of our feminine origins. We spend the first logarithmic third of life within our mother and the second third under her direct daily control. Our mothers are dominant in our entire being. I remember taking this up with male astrologers in England in the early 1980s. They were upset that my ideas placed so much importance upon our mothers and, by extension, the feminine. Indeed, it places getting in touch with the feminine on a level with understanding ourselves. We must understand our feminine origins—period.

We might refer again to the horoscope of Terence McKenna. He was a great advocate of initiation, especially through the use of psychedelic plants, and his Saturn and Pluto in Leo just after his Ninth House cusp, conjunct his conception point, bears this focus of his life out ever more forcibly. This is also the case in the horoscopes of those for whom sexuality is primary as a creative and expressive force in their lives. Planets conjunct the conception point show the increased importance of creativity and, depending on which planets, can either open the door or prevent access to us. Planets like the Sun, the Moon, Mercury, Venus, Jupiter, Uranus, and Neptune often open this door, while planets like Mars, Saturn, and Pluto can make the door a barrier to development. It is also significant where these planets are in aspect to the conception point. When they are opposite the conception, they represent a personification of the barriers and individuals who are gatekeepers preventing our access and are, of course, also those parts of us that counter our higher development.

THE HIGHER OCTAVE NINTH HOUSE

Gestation is a very potent metaphor: It symbolizes the ultimate stage of our life. This is our need to go beyond the physical, emotional, and mental bodies and come into contact and identification with our spiritual being. It is this for which we strive, a creative muse we can follow into eternity, if we can only find her.

A note here is that the Ninth House cusp archetypally registers at seventy-seven years old, although this varies widely due to the size of the houses. The farther north of the equator we are born the greater the likelihood the houses will vary considerably in size around the horoscope wheel. When the Seventh and Eighth Houses are small it is possible for us to pass into them, past the archetypal "death" point, as early as our forties. When this happens, we pass naturally into the higher Ninth and even Tenth Houses. As a spiral, the time scale has no end.

The higher octave of the Ninth House reflects the time when our mother comes to the realization that she is pregnant. Inklings of this occur as early as our first creative or sexual experiences. The feeling of pure life pulses through us, as though no one had ever made love, painted a picture, or realized the implications of their beliefs before. Our creative breakthrough can happen in seemingly accidental ways, and often do. It is difficult to legislate such profound influences. The Ninth House is our religious, philosophical, and psychological perspectives as we are able to create them. It is derived from the pattern of our behavior during our transcendent, creative, and sexual experiences. It is often symbolic of the process of realization we experience in first seeing glimpses of the transcendent world, and then our ability to follow the path farther. It often involves a training of our physical, energetic, or mental reality to purify and prepare for our higher states.

The horoscope of the late Swiss astrologer Bruno Huber shows the transcendent possibilities of the higher Ninth House. Bruno's mother conceived him with love, as shown by Venus just on the conception point, but in Scorpio; it was a short-term affair and his father left shortly afterward, when the Sun registered in Sagittarius, the sign of long journeys and foreign individuals. That the

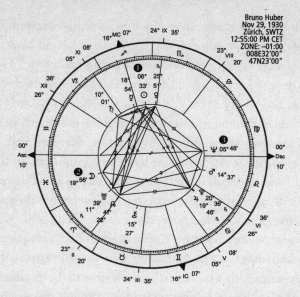

Bruno Huber
Nov 29, 1930
Zürich, SWTZ
12:55:00 PM CET
ZONE: −01:00
008E32'00"
47N23'00"

FIGURE 12.3: HOROSCOPE OF ASTROLOGER BRUNO HUBER

The important contemporary Swiss astrologer Bruno Huber lost his father soon after his conception ❶. We can see that the conception was enacted with love by the presence of Venus on the conception point. As a young child during the bonding process, he was often left alone, watching people pass by on the street ❷. He was highly sensitive. Neptune registers in his twenties when we can see his first access back to the Sun in the Ninth House and his first transcendent experiences ❸.

Sun is square the sensitive and illusory Neptune in the Seventh House of relationships further implies the effect of the separation on his mother, as well as the fact that there is no direct aspect between the Sun and the Moon. However, when Bruno passed Neptune in his early twenties he had the first of his transcendental realizations that he himself must become his father and guide himself because of its square ahead to the Sun in the Ninth House, which is also his psychological mentor Roberto Assagioli, creator of psychosynthesis. With the Sun in the Ninth House it is often necessary to assume the responsibilities of one's own father in creating a higher consciousness. The Sun is a guiding principle in such a life.

THE HIGHER OCTAVE MIDHEAVEN

This reflects the moment our mother realizes that she is pregnant. Our karmic heritage comes into being in that moment as our mother becomes conscious of her new life and objectives. It is also at this time that the soul enters our physical body. If our mother needed a doctor to confirm that she was pregnant, then we will seek such verification from a therapist, a spiritual guide, from our doctor, or from an authority figure in our life. The increased reliance on therapists rather than religious figures reflects the profound changes in our society in that previously the mother would have recognized her own pregnancy, but in our world women usually learn they are pregnant through chemical tests or a doctor's examination. A return to natural methods brings a more natural impetus to the higher awareness in us. If our mother initially kept her pregnancy secret due to confusion over paternity, then we would keep our life aims secret.

Our mother's reaction to pregnancy is a direct metaphor of our place in the world. We attempt to recognize and accept consciously the existence of our higher reality as we begin seeing the world clearly. This often involves a conscious acknowledgment of our new, higher goals, and we begin to specify how they will come into being in our world.

THE HIGHER OCTAVE TENTH HOUSE

The higher octave of the Tenth House reflects our parents' ability to organize things in their world after it has been determined that our mother is pregnant, and it also shows their ability to tell the world and their parents (Saturn and Jupiter), and also their deepest expectations of our role in their relationship and the world. The clearer our parents' motives and their expression just after the realization of gestation, the clearer is our path ahead in life. Elements and signs here show our potential ways to achieve position and fame in the world.

We must take our higher philosophy or psychology derived in the Ninth House into our physical reality of the Tenth House. It shows our ability to recognize that in order to bring our higher mind into being in physical form and manifest it in reality, we must learn to diminish our ego involvement in the outer world and its goals. Instead of higher consciousness being an alternative and rarely visited part of our being, it can become central to who we are and even may become an identification we carry. We convert ideas into reality here.

The horoscope of mathematician John Forbes Nash in Figure 11.2 shows that he has four planets in the Tenth House of outer world notoriety and fame. This shows a higher level of being and also that the focus of his life is really outside of this world, in a transcendent reality beyond time and space.

THE HIGHER OCTAVE ELEVENTH HOUSE

The higher octave of the Eleventh House is related to our mother's idealistic attitudes, which reflect her relationships at the time. Our higher ideals start with our immediate family and extend to local groups and then the public at large. The contrast between personal and collective ideals generates higher utopian aims, communal activities, and inventive social systems. We take our higher objectives into a collective realm by teaching, guiding, and acting as a leader or model for others to follow and understand. We join and become integral to groups and, in the process, sublimate our ego awareness manifested in the Tenth House.

THE HIGHER OCTAVE TWELFTH HOUSE

The higher octave of the Twelfth House reflects a receptive and sacrificial orientation of our mother in the last phase of gestation. Once we transmit our ideas into the world, we must reap the karmic consequences of our actions. These describe the spiritual impact of our life and its ideals upon others, inwardly and outwardly. This indicates to what extent we are willing to sacrifice ourselves, even physically, to higher aspirations. We can respond sympathetically to the finest spiritual values, and here they are so deeply embedded that we are able to release even them.

With the completion of this last house, life is complete on all four octave levels of existence: gestation, childhood, maturity, and transcendence. When we can translate all the potential we accepted at conception into actuality, the process of life is complete.

THIRTEEN

SYNTHESIZING OUR LIFE

When we reconstruct our life story, we inevitably begin to see patterns emerging that define us, others that we are only beginning to become aware of, and still others that are speculative. This is because the process of discovery is a lifelong pursuit. We will rediscover, analyze, and understand ourselves anew on a regular basis.

As we age, we transfer our energies into more complex and channels that are more challenging. When we reject or misunderstand opportunities, the focus shifts backward upon earlier stages about which we know and within which we are comfortable. Regression is a return to the habits and attitudes of an earlier time in life: If we cannot extend our involvement in the world, we retreat and channel it into something to which we do have access. When marriage (Seventh House) is too challenging there is a regression to the competition of secondary school (Sixth House), or when a child finds the demands of elementary school (Fifth House) overwhelming there is a regression to the baby talk and thumb-sucking of early home life (Third House). Regressions are not always permanent, but the principle operates in us all.

A case history will illustrate how early influences can be recreated, examined, and worked with to achieve a higher state of living.

A CASE HISTORY: THE CLASSICAL PIANIST
DAVID HELFGOTT

David Helfgott, the Australian concert pianist, is the subject of the Academy Award–nominated film *Shine,* which chronicled his early genius, mental breakdown, and marriage to an astrologer who nurtured his return to the concert stage.

In 1992 I traveled to Australia and taught a weekend workshop on my Life Time Astrology ideas to the Perth Astrology Group, founded and run by two wonderful women, Barbara Brackley and Gillian Helfgott. Gillian's husband, David, was staying in the hotel where the workshop took place. To say that David was a unique person would be an understatement.

A tall, fair man, he stood hunched over, moved way too rapidly, and continuously squinted and blinked his eyes, as though he had an aversion to the light. He constantly mumbled repetitive phrases to himself, yet loudly enough for others nearby to hear. He was separate from everyone, but always reminding us that he was there. And, characteristically, he continually admonished himself in an interior dialogue with phrases like: "Smile! It's important to smile! Always smile!" or: "Stay in control! Must always stay in control!"

When he swam in the pool, he thrashed about in an alarming way, as though he were about to drown, but one could see he was a strong swimmer well capable of supporting himself— maybe it was a will to live. Indeed, that is an accurate metaphor for David Helfgott's life. Gillian told us a story about a time when they were staying at this same hotel on Perth Bay, across which plies a large, paddle-wheel steamship, crisscrossing the two-mile-wide expanse of water. She had left David by the pool and went to get something in their room. When she returned, she could not find him. She noticed people looking toward the steamer in amazement and saw that David was swimming in its path, in the middle of the bay, half a mile away, oblivious to the danger.

When Gillian introduced David to us he came over and cuddled everyone, looked deeply into our eyes, and repeated our names in his bizarre rhyming slang, over and over again. He seemed to particularly like holding women, as though clinging to mother. Was there a sexual quality to that touch? It was clear meeting him that he was a deeply sensitive and fragile man. We eventually learned that he was a concert pianist. We heard an early CD he had recorded and saw filmed footage of him playing a concert in Australia. He was brilliant, and so alive, and yet also very disturbed. I wondered what could have created his life.

Gillian stated that one reason she had come to my workshop was to explore David's horoscope to see if there were significant influences before birth that could have been significant in forming his unique being. As we will see, this is definitely the case. According to Gillian, David Helfgott was born in Melbourne, Australia, at 08:28 A.M. GST (−10E) on May 19, 1947 (see Figure 13.1 for David's horoscope).

The earlier in life critical events happen to us, particularly traumatic events, even if they are very subtle, the more energy they carry, the greater their impact on our psyche and life, and the more important they are astrologically. Life is a cascade of mathematical and rhythmically pulsing planetary events and experiences, measured by their aspect patterns around the horoscope circle. When early events happen, they are triggered regularly as if to reinforce their influence on us, again and again. As we get older their recurrence is less and less frequent, but also more powerful. We have the opportunity to experience it all again, but the influences repeat in a logarithmic pattern in time. The intervals get longer and we have less energy to change. As we will see in David's horoscope, early influences in gestation remain a profound and critical force in later life.

The time scale allows us to see at a glance when critical times of life happen, as a guide and context for discovering what they mean and when they will next recur. We learn where to look, which informs our questions about what happened. In cases where therapeutic work is necessary they point to times when episodes recur, and those are the times when it is best to work with them. When we look at David Helfgott's horoscope, we immediately notice that five (half) of the planets and the Moon's North Node are in the gestation, when he was developing within his mother. This signals that early influences are powerful and inherent in his physical body, which is certainly true.

In his artistic expression, David Helfgott could be characterized as bound by deep, rigid, inherited patterns and also the ability to transcend his difficult outer situation.

In David's case the personal planets are concentrated in gestation—both the Sun and the Moon are conjoined there with the three other personal planets, Mercury, Venus, and Mars. During gestation outer influences are transmitted to (and stored in) our developing fetus through the psyche and body of our mother, and they interact with the inherent karma of our developing soul. The interaction of outer influences and inner karmic development during gestation and birth has been described by Stan Grof as *perinatal matrixes* that correspond to our spiritual and psychological development.[29]

The deepest influences will always define the inner life of David Helfgott in profound ways, will be physical (somatic) in their expression of form and quality, and are traits he will believe to be inherent and unchangeable in him. It may be impossible to modify such deeply held patterns. Because these influences happen before birth, we feel as though they have always been there, and in some ways they have always been there. It is the patterns found during gestation that are the foundation of our lives, both physically and psychologically.

A TRAUMATIC GESTATION

The question we first ask is: Which of his parents was responsible for the urge to conceive him? Since the Ninth House is the conception point, we move backward (against the signs) in a clockwise direction until we reach the Sun or the Moon. We first come to the Sun in Taurus, showing David's father, Peter, in the Twelfth House, at the end of gestation. He felt "fated" to have a child and was also a man who found it difficult to express his own talents and artistry in the world. Peter grew up in an intensely Jewish socialist family in Russian-occupied Poland. As a boy, he secretly saved up and bought a violin, which his father then smashed into pieces, exclaiming that he should instead become a rabbi. Already, before David's conception, his father saw him as a creative surrogate of himself in the world. His (male) child would express all the creative musical qualities he (the father) was unable to express, due to circumstances beyond his control (Twelfth House). This is a great karmic burden for any child to carry and characteristic of the Sun in the Twelfth House.

David's mother's role in his conception is shown by the lack of direct aspect between the Sun and the Moon. The two parents had little in common apart from the need to survive. Rachel was twenty-four years old and Peter was forty-one when they were married, having been introduced by a business associate of Peter's. Both luminaries in the earth element show that their relationship was very physical, and that their love derived from the physical as well. Venus in Aries disposes the Taurus Sun and Moon and shows the combined parental drive and need for self-assertion. They saw their life in Australia as a new beginning. They already had a daughter, but David was the first son among five children. As Judaism is a patriarchal religion, this was extremely important to his father. This is supported by the opposition to Jupiter in Scorpio from the Sun.

The relationship between father and mother is an apt metaphor for David's relationships. His father lived within himself, apparently constantly tortured by inner demons from his past, and he almost certainly passed these on to his son, who then carried them within himself. The mother, shown by the Moon in the Eleventh House, was more gregarious, open, friendly, and outwardly loving, yet the square to Saturn in Leo shows that she too felt inhibited and was possibly depressed by her past and unable to communicate freely in her life. It is clear that both parents carried within themselves the troubles and pains of persecution in the ghetto, awaiting resurrection in and through David.

The sexual act of conception is indicated by the Aquarius Ninth House cusp that is exactly squared by Jupiter in Scorpio. The Aquarius, airy quality of their sexuality belied their mutually earthy nature. David's mother's sexuality was quite detached and abstract, and she probably considered it a duty, whereas it emanated from a passionate and expansive, but blocked, father. Such sexuality is bittersweet at best and can often be unconscious or hidden in its expression (Jupiter is below the horizon).

The Midheaven is the moment, some seven weeks after conception, when David's mother realized that she was pregnant, when the developing embryo became a fetus, and when the soul entered the physical matrix of the evolving body. David's Midheaven is in Pisces, showing that his mother "felt" she was pregnant, and that something deep within her was stirred by this process, a symbol of the feeling-toned playing and even ego consciousness of David. The sextile to the Sun shows that David's father was expansive about the pregnancy and indeed could have claimed the impulse as his own. There is no direct aspect to the Moon; therefore David's mother might have felt more like the vehicle through which father expressed himself, rather than an equal partner in the process. This early fact is almost certainly a characteristic of their relationship. (David's mother barely exists as a formative influence in the movie.) The Sun/Midheaven aspect also shows that the son receives the projections and expectations of the father even before his birth, which ingrains them in his very body.

The exact Mars-Venus conjunction in Aries registers in December 1946, three months after conception. This is a highly creative and spontaneous combination and shows both strong sexuality and creativity, qualities that are almost always related to each other—the masculine Mars just precedes the feminine Venus in the self-assertive sign. David himself carries a strong feminine quality in his nature, and the mixture of aggression and beauty in his piano-playing also reflects this powerful combination. While the conjunction is only semisextile to the Midheaven and the Sun, it is also at the midpoint of Sun/Midheaven, which corresponds to vibrant creative individuality and a strong relationship between ego, sexuality, and body consciousness. David's creativity is what holds him together, and it may also be that his sexuality is equally strong. In the context of gestation, it is as though his father continued to express himself sexually as a way of programming the coming child with his own creative aspirations.

The Moon in Taurus registers in January 1947, four months before David's birth. This is a fascinating position because the Moon square Saturn is associated with inherited physical diseases as a reflection of feelings of estrangement and separation.[30] David's mother must have felt quite alone and isolated at this time, in a strange, new country, and was probably often alone during her pregnancy. The Moon is also quincunx Jupiter, bringing a slightly more optimistic view to the situation, but the mother's heart was abroad. This aspect shows the frustration she felt at being separated from her family physically, emotionally, and psychologically. This is a major factor in David's great need to travel away from the family in 1961, which was prevented by his father, and later in 1966, when he disobeyed his father and left for London.

David's father as the Taurus Sun in the Twelfth House is a powerful but diminished influence in the horoscope. He carries a powerful, fixed, and emotional force probably regularly translated into physical terms, but he feels inexorably trapped by his fate. The Mars sextile Venus aspect is so exact that it probably transmits the simultaneous and inseparable anger and love that he later channeled to David. This may later influence the father's relationship to David and his daughters: They are Venus and he is Mars; they receive love from him, David receives anger. The Jupiter opposition shows the father's foreignness, his sense of religious isolation, a natural pessimism, and probable depression at this time. (It is fascinating to see that Jupiter registers later in 1963, when David's opportunities to travel to study with Isaac Stern have been soundly rejected by his father, who states that he refuses to allow his family to break up.)

Mercury falls just into the sign Gemini in April 1947, showing great mental abilities, mimicry, and communicative skills, paradoxically in the Twelfth House of introversion, psychism, and unconsciousness. In its sextile to Saturn, Mercury is very deep and thoughtful, though. We can picture David's father brooding, awaiting the child in the month before his birth, planning his saturnine role as teacher and disciplinarian. Mercury is the trickster and rebel, and it may be a guiding principle in David Helfgott's life. The exact opposite point to Mercury, when it culminates in the first degree of Sagittarius, registers in 1966 when he does leave his father to study with the celebrated music teacher Cyril Smith at the Royal College of Music in London.

The birth is governed by Gemini and its ruler, Mercury, which disposes easy births, although the exact sextile to Pluto shows that there is something extraordinary about David's personality. As the only aspect to the Ascendant, Pluto brings a force, destiny, and awesome power to him, yet also a cruel fate. His nervous breakdown, in 1970, happens exactly on the Descendant, twenty-three and a half years later, and Pluto is again involved intimately.

DAVID'S CHILDHOOD

The four houses of childhood are the First through the Fourth, during which time the emotional body is formed in the context of home and family, just as the physical body was formed during gestation. That this time is extraordinary for David is indicated by the presence of Uranus, Saturn, Pluto, and Neptune, the four outermost planets. As his physical heritage is occupied by personal planets, his emotional reality is entirely influenced by the collective planets.

Uranus registers in July 1947, when David was just one month old. It shows unique creative and communication skills, but also an instability focusing on the instinctive mind. This is further indicated by the trine to Neptune in November 1953, by which time he was playing the piano with great skill. This combination is extremely psychic to the extent of being enlightened, yet is so emotionally sensitive and unstable that there is a decided lack of mental balance. The semi-square from the gestation Moon can mean that this psychic sensitivity derives from his mother or her side of the family.

By the time Saturn and Pluto register in Leo, it can be easily seen that most of the aspects move back toward the gestation time. David is under the influence of his heredity and the difficulties of an emotional nature carried by his father. There is an element of cruelty about his relationship with his father that one cannot fail to see when you meet him to this day. In my estimation this could even have been a time of domestic violence that has left its impact on his emotional body and psyche. Terrific skills and concentration are added to the brew, and they produced the emotional power to play Rachmaninov piano pieces in the early years of his career.

Neptune in Libra (November 1953) shows the family move from Melbourne to Perth, caused by Peter's increasing financial instability. Their sea voyage (Neptune) was disorienting to David, and he mentions having been beaten by his father regularly. This time also signals the onset of his mental instability and the stress caused by his father. The pathos and tragedy of the situation gives an eventual insight and delicacy that is evident in David's playing. In some ways it seems that he was able to get into the emotional space of the composers and "become them." This may have been an attempt to escape from his outer life. His psychic ability again is derived from his mother via the quincunx from the gestation Moon, which indicates frustration and estrangement from his mother. He describes her status at the time as being "crushed completely [by his father. She had] absolutely no say in the house at all."

ON MY OWN-SOME AND SORT OF LONESOME

When investigating times in life between the age point registrations of natal planets, we can date and describe the aspect sensitive points. Using the Matrix ASPRING (Aspect Ring) chart, from the commonly available astrological program Winstar 2, one can see these points all around the circle. It is obvious that oppositions to prominent natal planets will generate such times, when there is a rejection of the qualities represented by the planet itself—as it

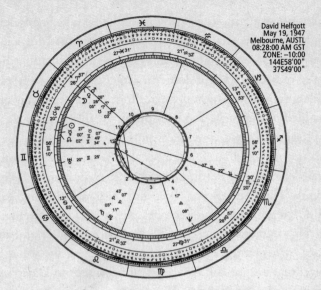

FIGURE 13.1: HOROSCOPE OF DAVID HELFGOTT

David Helfgott's horoscope with the ASPRING (Aspect Ring) shows the sequence of sensitive aspect points (SAPs) inside the ring of the twelve signs. These SAPs show the astrological texture of his life.

were, an opposing energy in life pressuring an essential quality. When one passes the Moon in the time scale one identifies with the father, but when opposing the Sun, one will naturally reject qualities associated with the father (or vice versa).

In 1961 the great violinist Isaac Stern was so impressed with David that he invited him to come to the United States, but his father refused to let him leave. The frustration is shown by the sensitive points (aspect points) of 135° from the Midheaven and 150° from Uranus in 1961 and 1962. Over the next years he won the state finals of the ABC Concerto Competition in Australia six times. But this time also signaled his increasing introversion. He simply withdrew from the outer world and felt rejection in his day-to-day life. He got angry at this rejection and elicited outbursts from teachers and friends at what they perceived as arrogance.

The great break of his career was when he received a scholarship to the Royal College of Music in London (which David called "college-knowledge") in September 1965, and against the wishes of his father, he left home. This registers as the opposite sensitive aspect point to the Sun, indicating both an expression of his individuality and also the resistance and separation from his father. Although his father relented to pressure from college professors to allow David to leave Australia, he refused to allow him to leave willingly, claiming he was forced to "sign his son away." Curiously, this coincided with an acrimonious visit from his mother's father. Predictably, David's "fathers" fought over him. In the end David packed and left his father's house for many years.

The transition from one sign to another in maturity is often traumatic and powerful in its impact. David made the transition from Scorpio (frustration and denial) into Sagittarius (foreign influences and new opportunities) in February 1966, when he met and worked with the famous piano master-class teacher Cyril Smith in London. Smith described him as the most gifted student he had seen in twenty-five years and said that he was "technically and temperamentally in the Horowitz class." His experiences at the school produced great tensions, and these can be seen in the South Node registering in 1967. The North Node is our ability to be part of a family or other emotional structure. Its opposite point is the South Node, directly opposite it in the zodiac; the South Node represents our inability to fit in. David's South Node is in the sign Sagittarius, showing that he was in a foreign country and a foreign situation, away from the structure his father had created for him.

He experienced a quincunx sensitive aspect point from his Moon (separation and frustration from the mother) in 1968. The

Moon signifies not only our actual mother, but also our ability to feel connected with others and to accept or give nurturing. The quincunx aspect of 150° shows frustration. He didn't feel like fitting in at this time.

The greatest and most extreme transformation happened in 1970, just after he returned in triumph to Australia. His father refused to see or speak to him, and he became subject to the mental illness that still affects him. It is directly timed by the Descendant (opposite the great expectations placed on him by his father at birth) and the trine sensitive aspect point from Pluto. He was coerced into marrying his first wife, Clara, who seemed to be more interested in the money he might make than in David himself. The relationship ended rapidly with him retreating into an institution in 1974. He spent the next ten years in a succession of mental institutions. In the time scale between 13° and 28° Sagittarius the sequence of sensitive points reads 135° Mars, 135° Venus, 135° Saturn, 135° Moon, 180° Uranus, 30° Jupiter, 135° Pluto, and 150° Sun, all of which show disorientation and tension. Near the time when he was at last released, the 90° Midheaven sensitive aspect point signifies a dramatic shift in ego consciousness.

In 1981, coinciding with the transition out of Sagittarius and into Capricorn (from expansion and duality into contraction and order, and the development of ego), David began playing the piano at restaurants in Perth. It was here that he began performing again and gradually came back into the world.

In 1984 he met and then married his astrologer wife, Gillian, signified by sensitive point quincunxes from Saturn and the Node (making a destined *yod* shape, a triangle formed by two 150° quincunxes completed by a semisextile of 30°) followed by a sensitive trine to the Moon. Gillian and Barbara Brackley selected their marriage time as August 26, 1984, 11:57 A.M. in Perth. David subsequently had a triumphant return to the concert platform and has improved ever since. He still is subject to his illness, but the loving attention of his wife has kept him playing and performing.

The Australian actor Geoffrey Rush won the Best Actor Oscar for his performance as David Helfgott in the movie *Shine*. This is a fitting acknowledgment for a man whose brave efforts to overcome the "dark night of the soul" have given such pleasure to so many people. His piano-playing is sublime, sensitive, and still unpredictable, and he is a pleasure to hear. It makes one appreciate how apt it is that his surname Helfgott means "help from God."

FOURTEEN

UP THE GOLDEN PATH

The breeze at dawn has secrets to tell you.
Don't go back to sleep.
You must ask for what you really want.
Don't go back to sleep.
People are going back and forth across the doorsill
where the two worlds touch.
The door is round and open. Don't go back to sleep.

RUMI, TRANSLATED BY COLEMAN BARKS

O ur lifetime of movement around the horoscope circle is an upward spiral through and around the periphery and into the center of the cylinder that contains layers of memories, our cast of characters, the stages of our life drama, and the myriad components of our being. In psychotherapy we reach down from the surface of consciousness into this rich pool of life, grasping ever-deeper feelings and seeking their messages, and yet here we recreate our own life sequence from the bottom up. In recapitulating our progress, we illuminate the structure of astrology as we explore our own being through our relationships. When you think about it, who are we without our relationships? What is the sound of one hand clapping?

The process brings a new vitality and understanding to all our relationships. We discover that "ever-deeper" also means greater trust in the profound mysteries of relationship. Attaining an overview of life rewards us by allowing us to know and act in the

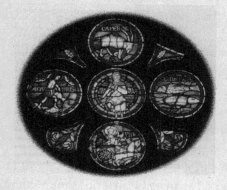

FIGURE 14.1: CHURCH ZODIAC

This rose window in Lausanne Cathedral, Switzerland, depicts the zodiac signs Capricorn, Aquarius, and Pisces, and the Moon (Luna) being drawn across the sky in a chariot. *Photograph by Painton Cowen.*

fullness of who we are. Then we can release our bondage to the past and live in the present, which is the only time that exists. We fail only when we cannot recognize that our true self is always here, awaiting acknowledgment and living in love.

When we reexperience our own life in time we begin to accept that what we often perceive as the greatest difficulties are gifts of light and insight, and our travails are the best stimuli for growth. Seeing it written in the stars brings the next boundary into view—have we been directed to develop this vision all along or are we free to define ourselves? Are we directors of our own being or merely actors in our personal drama? It is the old issue about fate versus free will. Are we fated to live a particular life? I invite you: Come on a journey through life, and by extension the lives of all who travel with us, and discover that the most valuable guide is our own awakened intuition, and the best companion is our truth of being. We may understand the whole and free ourselves by identifying with our process. Understanding is always provisional. It changes just as we change, but we must make the effort and yet allow our reality to be flexible, to mutate with our life's urges and spiritual heights. Astrology is a most valuable language and tool for accomplishing this necessary task.

PREDICTIONS AND RELATIONSHIPS

Within the context of our new vision of astrology, traditional prediction takes on an added depth and flavor. There are a number of major predictive techniques that more advanced astrologers use on a regular basis. They are transits, progressions, and solar arc directions. I have created an additional technique based on the logarithmic time scale that I call *log arc directions*.

Transits are the continued movement of the planets after our birth. They are usually represented as an additional ring around the birth horoscope so we can see the relationship of the transiting planets relative to the planets in our birth horoscope. What becomes immediately clear is that as the transiting planets pass around the circle they occupy and activate particular times in our life. When a transiting planet passes our Ascendant, which is the birth moment, it naturally triggers our actual birth and the bonding process with our mother, but on a higher level. It might signify a new residence, a movement in our personality, or a change in our appearance, but all are qualified by the nature of our original birth experience as shown in the horoscope. Transits of the gestation octave signify qualities gestating within us; within the childhood octave, we are awakening our inner child on a higher level; and within the maturity octave, we are undergoing a mental revival and reconsideration of our life.

Progressions are determined according to the equation that all planets move ahead with each day after birth corresponding to one year of our life. Therefore, if we look at the positions of the planets thirty days after our birth, one month later, they represent the progressions at the age of thirty. Solar-arc directions use the same formula, but all the planets advance the same distance as the Sun moves, which is about one degree per year. Again the positions of progressions and solar arcs reflect the stage of our life that is being activated at a given present moment.

These predictions can be very accurate and allow us to place the present time in the context of our life as a whole.

Relationships between individuals take on a different and deeper dimension within the context of our new vision because we can compare the stages of our lives with others and see how we mirror, shadow, and reflect each other in life.

Both predictive astrology and relationships are areas of further study and will be the subject of future books.

A *New Vision of Astrology* is a seed planted in our souls and can only enliven our spirit.

SYMBOL KEYS FOR ZODIAC SIGNS, PLANETS, AND ASPECTS

ZODIAC SIGNS

Symbol		Sign	Dates
♈	AR	Aries the Ram	Mar 21 to Apr 21
♉	TA	Taurus the Bull	Apr 21 to May 22
♊	GE	Gemini the Twins	May 22 to Jun 22
♋	CN	Cancer the Crab	Jun 22 to Jul 23
♌	LE	Leo the Lion	Jul 23 to Aug 24
♍	VI	Virgo the Virgin	Aug 24 to Sep 23
♎	LI	Libra the Scales	Sep 23 to Oct 23
♏	SC	Scorpio the Scorpion	Oct 23 to Nov 23
♐	SG	Sagittarius the Centaur	Nov 23 to Dec 22
♑	CP	Capricorn the Goat	Dec 22 to Jan 21
♒	AQ	Aquarius the Waterbearer	Jan 21 to Feb 19
♓	PI	Pisces the Fishes	Feb 19 to Mar 21

PLANETS

Symbol		Planet	Principle	Cycle
☉	SU	Sun	Spirit	1 year
☽	MO	Moon	Soul	29½ days
☿	ME	Mercury	Mind	88 days
♀	VE	Venus	Harmony	225 days
♂	MA	Mars	Conflict	687 days
♃	JU	Jupiter	Expansion	12 years

Symbol		Planet	Principle	Cycle
♄	SA	Saturn	Contraction	29½ years
♅	UR	Uranus	Rhythm	84 years
♆	NE	Neptune	Sensitivity	165 years
♀	PL	Pluto	Regeneration	270 years
☊	NO	Node	Association	19 years

	Aspects			Degree
☌	CJN	Conjunction	Unity-integration	0°
⚹	SXT	Sextile	Mental connection	60°
□	SQU	Square	Tension-change	90°
△	TRI	Trine	Harmony-balance	120°
☍	OPP	Opposition	Contradiction-duality	180°
⊻	SSX	Semisextile	Surface connection	30°
⊼	QNX	Quincunx	Frustration	150°
∠	SSQ	Semisquare	Conditioned tension	45°
⚼	SQQ	Sesquiquadrate	Released tension	135°

TABLE FOR CONVERTING AGE IN YEARS INTO DEGREES FROM THE ASCENDANT

Age	Degrees from Ascendant	Age	Degrees from Ascendant	Age	Degrees from Ascendant
01	043.29	23	178.57	45	213.06
02	066.52	24	181.06	46	214.13
03	082.57	25	183.09	47	215.19
04	095.13	26	185.08	48	216.24
05	105.08	27	187.03	49	217.28
06	113.28	28	188.54	50	218.30
07	120.39	29	190.41	51	219.31
08	126.58	30	192.24	52	220.30
09	132.36	31	194.04	53	221.29
10	137.41	32	195.41	54	222.27
11	142.18	33	197.15	55	223.24
12	146.33	34	198.46	56	224.19
13	150.29	35	200.15	57	225.14
14	154.09	36	201.41	58	226.07
15	157.33	37	203.05	59	227.00
16	160.46	38	204.27	60	227.52
17	163.47	39	205.46	61	228.43
18	166.38	40	207.04	62	229.33
19	169.20	41	208.20	63	230.23
20	171.55	42	209.34	64	231.11
21	174.22	43	210.46	65	231.59
22	176.42	44	211.57	66	232.46

Age	Degrees from Ascendant	Age	Degrees from Ascendant	Age	Degrees from Ascendant
67	233.33	79	242.03	91	249.21
68	234.19	80	242.42	92	249.55
69	235.04	81	243.20	93	250.28
70	235.48	82	243.58	94	251.02
71	236.32	83	244.36	95	251.34
72	237.16	84	245.13	96	252.07
73	237.58	85	245.50	97	252.39
74	238.40	86	246.26	98	253.11
75	239.22	87	247.02	99	253.42
76	240.03	88	247.37	100	254.14
77	240.43	89	248.12		
78	241.23	90	248.47		

To find the age equivalent for degrees from the Ascendant, take the degrees opposite the age in the table and add them to the Ascendant. Use the degree equivalent from 0 to 360 in a counterclockwise direction from the Ascendant. When the sum is greater than 360, subtract 360 for the correct result.

Example:

An ASC of 19 Leo	= 139°	true longitude from 0° Aries
at 57 years old	+ 225°	
	364°	
	−360°	
	004°	004° true longitude is 4° Aries

Asc 11 ma = 221°
228.43
449°·43
- 360
89° = 288

BIRTH TIME SOURCES

The astrologer Lois Rodden has created and continues to maintain AstroDatabank (www.astrodatabank.com) as a reference source for accurate birth information of prominent individuals. It includes her Rodden Ratings and Source Notes. I thank Lois for verifying the accuracy of the public domain horoscopes I have used as examples in the book. The following is her accepted rating system.

AA	Accurate data as recorded by the family or state
A	Accurate data as quoted by the person, kin, friend, or associate
B	Biography or autobiography
C	Caution: no source
DD	Dirty Data: two or more conflicting quotes that are unqualified
X	Data with no time of birth
XX	Data without a known or confirmed date

Yoko Ono Lennon
February 18, 1933, 8:30 P.M. JST, Tokyo, Japan
A: Roger Elliott quotes her, client.

John Forbes Nash
June 13, 1928, 7:00 A.M. EST, Bluefield, West Virginia
AA: Barbara C. Taylor, an astrologer in Roanoke, Virginia, quotes Nash's sister, Martha Legg, from John's baby book.

John Lennon

October 9, 1940, 6:30 P.M. GMD, Liverpool, England

A: Lois Rodden quotes his stepmom, Pauline Stone, by correspondence, "from Lennon's aunt who was present at the birth." Aaron Fischer quotes his Aunt Mimi in Ray Coleman's *Lennon,* McGraw-Hill, 1985, New York: "At 6:30 on 9 October I phoned and they said Mrs. Lennon had just had a boy." This would put the time somewhat before 6:30 P.M. Marion March reported that Lennon was born during an air raid, and London papers reported a raid that night, not in the morning.

David Helfgott

May 19, 1947, 8:28 A.M. GST, Melbourne, Australia (AEST: 10 hours)

C: Family records with time rectified by his astrologer wife, Gillian Helfgott.

Oprah Winfrey

January 29, 1954, 4:30 A.M. CST, Kosciusko, Mississippi

A: East Coast astrologer Robert Marks quotes her from the time he was on her show in 1988, reported to LMR on October 2, 2000. (Formerly, Frank C. Clifford gave 7:50 P.M., taken from the "life-clock," given on her show.)

Neil Armstrong

August 5, 1930, 0:30 A.M. EST, Wapakoneta, Ohio (0:31 on B.C. Washington, Ohio)

AA: Birth certificate in hand gives Washington township, Auglaise Co. GBAC gives 0:10 A.M. CST, St. Mary's, Ohio, CST.

Terence McKenna
November 16, 1946, 7:25 A.M. MST, Hotchkiss, Colorado
AA: Erin Sullivan quotes his brother Dennis, citing his birth certificate and family records. Same data is given by three other astrologers, quoting him.

Bruno Huber
November 29, 1930, 12:55 P.M. CET, Zurich, Switzerland
A: Jayj Jacobs quotes him.

Albert Hoffmann
January 11, 1906, 3:00 P.M. CET, Baden, Switzerland
A: Ray Mardy quotes him, October 1988.

All other horoscopes are partial horoscopes derived from the author's archives.

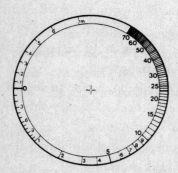

DATING DISK

ENDNOTES

1. I am on the Advisory Council of Kepler College. The college can be contacted through its website: www.keplercollege.org.
2. See a further discussion in my book *The Round Art,* pp. 38–40.
3. All purchasers of this book are eligible to receive, via the Internet website www.newvisionastrology.com, a series of horoscope diagrams that will allow the interpretation sequence described in the book to be followed.
4. Tables of correspondences of signs, planets, and houses appear in a box titled "The Zodiac Signs" in chapter 1.
5. *Synchronicity* is a term used by Carl Jung to describe an acausal connecting principle that brings the psyche into contact with information and events that resonate with meaning.
6. Middle English *microcosme,* "man as a little world"; from the Greek *mikros,* "small" + *kosmos,* "world, order."
7. Dr. Percy Seymour, from "Astrologers by Nature," in *The Mountain Astrologer,* February 2002, and his book *Astrology: The Evidence of Science.*
8. Called "le petite mort."
9. See the work of the biologist Rupert Sheldrake on morphogenetic fields, such as *A New Science of Life.*

10. See Rodney Collin's books, *The Theory of Celestial Influence* and *The Theory of Eternal Life.*

11. See particularly the work of the Swiss child psychologist Jean Piaget, who defined the stages of childhood development. See Ruth Beard's *An Outline of Piaget's Developmental Psychology.*

12. See particularly the work of Liz Greene, Howard Sasportas, and Demetra George.

13. *Dharma* is an Indian Vedic term usually defined as the characteristic property of an individual action or life.

14. For a psychological view of the houses, see Howard Sasportas, *The Twelve Houses.*

15. See the Bibliography for books about subpersonalities and psychosynthesis by Roberto Assagioli and Piero Ferrucci.

16. Ferrucci, Piero, *What We May Be,* p. 47.

17. *Astrology and the Art of Healing,* pp. 64–68.

18. Eileen Nauman, *The American Book of Nutrition and Medical Astrology,* San Diego: Sound Horizons, 1982.

19. Available from the American Federation of Astrologers, Tempe, Arizona.

20. See *The Tibetan Book of the Dead* for descriptions of the Bardo state, and also my book *Elements of Reincarnation.*

21. For example, see the work and dating systems of Dane Rudhyar and the Huber from Switzerland. Neither of their systems includes the gestation time. Both Bruno and Louise associate each house with a set number of years (for Rudhyar, six years; for the Hubers, seven years).

22. Michael Derzak Adzema, "The Emerging Perinatal Unconscious: Consciousness Evolution or Apocalypse?" *The Journal of Psychohistory,* V. 25, N. 3, Winter 1998.

23. I have adapted this from Lorna Clay's master's thesis on psychosynthesis, "Theatre: The Healing Art," which was written

and accepted in 2001 by the Psychosynthesis and Education Trust, London.

24. Rudolf Steiner believed that early childhood illnesses coincided with our soul development.

25. Liz Greene, *Relating,* London: Coventure Books, 1977.

26. See Sogyal Rinpoche, *The Tibetan Book of Living and Dying,* San Francisco: Harper, 1992.

27. See my book *Sacred Sexuality,* written with Jane Lyle, London: Vega Books, 2002 (originally published by Element Books in 1995), for a view of sexuality that evokes the sacred.

28. Based on my book in progress, *The Spiritual Potential of Junk DNA: Accessing the Akashic Record.*

29. Grof, Stanislav, *Beyond the Brain: Birth, Death, and Transcendence in Psychotherapy,* Albany, New York: State University of New York Press, 1985.

30. See Reinhold Ebertin, *The Combination of Stellar Influences,* especially the Biological Correspondence of the Moon/Saturn combination.

BIBLIOGRAPHY

Assagioli, Roberto. *The Act of Will.* New York: Viking Press, 1973.

Beard, Ruth. *An Outline of Piaget's Developmental Psychology.* London: Routledge & Kegan Paul, 1969.

Collin, Rodney. *The Theory of Celestial Influence.* London: Shambhala, 1984 (1953).

Collin, Rodney. *The Theory of Eternal Life.* New York: Random House, 1984 (1950).

Davison, Ronald C. *Astrology.* New York: Arco, 1975.

Ebertin, Reinhold. *The Combination of Stellar Influences.* Tempe, Arizona: American Federation of Astrologers, 1997 (1940).

Ferrucci, Piero. *What We May Be: The Vision and Techniques of Psychosynthesis.* London: Mandala, 1990.

Mann, A. T. *Astrology and the Art of Healing.* London: Unwin Hyman, 1989.

————. *The Elements of Reincarnation.* Shaftesbury: Element Books, 1996.

————. *Life Time Astrology.* London: Allen & Unwin, 1984.

————. *Sacred Sexuality.* Shaftesbury: Element Books, 1995.

————. *The Divine Life: Astrology and Reincarnation.* London: Vega, 2002.

————. *The Divine Plot: Astrology, Reincarnation, Cosmology and History.* London: Allen & Unwin, 1986.

————. *The Future of Astrology.* London: Unwin Hyman, 1989.

————. *The Mandala Astrological Tarot.* San Francisco: Harper & Row, 1987, 1997.

————. *The Round Art: The Astrology of Time and Space.* London: Dragon's World, 1979.

Sasportas, Howard. *The Twelve Houses.* London: Aquarian Press, 1985.

Seymour, Percy, Ph.D. "Astrologers by Nature," *The Mountain Astrologer,* February 2002.

————. *Astrology: The Evidence of Science.* London: Penguin, 1990.

Sheldrake, Rupert. *A New Science of Life.* London: Blond & Briggs, 1981.

INDEX

Note: Page numbers in italics refer to illustrative materials.

Venus during, 244
medical astrology, 105
meditation, 280
memory, 19–20
  of early childhood, 20, 40, 44
menstruation, 278, 279
mental body, *see* maturity
Mercury, 70, 78, 82–83
  characters in our life and, 15, 82–83
  during gestation, 176
    interpretation tables:
    aspects, 146–47
    personifications (Mercury in
      houses), 125
    principles (Mercury in signs), 124
  during maturity, 244
"microcosm is the macrocosm," 29–30,
  30
middle age, *see* Eighth House (forty-
  two years old until death)
Midheaven (MC) (seven weeks after
  conception or thirty-three
  weeks before birth), 119, 181–87
  aspect interpretation, 154
  higher octave, 285
  Tenth House cusp and, in the signs,
    183–87
midpoints, 117
Milky Way galaxy, 31
minor aspects, 104–08
Minuchin, Salvadore, 220
Moon, the, 59, 81–82, 99
  characters in our life and, 68, 81–82
  during childhood, 221–22
    feminine symbolism of, 2, 15, 67
    geometric relationship to the Sun
      in our horoscope, 16–17
  during gestation, 176
    interpretation tables:
    aspects, 144–45
    personifications (Moon in
      houses), 123
    principles (Moon in signs), 122

  during maturity, 243
  North Node of, *see* North Node of
    the Moon
mother, 69, 70
  conception and, *see* conception
  Fourth House's association with, 236
  gestation and, *see* gestation
  relationship with your father, 100
  Tenth House's association with, 236
  see also Moon, the
mutable signs, 6

Nash, John Forbes, horoscope of, 254,
  254, 286
Natural Zodiac, 5, 62, *63*
  time scale and, 13–15, *14*
Nauman, Eileen, 103
near-death experiences, 52, 279
Nelson, John, 98
Neptune, 70, 78, 88–89
  characters in our life and, 88–89
  during childhood, 223
  during gestation, 178
    interpretation tables:
    aspects, 152
    personifications (Neptune in
      houses), 137
    principles (Neptune in signs), 136
  during maturity, 245–46
  as outer planet, 15
newspaper astrology, 4–5, 29
new vision of astrology, 18–19
  aspects of relationship, *see* aspects of
    relationship
  the four octaves, *see* childhood; ges-
    tation; maturity; transcendence
  life as a spiraling process in time, 34
  the planets and, *see* planets; *individ-
    ual planets*
  predictions and relationships,
    304–05
  recreating our life from the begin-
    ning, 24, 46

Second House (seven months old until
one year eight months old), 47,
61, 225–29
the signs in, 226–29
semisextile aspect, 105, 107
semisquare aspect, 104–05
sensitive points, 114–17, *115*
September 11, 78
sequence of events, importance of,
158–59
sequence of planets, release of, 269, *270*
sequence of the planets:
aspects of relationship and, 106–07,
107
sesquiquadrate aspect, 104–05, 107
Seventh House (twenty-three years and
five months until forty-two
years old), 50, 62, 258–65
horoscope of cross-dresser, *261,*
261–62
signs in the, 262–65
sextile aspect, 102, 107, 119
sexuality, 280
conception and, 159, 162
Seymour, Dr. Percy, 33
shadow quality, 22
Sixth House (thirteen years old until
twenty-three years and five
months), 48, 50, 61, 252–58
horoscope of John Forbes Nash,
254–55, *255,* 286
horoscope of John Lennon, 254–55,
255
signs in the, 255–58
Smith, Cyril, 299
solar system, spiral movement of the,
31–34
spirals of life, 31–34
square aspect, 103–04, 119
Stern, Isaac, 298
strange attractor, 107–08, *108*
Sun, the, 59, 79–81, 99
characters in our life and, 68, 79–81

during childhood, 221
geometric relationship to the
Moon in our horoscope, 16–17
during gestation, 175–76
interpretation tables:
aspects, 143–44
personifications (Sun in houses),
121
principles (Sun in signs), 120
masculine symbolism of, 2, 67
during maturity, 243
sun signs, *see* zodiac signs; *individual
signs*
superficiality, 111
synthesizing our life, 288–301
case history, *see* Helfgott, David,
case history of

tai chi, 280
tarot card, High Priestess, 235, *235*
Taurus the Bull:
Ascendant birth in, 206–07
body parts associated with, 2–3
Eighth House cusp in, 270
Eleventh House cusp in, 191
Fifth House cusp in, 250
Fourth House cusp in, 238
Midheaven in, 184
planets in, *see* interpretation tables
qualities of, 8
Second House cusp in, 227
Seventh House cusp in, 263
as single sign, 11
Sixth House cusp in, 256
Third House cusp in, 232
Twelfth House cusp in, 197
Tenth House (thirty-three weeks to
twenty-eight weeks before
birth), 47, 60, 187–90
Theory of Celestial Influence, The
(Collin), 38
Third House (one year and eight
months until three years and

ABOUT THE AUTHOR

A. T. Mann devised Life Time Astrology in 1972 and has practiced astrology for thousands of clients worldwide. A graduate of the College of Architecture at Cornell University, he practiced as an architect in New York City and Rome. He lived in England and Copenhagen for twenty-five years and now lives in New York. His website is: www.atmann.net.